THE NOVELS OF F. SCOTT FITZGERALD

The Novels of
F. Scott Fitzgerald

John B. Chambers

Academic Dean
Tennessee Wesleyan College

St. Martin's Press   New York

PS 3511
I9
Z575
1989 © John B. Chambers, 1989

First published in the United States of America in 1989

Printed in Hong Kong

ISBN 0–312–02803–2

Library of Congress Cataloging-in-Publication Data
Chambers, John B., 1931–
The novels of F. Scott Fitzgerald/John B. Chambers.
p. cm.
Bibliography: p.
Includes index.
ISBN 0–312–02803–2: $35.00 (est.)
1. Fitzgerald, F. Scott (Francis Scott), 1896–1940 — Criticism and
interpretation. I. Title.
PS3511.I9Z575 1989
813'.52 — dc 19   88–8014
                                                                       CIP

For my father

Contents

Acknowledgements	ix
1 **Scott Fitzgerald's Novels**	1
2 **From *The Romantic Egotist* to *This Side of Paradise***	17
3 ***The Beautiful and Damned***	67
4 ***The Great Gatsby***	91
5 **The Wise and Tragic Sense of Life**	127
Notes and References	190
Selected Bibliography	204
Index	209

Acknowledgements

I am very lucky to have had the support of many friends while writing this book. However, for my career as a teacher of Literature, and as a specialist in American studies I am indebted to the excellent teaching I received at St John's College, York, notably from Canon Philip Lamb and Roy Stevens.

If the book has a single originating idea it came from work done with Dennis Welland in my undergraduate days at the University of Nottingham. I can never thank him sufficiently for his encouragement.

Mark Leaf at the University of Durham was a sympathetic guide in the early stages of my work and I was immensely lucky to have at the same time the wise aid of Peter Ure at the University of Newcastle upon Tyne. With his assistance and the generosity of that university I was able to make the first of many trips to the USA. In that first venture I received the life-line of an award from the American Embassy in London, made possible by the then Cultural Attaché, Cleanth Brooks. That generosity enabled me to take up a Visiting Research Fellowship at Princeton University, where, among many advantages, I enjoyed the privilege of the friendship of Alexander P. Clark, Curator of Manuscripts in the Rare Book Department of the Firestone Library.

My award allowed me to travel through the USA visiting Fitzgerald scholars. Two, especially, listened patiently to my questions, offered sound advice and also took me into their homes with warm hospitality. The late Andrew Turnbull's courteous welcome made Brattle Street feel shorter and cooler than it really was and Matthew Bruccoli's great enthusiasm reinvigorated mine. It was at this time that I was fortunate to meet George Connor at the University of Chattanooga. George is simply the best friend one could ever hope to have. He has been a true support in so many ways that it is hard to imagine where this book would be now without him. Thank you George for many pleasant hours.

I want to thank the Open University of Great Britain for research time and funds which enabled me to complete the project and also my new colleagues at Tennessee Wesleyan College for their valued support. I also want to thank my friend and ex-colleague at the University of Newcastle upon Tyne, Ernst Honigmann, for his patient support during the last stages of the research.

I have been unusually lucky in the fact that I have had the great benefit of two excellent typists: Susan Dowson in England and Evelyn Saunders in America. They have both endured the difficulties of my corrected manuscripts with great fortitude. Many thanks to you both.

Finally, I thank many students in Britain and America whose lively interest has always stimulated my efforts – especially that amazing graduate class in Chattanooga – Nelson, Joan, Jim, Butch. I also thank the many friends who have wished me well, indicating by their quiet support that they knew the book would eventually appear. And, of course, the author's long-suffering family whose patience is finally rewarded: Muriel my wife; John, Cathy, Helen and Rachel, my wonderful children.

The author and publishers wish to thank the following for kindly granting permission to use copyright material:

Princeton University Library for extracts from F. Scott Fitzgerald, Box 17, *The Romantic Egotist*, typescript.

Harold Ober Associates Incorporated for extracts from manuscript of F. Scott Fitzgerald's *The Romantic Egotist*. Compilation Copyright © 1988 by Eleanor Lanahan Hazard, Matthew J. Bruccoli, R. Andrew Boose, Trustees u/a 7/3/75 by Frances Scott Fitzgerald Smith.

The Estate of F. Scott Fitzgerald for extracts from *This Side of Paradise* (The Bodley Head Scott Fitzgerald Volume Three), from *The Beautiful and Damned* (The Bodley Head Scott Fitzgerald, Volume Four), from *The Great Gatsby* (The Bodley Head Scott Fitzgerald, Volume One), from *Tender is the Night* (The Bodley Head Scott Fitzgerald, Volume Two).

1
Scott Fitzgerald's Novels

Few readers approach the novels of Scott Fitzgerald unacquainted with details of his life story. That story has been told many times and in many ways. There have been novels based upon it, documentary films and television programmes illustrating it, and affectionate reminiscences which praise Fitzgerald as teacher, friend, laureate of The Jazz Age, discoverer of The Flapper, or as the doomed artist who lived life on a grand scale. Few years seem to pass without a new critical biography. These and all other documentations of the life story are usually well received by a wide public. The number and variety of these items over the past forty years testify to the undeniable fact that Fitzgerald's life story is equally as popular as his fiction. The media hype which attended the expensive television dramatisation of *Tender is the Night* usefully illustrates the position which has been reached. In the extensive publicity which preceded the actual transmissions, and in the subsequent reviews, the subsuming theme – often implicit – was the intimate link between the novel and the life of the Fitzgeralds. This has always been a characteristic of Fitzgerald criticism. The consequences of this linking have been enormous: on the one hand it has provoked and sustained wide public interest; and on the other, it has severely constrained literary appreciation.

The first major study of Fitzgerald's work was Arthur Mizener's book *The Far Side of Paradise*.[1] Mizener is quite explicit about the link. In his Introduction he asserts: 'His life is inextricably bound up with his work.'[2] Indeed, he makes this the basis of the whole study, using excerpts from Fitzgerald's writings alongside details from the real-life story to produce mutual understanding. After Mizener, this form of biographical approach has been the critical norm. Crucially, Mizener's method was founded upon a quasi-psychological explanation of Fitzgerald's personality and intellect. The use of the same method by other critics posits their agreement with Mizener's understanding of the man.

1

It should be remembered that Mizener was writing in the late 1940s when Fitzgerald's reputation was not high. His major task was to rescue Fitzgerald from the clearly expressed public disapproval which had been growing in the later years; at least since the publication of his various confessional essays. Mizener's biography illustrates in minute detail the stresses and strains at work on the man. That was absolutely necessary to his purpose because his thesis is that Fitzgerald was able to create great art *because* he was the man he was. In the following passage Mizener presents the kind of paradox which is central to his explanation.

> If the insight and heroism Fitzgerald possessed are to be seen for what they are, they have to be known in the context of his characteristic . . . ignorances and irresponsibilities. They existed in inextricable involvement with these defects and cannot, without serious distortion, be abstracted from them.[3]

Believing this, *The Far Side of Paradise* attempts to chronicle the development of Fitzgerald's mind. It attempts to show how he came to write as he did rather than to evaluate the writings.

Mizener succeeded in his main task because he moved discussion away from the area of moral judgements about real-life incidents by making such incidents an integral part of the creative process. His method was to insist upon the representative nature of Fitzgerald's experience.

> It has always seemed to me that Fitzgerald's greatest value for us is his almost eponymous character, the way his life and his work *taken together* represent what, in the very depths of our natures, we are – we Americans, anyhow, and – with some variations – perhaps most men of the western world.[4]

This not only condones the behaviour, it elevates it: this kind of assertion paved the way towards an epic dimension.

Lionel Trilling added his own considerable critical authority to this line by extending the idea of Fitzgerald's exemplary role. In *The Liberal Imagination* he speaks of the 'heroic quality' of the *Crack-Up* essays and makes use of a Miltonic comparison; claiming that it applies as far as Samson's 'sojourn among the Philistines and even to the maimed hero exhibited and mocked for the amusement of the crowd'.[5] That such encomium could be uttered after so much earlier disapproval is a tribute to Mizener's method.

This explanation which gives Fitzgerald's experience a national, or even universal significance, inevitably creates an heroic context for his attempt to write. The idea of *necessary suffering* on this plane has been immensely attractive. The tendency is to see Fitzgerald as a tragic literary figure. As well as the Milton comparison, Trilling relates Fitzgerald to Racine's Orestes. The image which is created is of a specially sensitive man who, as well as suffering the peculiar and complex fate of being American, is also a writer with an heroic awareness which enables him to hold fast to his determination to write and 'to utter his vision of his own fate publicly'.[6] In this way, the very act of writing about himself is thought to approach the epic dimension.

Although it has been capable of a degree of variation, this notion of Fitzgerald as exemplar with the consequent ennobling of his own experience, has been a major strand in critical assessment since Mizener's biography. Curiously, when adverse criticism has been offered, it too has accepted the Mizener line of the inextricable linking of life and art. However, some critics have seen a different quality in the nature of Fitzgerald's sufferings. Unlike Mizener, they do not see his characteristic defects as the basis of great art; instead, they see them as the reasons why he could never attain excellence. F. R. Leavis has put the extreme case.

> The extremity of the destitution that disqualifies [Fitzgerald] as a novelist and a creative writer . . . is what can be seen in the accounts of his life; . . . The state of dispossession they illustrate – dispossession of the interests, the awarenesses, the impulsions and the moral perceptions out of which a creative rendering of human life might come – is such that he seems to have had hardly any sense of even the elementary decencies that one had thought of as making civilised intercourse possible.[7]

Other, similarly hostile critics such as Norman Podhoretz, vary this by suggesting that serious moral and personality defects simply delayed Fitzgerald's development as a writer.

For both hostile and favourable critics then, the key to the literature is to be found in the personality and intellect of the man. For one line of criticism Fitzgerald had the heroic awareness to face his representative suffering and to find the means to write about it; for another his adolescent fantasies prevented a courageous self-confrontation until almost the end of his writing career. These are the poles of critical opinion about Fitzgerald and they are both founded upon assertions about the man himself. In the contemporary consensus by far the greater number of critics incline to the line of heroic suffering.

There have been, of course, minor variations upon the theme but Mizener's seminal formulation gave little opportunity for anything but elaboration. The main constraint has been that corner-stone of the whole Mizener edifice: the nature of Fitzgerald's intellect. Despite the attempt to present it as a romantic theory of composition, Mizener's insistence upon the subjective nature of Fitzgerald's manner of comprehension has led to the widely held view that he was an emotional rather than a conceptual thinker. The consequence for criticism has been the predilection to view Fitzgerald's artistic development as a slow and painful one which was consequent upon his slow and painfully won comprehension of real-life issues.

Milton R. Stern's study of Fitzgerald, *The Golden Moment*,[8] typifies recent criticism owing allegiance to this popular belief. Like Mizener, Stern believes that Fitzgerald needed to suffer disillusionment, failure, ill-health, etc., before he could write well. Like Mizener, he believes that Fitzgerald's sufferings were paradigmatic. However, in Stern's method of viewing life and art together there is special emphasis given to the way Fitzgerald learned. Perhaps even more than Mizener, Stern is devoted to the notion that Fitzgerald tried to work out the meaning of his life in his fiction. From this belief Stern creates an image of a 'dark, destructive reconnaissance'[9] to stand for Fitzgerald's alleged real-life struggle to come to terms with real-life issues. Stern closes his study on the metaphor of a difficult journey to a golden land with the ironic twist that Fitzgerald finally discovered that the real gold was his own artistic talent.

Such imagery indicates a high degree of affectionate attachment to an idea of Fitzgerald the man. As with Mizener's closing paragraphs, the effect is to create great pathos and powerful sympathy. The mingling of life and art in this fashion intimately involves Fitzgerald in the artistic versions of tragedy. The important factor at work here is the easy acceptance of the idea that at least in his early fiction Fitzgerald was not really in control of his writing. Apparently, the heroic struggle is sufficient excuse.

In Robert Sklar's study of Fitzgerald, *F. Scott Fitzgerald: The Last*

Laocoön,[10] basically the same position is taken but here the notion of struggle concerns Fitzgerald's alleged subjective attempts to create a contemporary hero rather than to rely upon the stereotyped genteel heroes of older works. In the very title, taken from Malcolm Lowry, Sklar enshrines the familiar notion of tragic heroism. He too sees Fitzgerald's development as a struggle for control; an artistic struggle which could only be won when the real-life comprehension had been achieved.

> Throughout his career Fitzgerald never rested content with his intellect and accomplished artistry, but struggled always in his novels toward a firmer understanding of the moral qualities and values he dramatized in conflict, toward a finer control over his art.[11]

This kind of assessment has been bolstered by confident assertions about Fitzgerald's weak analytical abilities. Henry Dan Piper makes a typical statement.

> Intellectually, he was no match for [his] friends. He never achieved those analytical habits of mind that characterize the typical intellectual. Indeed, his inability to discuss ideas rationally was to be the lifelong despair of his friends.[12]

Similar dicta have come from most of Fitzgerald's critics; the most influential opinions, perhaps, coming early from Alfred Kazin and Malcolm Cowley.[13] The most amusing one which Piper actually quotes but does not allow to influence his own position, comes from one of Fitzgerald's Princeton professors who, apparently, 'went to his death maintaining that Fitzgerald had not written *The Great Gatsby* ... because his English grades were never good enough'.[14]

It is evident that several other contemporaries felt similar disbelief when they tried to relate their idea of the man they knew to the work he began to publish. The shock is most marked in the reaction of Edmund Wilson. His rationalisation of the issue deserves study: it has had an immense effect on succeeding criticism. Commenting on the manuscript of *This Side of Paradise*, he wrote:

> Your hero is an unreal imitation of Michael Fane of *Sinister Street*

who was himself unreal ... as an intellectual Amory is a fake of
the first water and I read his views on art, politics, religion and
society with more riotous mirth than I should care to have you
know ... in the latter part of the book, you make Amory the hero
of a series of dramatic encounters with all the naive and romantic
gusto of a small boy imagining himself a brave hunter of Indians
... Cultivate a universal irony and do read something other than
contemporary British novelists.[15]

The sense of intellectual superiority in this advice is unmistakable.
Here is amused contempt for his friend's novelistic efforts.
Whether or not this opinion was justified is a matter of speculation
but what is beyond dispute is the important effect such assertions
have had on following critics.

Wilson's arrogant dismissal of Fitzgerald's intellectual preten-
sions was continued in a published – but unsigned – article in
March 1922.[16] The essay deals with Fitzgerald's first two novels
and is extremely significant for the powerful and lasting influence
it has had on Fitzgerald criticism.

Until the publication of Wilson's essay, the great majority of
critical reviews of Fitzgerald's first two novels had been
favourable.[17] Curiously, in view of the later consensus, there had
been the frequent use of the word 'clever'. However, reviewers of
The Beautiful and Damned and Flappers and Philosophers did tend to
praise the technique rather than the content and by the time of
Wilson's essay it appears that the prevailing critical opinion was
that Fitzgerald had a brilliant prose style that produced a 'spirited
narrative', and work which 'fairly scintillates with clever
sayings'.[18] At this point Wilson brought his personal idea of the
author into discussion and added an element which has remained
constant. His explanation effectively shaped the prevailing tendencies and, in so doing, created such authoritative terms of reference
that succeeding critics can see Fitzgerald only through Wilson's
eyes.

The awkward problem that Fitzgerald's early work posed for
Wilson was to account for the way someone with as little talent as
Fitzgerald could write something which, while obviously imma-
ture, did not fail to live. Here is his opening paragraph.

It has been said by a celebrated person that to meet F. Scott
Fitzgerald is to think of a stupid old woman with whom

someone has left a diamond; she is extremely proud of the diamond and shows it to everyone who comes by, and everybody is surprised that such an ignorant old woman should possess so valuable a jewel; for in nothing does she appear so stupid as in the remarks she makes about the diamond.

Wilson claimed a symbolic truth for this story. For him, Fitzgerald's jewel was the prose talent: the stupidity was just that Fitzgerald simply did not know what to do with his talent. 'He has been given imagination without intellectual control of it . . . he has been given a gift for expression without many ideas to express.'[19]

In Wilson's eyes, Fitzgerald's talent was, essentially, fortituous: it was something not worked for; something, even, undeserved. It is curious that this view should have proved so durable. Instead of becoming completely damning, this maliciously patronising judgement has been accommodated into the thesis of a slow and painful journey toward maturity. Even the hostile Podhoretz has been able to explain Fitzgerald in these terms. His view that Fitzgerald 'was a highly gifted natural whose intelligence was not always equal to his talent'[20] might have come straight out of Wilson's essay. Ernest Hemingway probably did as much as any critic to help popularise the notion of the talent as a fortuitous gift. Although kinder than Wilson's, his image is still patronising.

His talent was a natural as the pattern that was made by the dust on a butterfly's wings. At one time he understood it no more than the butterfly did and he did not know when it was brushed or marred. Later he became conscious of his damaged wings and of their construction and he learned to think and could not fly any more because the love of flight was gone and he could only remember when it had been effortless.[21]

Here, despite Hemingway's instinctive dislike for artistic cerebration, is another sentimental image of Fitzgerald to fit into the pattern of an agonised struggle towards understanding and control.

There is another important element in Wilson's attempt to reconcile stupid author and animated narrative and which, given their acceptance of the initial premise, has been axiomatic for following critics: this is the notion of author participation in the fiction. Wilson claimed that Fitzgerald's lack of intellectual comprehension of the things about which he wrote could be a positive advantage. For, 'in the very bewilderment of his revolt, he is typical of the war generation'. Thus, his very immaturity was a useful tool. 'There is a profounder truth in *The Beautiful and Damned* than the author perhaps intended to convey.'[22] Mizener, who has acknowledged his debt to Wilson's criticism, clearly draws a great deal from this idea.[23] It became the key to his explanation of the special emotional intensity which he detects in Fitzgerald's work. 'The events of his stories are nearly always events in which Fitzgerald has himself participated with all his emotional energy.'[24] This becomes for Mizener the vital element in his notion of Fitzgerald as a romantic. By this means, it takes its place in the pattern as the phenomenon which determined the sad note in all Fitzgerald's fiction. 'There is, finally, cast over both the historically apprehended event and the personal recollection embedded in it, a glow of pathos, the pathos of the irretrievableness of a part of oneself.'[25]

In his development of the Wilson idea Mizener opened up a rich seam for further working. His claim that in Fitzgerald's best work there is a balance struck between the view of a participator and that of the detached outsider has led to the popularisation of a double vision theory; of an alleged struggle between subjectivity and objectivity. Mizener had been struck by John Peale Bishop's remark. 'He [had] the rare faculty of being able to experience romantic and ingenuous emotions and half an hour later regard them with satiric detachment.'[26] He quotes Bishop in support of his own thesis that there was a dualism in Fitzgerald's nature: he was partly a romantic in the way he wished to plunge into life and partly 'a spoiled priest' who wanted to remain detached and to analyse life.[27] Later critics, notably Alfred Kazin, perhaps feeling the need to defend Fitzgerald from accusations of an undue admiration for the rich, developed the same form of explanation. 'He was innocent without living in innocence and delighted in the external forms and colours without being taken in by them; but he was pre-eminently a part of the world his mind was always disowning.'[28] This dichotomy identified by Kazin – after Wilson, Bishop and Mizener – was picked up by Malcolm Cowley and popularised by him in a widely-known image of Fitzgerald at a dance with a pretty girl; 'and as if at the same time he stood outside the ballroom, a little Midwestern boy with his nose to the glass, wondering how much the tickets cost and who paid for the music'.[29] This may be affectionately meant but it takes its place with many other sentimental images which belittle Fitzgerald's intelligence.

The alleged subjectivity/objectivity dilemma has been very popular. Henry Dan Piper, for example, is a leading proponent of the notion. In his *Critical Portrait* of Fitzgerald he asserts that 'the secret of his art . . . had been his skill in writing about himself with objective detachment'.[30] He also turns to another form of romantic theory when he adduces Keats' idea of negative capability as an example of a similar phenomenon. Other critics too have made the same link. Even a critic like John Kuehl who begins with the intention of proving an early seriousness in Fitzgerald's critical opinions eventually succumbs to the seductively plausible subjectivity/objectivity dilemma. 'Like Keats, Scott Fitzgerald struggled between "objectivity" and "subjectivity," and, again like Keats, he was primarily a "subjective" writer.'[31]

It should be clear that there is a curious unanimity about the critical approach to Fitzgerald. The reason for this being that for some forty years all criticism has started from the unquestioned premise that he was an emotional rather than a conceptual thinker. This belief has led to a special interest in his life story because it is felt that life and art must be taken together in order to see him clearly. Whether he is seen as the tragic or the pathetic exemplar, the method of his critics is the same: they proceed from the assumption that his whole life was a struggle for personal understanding and artistic control. Even those critics who have sought to establish the idea of Fitzgerald as a careful craftsman have done so while maintaining the notion of the precarious subjectivity/objectivity balance. James Miller and Sergio Perosa for example, produced early studies of this nature.[32] Their criticisms of *The Beautiful and Damned*, for example, show their allegiance to that particular explanation. Miller claims that 'in actuality, nothing at all separates him from his subject'. Perosa asserts that, on the one hand Fitzgerald tried to pass a moral judgement on his characters, but that on the other 'he sympathized with his characters and shared some of their illusions'.[33]

Given the universal acceptance of only an emotional learning process, the idea of a slow and painful journey toward maturity follows naturally. The implications for critical evaluation are obvious: there is little scope for disagreements; only the precise dating of mature vision is open to question. *The Great Gatsby, Tender is the Night* and the unfinished *The Last Tycoon* all have their champions who variously claim them as the high point of Fitzgerald's personal maturity and artistic control. Although even these undoubtedly major works suffer from the restricting pattern forced by the inherited opinion about Fitzgerald's intelligence, perhaps the greater injustice is inflicted upon the first two novels. Conventionally they are slighted under the impression that it was not until he was writing his third novel, *The Great Gatsby*, that he began to take imaginative and artistic control over his material, that is, his own life story. Before *The Great Gatsby*, the presence of a sad note in his writing, could only come from his emotional sense that he was living a tragic story. It was, claims Mizener, intense personal experience of humiliation and failure which gave Fitzgerald 'his essentially tragic sense of human experience'; necessarily, it was a slow process; there were no intellectual shortcuts to understanding; it was all proved through the emotions.[34]

The consequences of this kind of explanation are all too clear in the critical consensus regarding *This Side of Paradise*. It must be hard for anyone coming to it for the first time to read it as anything more than Fitzgerald's reworking of his own youthful experiences – in the main a nostalgic look at college life. After the work of James Miller, that belief about the springs of the book has been given a modicum of artistic respectability by reason of his claim that the work falls into the category of the 'saturation' type of novel as distinct from the novel of 'selection'. Miller believes that, within its discursive form, Fitzgerald could write movingly of experiences which paralleled his own without possessing an intellectual understanding of them. In this ingenious explanation several strands of received opinion about Fitzgerald come together. It serves Mizener's notion of delayed maturity as well as the idea of emotional participation. The sad note came from deeply felt but essentially 'unassimilated emotion'.[35] Or, to use Kazin's terms, Fitzgerald managed to capture the 'welling inaudible sadness' of the tinselly world of his youth without ever coming to terms with the basic subjectivity/objectivity conflict.[36]

Miller's study of Fitzgerald purports to be of 'His Art and His Technique'; it is in fact based upon extra-literary judgements inherited from others. He does not investigate the texts of the two first novels in search of patterns of thought and/or control so much as to find evidence for a thesis already assumed. Unfortunately, his lead has been followed many times since. Today's typical reaction to *This Side of Paradise* will ignore the possibility of intellectual and artistic coherence and, instead, stress its 'honesty' or its 'sincerity'. K. G. W. Cross summarises the alleged naïvety of the novel by describing it as being 'a young man's book, immaturely imagined, and, as Edmund Wilson complained, always just verging on the ludicrous'.[37] The recourse to Wilson as authority is characteristic and illuminating. It indicates that his early explanation of a prose talent without intellectual control still stands as the basis for critical evaluation.

Wilson's 1922 essay was his attempt to reconcile the (slight) qualities he discerned in Fitzgerald's first two novels with the man of undistinguished mind he called his friend. Since the assertion of intellectual immaturity was the bed-rock for his conclusions, it was inevitable that he would have a low opinion of Fitzgerald's attempts at seriousness of content. This is particularly apparent in his mocking dismissal of Fitzgerald's idea of tragedy. The following passage has had an extraordinary influence on this issue.

> Since writing *This Side of Paradise* – on the inspiration of Wells and Mackenzie – Fitzgerald has become acquainted with another school of fiction: the ironical-pessimistic. In college, he supposed that the thing to do was to write biographical novels with a burst of ideas toward the close; since his advent into the literary world, he has discovered that there is another genre in favor: the kind which makes much of the tragedy and 'the meaninglessness of life'. Hitherto, he had supposed that the thing to do was to discover a meaning in life; but he now set bravely about it to contrive a shattering tragedy that should be, also, 100 per cent meaningless.[38]

If this cynical analysis is accepted, there is no point in looking for what Mizener calls 'maturity of judgment' or intellectual control in either *This Side of Paradise* or *The Beautiful and Damned*.

Unfortunately for Fitzgerald criticism, Wilson's assertion has been so attractive that it has become one of the most famous critical dicta: so much so that, far from being examined, it is widely quoted as though it is its own proof. Here is Miller turning his attention to an alleged change in Fitzgerald's attitude after his first novel.

> Edmund Wilson has suggested somewhat precisely the cause and nature of the change in Fitzgerald's attitude toward the

novel between *This Side of Paradise* (1920) and *The Beautiful and Damned* (1922): 'Since writing *This Side of Paradise* – on the inspiration of Wells and Mackenzie – Fitzgerald has become acquainted with another school of fiction: the ironical-pessimistic.'[39]

Professor Sergio Perosa's study, *The Art of Scott Fitzgerald* is another work which shows confidence in Wilson's explanation. Once again the seriousness is devalued. 'Edmund Wilson . . . claimed that *The Beautiful and Damned* was an attempt in which Fitzgerald had tried to use the principles of a new school of writing that he called "ironical-pessimistic".'[40] Milton Stern also acknowledges a debt to Wilson when he too detects evidence of a change in attempted seriousness in Fitzgerald.

The change is what Edmund Wilson referred to when he said: 'Since writing *This Side of Paradise* – on the inspiration of Wells and Mackenzie – Fitzgerald has become acquainted with a different [sic] school of fiction: the ironical-pessimistic.'[41]

K. G. W. Cross approaches the idea of the appearance of a serious note in Fitzgerald's fiction via an assertion about his 'many illusions about youth and money', and then adds: 'As if this were not enough, Fitzgerald adopted the attitudes of what Edmund Wilson called the "ironical-pessimistic" school of fiction.'[42] Mizener, too, has followed the same evaluation of an author grasping after literary vogues rather than expressing his own vision and, in consequence, becoming hopelessly muddled. 'About this muddle his friend Edmund Wilson was very severe: ". . . since his advent into the literary world . . ." ', etc. Mizener quotes the whole of the Wilson passage with clear approval. Although he qualifies the criticism a little, suggesting there is 'more than the fashionable Fitzgerald in it' (*The Beautiful and Damned*), the use of the original words discredits Fitzgerald's intelligence and motive in writing the novel.[43]

Demonstrably then, the keynote of the critical consensus about the seriousness, or lack or seriousness, in the first two novels was struck by Edmund Wilson as long ago as 1922. By now, the simple repetition of his claim can be presented as proof of what should be a very contentious statement. In the most recent biography of Fitzgerald, James R. Mellow's *Invented Lives*, the famous paragraph is paraphrased but the criticism is clearly accepted. And in another recent work, André Le Vot's biography *F. Scott Fitzgerald*, although Wilson's words are not explicit, the concentration upon the influence of Mencken betrays the familiar explanation: 'Fitzgerald seems merely to be playing scales, reciting without conviction a lesson he has not quite learned.'[44] Thus, almost sixty years after its first formulation, the idea that there is very little meaning in *This Side of Paradise* and that the serious note in *The Beautiful and Damned* is bogus has achieved the authority of fact.

It should now be clear why the so-called 'saturation' novel has become such an appropriate categorisation for *This Side of Paradise*. If the conventional line on Fitzgerald's intelligence is accepted, if it is believed that essentially he had nothing to say – that all he had was 'a gesture of indefinite revolt'[45] – then, certainly, a novel form which requires no intellectual coherence is the ideal vehicle. As Miller says: 'By definition the saturation novel is not about any one thing: it is about "life" and must, therefore, include those irrelevancies which prevent life itself from coming to a focus and being *about* something.'[46] Although it was Miller's intention to see *This Side of Paradise* in the best possible light, since he has so clearly accepted the first premise of Fitzgerald's intellectual immaturity, it would be impossible for him to find much to praise. And so, inevitably, he falls back to the Wilson position of 'undeniable charm'. The best he can do is to quote the vague approvals of three other critics and then to offer his own version of its immaturity, honesty and sincerity.

> In spite of its faults, perhaps in part because of them, *This Side of Paradise* continues to appeal. In its very immaturity lies its charm; it is an honest and sincere book by youth about youth, containing the emotions, ranging from ecstasy to despair, of the immature which the mature can neither easily recall nor evoke.[47]

Clearly, there is no place for a controlling intelligence in Miller's critical view.

Sklar is explicit about the lack of what he calls an 'intellectual foundation' for the work.

> The 'saturation' form of the novel suited his needs because he had not yet acquired a point of view firm enough to take advantage of the 'selection' form; he did not possess the

intellectual foundation, that is, to know what to include and what to exclude. In *This Side of Paradise* Fitzgerald seeks to discover that foundation.[48]

Cross goes further in the direction of author self-projection into the fiction.

Amory Blaine – clearly an idealised projection of the young Fitzgerald – embarks on his quest endowed with looks, intelligence, and wealth; he undergoes a series of emotional and spiritual crises, ... to attain finally a degree of self-knowledge. His quest, however inconsequential and, at times, absurd, epitomised that of the rising generation.[49]

This, of course, takes Cross close to the exemplary role. Stern follows the line of self-idealisation and is explicit again about his authority. 'The young Edmund Wilson, writing to the young Scott Fitzgerald shortly after the publication of *This Side of Paradise*, hit exactly upon Fitzgerald's adolescent posing as the force behind Amory's posing.'[50]

Statements of this kind typify the conventional elaborations of one of the earliest critical views. Quite obviously, there is no place in such assessments for the consideration of a possible serious centre for the novel. Conventionally, if a serious note is faintly heard in this allegedly immature book, it is always explained as deriving from the subjective/objective dilemma which it is believed so confused the young author. His deeply felt but inchoate emotional involvement is felt to be at one and the same time the reason for his first novel's power and its great weakness. 'Taking things hard' gave the book its life and vigour but also brought it to the verge of the ludicrous.

What has never been seriously considered is the possibility that everything Fitzgerald wrote was drawn from a firm intellectual centre; that he had a consistent point of view which determined all the fiction. The curious fact is that this point of view is easily apparent. Although it operates in the manner of James' celebrated image of the figure in the carpet, it is not the expression of an arcane philosophy. It has been passed over simply because the notion that Fitzgerald lacked a conceptualising intelligence has determined that his critics have searched for an emotional 'primal plan' rather than an intellectual plan. Far from stemming from a vaguely romantic predisposition toward subjective melancholia, the sad note in his later fiction had its origin in the same comprehensive and rational view of life which controlled the first novel. In other words there is no change to a new seriousness of the kind alleged by Wilson *et al*. There was no painfully slow progress towards personal maturity which eventually gave him greater artistic control. The essential features of what all critics agree is a 'tragic sense of human experience' in his later work are to be found in *This Side of Paradise*. That novel, like all his others, is demonstrably a novel of selection rather than of saturation.

In a letter to his daughter written shortly before his death Fitzgerald offered a piece of advice which leaves no doubt about his own point of view. He outlines three areas which should concern a 'nascent mind', making it perfectly clear which had pre-eminence in his own mind. He first refers to the way that the material world allows little time for a person to 'form a literary taste', secondly 'to examine the validity of philosphic concepts for himself', and thirdly 'to form what, for lack of a better phrase, I might call the wise and tragic sense of life.' His expansion of this phrase indicates its importance to him as an explanation leading to a code.

> By this I mean the thing that lies behind all great careers, from Shakespeare's to Abraham Lincoln's, and as far back as there are books to read – the sense that life is essentially a cheat and its conditions are those of defeat, and that the redeeming things are not 'happiness and pleasure' but the deeper satisfactions that come out of struggle.[51]

Although this explicit formulation came at the end of his life, it is a point of view which is powerfully present in *This Side of Paradise*. Indeed, in James' terms, it acts 'something like a complex figure in a Persian carpet'. In other words it governs both content and technique.

There have been two major obstacles blocking a clear view of this 'complex figure' and both were erected on the unreliable foundation of assertions about Fitzgerald's intellectual competence. In the first instance, because they have been so firmly convinced of Fitzgerald's emotional involvement within the work, critics have neglected to look beneath Amory Blaine's apparent solipsism, preferring instead the explanation of the author's subjectivity/

objectivity dilemma. In the second place, being firmly wedded to the notion of the 'saturation' form, critics have failed to recognise a controlled ironical presentation. Although the present consensus renders it almost unthinkable, an approach which ignores biographical speculations will soon discover that not only did Fitzgerald have a coherent point of view but also that it was early in formulation and, above all, that it was ironic.

The essence of the ironic vision is contained in the advice to his daughter. The important area is the gap between the perception of the inevitable defeat of hope and the exhortation to struggle. It was this area which he had explored as the basis of his double vision theory in the first *Crack-Up* essay in 1936. The story of Amory Blaine was his first ambitious attempt to construct a novel from this 'wise and tragic sense'. Amory's cry at the end of *This Side of Paradise*: 'I know myself . . . but that is all', might be seen as the author's collapse into a subjective 'gesture of indefinite revolt',[52] but it is in fact firmly tied to his growing sense that the struggle through illusions was worth while. The 'redeeming' understanding which has replaced his pursuit of happiness is that 'deeper satisfactions' will come from a life of service to others. The crucial factor which carried him through his struggles was his egotism; his apparently ridiculous sense of election. It is in this area that the issue of irony needs most to be addressed. As will be seen, it is a matter of content and technique.

2

From *The Romantic Egotist* to *This Side of Paradise*

'Cultivate a universal irony.'
(Edmund Wilson to F. Scott Fitzgerald.)

I

Fitzgerald started to put together material for the first draft of what was eventually to become *This Side of Paradise* in the summer of 1917 when he was in his final year at Princeton University. He completed that first draft under the title *The Romantic Egotist* in the autumn of that year while stationed at Fort Leavenworth officer-training camp. In March 1918 he sent it to Scribner's but they rejected it in August. He immediately set about revising the manuscript and the second draft was quickly re-submitted only to be returned in October. During the summer of 1919 he worked on a third version, this time under the title *This Side of Paradise*. It was this draft which was finally accepted by Scribner's on 16 September 1919.

Unfortunately, only a fragment of those early attempts appears to have survived. There is, however, enough to provide evidence of an informing idea which was shaping the material. The misleading feature of this central idea is that it was developed from an ironic concept of egocentricity: a concept which has proved to be highly susceptible to biographical speculations. Over the years, following Mizener's lead, a certain kind of critical viewpoint has grown. By now it is almost commonplace that the young Fitzgerald pored over his Princeton writings struggling to understand himself. The belief that he failed to reach that understanding is reflected in critical exegeses of *This Side of Paradise* which claim to discern only a random selection and ordering of the incidents of the novel.

The following passage illustrates the difficulty faced by the critic

17

influenced by biographical explanations. It is taken from the second draft of *The Romantic Egotist*[1] where it appears early in Chapter 1. the story is narrated by Stephen Palms who calls himself 'the supreme egotist'. His ambition is to be a novelist and at this point he is reflecting upon the apparently desultory nature of the novel he is writing.

> I realise that in the history of a human being there must be, especially at first, a pile of detail which, no matter how relevant it may seem to the individual in the complexities and subtleties of his development, appears unnecessarily disjointed and discon- nected to anyone else.

This could be Fitzgerald's signal that the material did have an organising principle or it could indicate his awareness of his own shortcomings. If it is the latter, then the next sentence is an even more impudent way of brazening out those shortcomings. 'These details stand in place of a point of view and are really juvenile indexes to it.' Clearly, a critical approach which starts from the received opinion of the relatively late development of Fitzgerald's intellect will find it easy to interpret these lines as a rather slick – if novelistically cheap – way out of a difficulty. Such a reading suggests that Fitzgerald was hoping the reader would be able to do something which he could not do, namely, to piece together the fragments of Palms' experience so that a coherent whole is revealed. It is this kind of rationalising which lies behind the notion that Fitzgerald tried to learn about himself by studying what he had written.

The only completely satisfactory answer to this kind of explana- tion would be a careful study of *The Romantic Egotist* to see if 'a point of view' is to be discerned behind the 'pile of detail'. Unfortunately, since only five chapters of that work appear to have survived, that is not possible. However, for the light it sheds upon the process by which *This Side of Paradise* was created, that earlier draft is extremely valuable. As the above quotation shows, there is some evidence that Fitzgerald was at least aware of some of the difficulties involved in the writing of his story. And in this respect Fitzgerald's decision to use the first person form of narrative is particularly significant. If that method is chosen to indicate a final point of view which makes relevant the complexities and subtleties of Palms' development', then the writer is inevitably involved in the technical difficulties of a double story-line. First there will be what might be called the outer structure formed of 'a pile of detail' which establishes the sequence of action in the outer public world, but, arising from this will be the vital inner structure of a philosophical/psychological story-line which indicates the narrator's inner, private progress towards the final 'point of view'. This essentially indirect method of establishing the mature point of view will frequently make use of the device of irony. This is most frequently the case when the chosen persona for the narrator is characterised by a very obvious naïvety. When that is the case, as for example in *Huckleberry Finn*, the reader has to see all the incidents on two levels of meaning: that of the relatively undeveloped narrator, and that of the author. The danger as always with the use of irony is that the inner level of meaning can be missed. Technical skill of a high order is required to establish the inner story as the true norm of the work. It is often too easy for the reader to accept the first-person voice as authoritative and to imagine it to be the author's own voice.

The following passage can illustrate the difficulty. It too comes from Chapter 1 of *The Romantic Egotist*.

A week has gone here in the aviation school – just hurried by with early rising by the November moon, and here I am with not one chapter finished – scrawled pages with no form or style – just full of details and petty history. I intended so much when I started, and I'm realizing how impossible it all is. I can't rewrite and all I do is form vague notes for chapters that I have here beside me and the uncertain channels of an uneven memory. I don't seem to be able to trace the skeins of development as I ought. I'm trying to set down the story part of my generation in America and put myself in the middle as a sort of observer and conscious factor.

But I've got to write now, for when the war's over I won't be able to see these things as important – even now they are fading out against the background of the map of Europe. I'll never be able to do it again; well done or poorly. So I'm writing almost desperately – and so futilely.

What must never be forgotten about this kind of passage is that the narrator is himself an actor in the unfolding events of the novel. His desperation and sense of inadequacy must be seen against the fact that he did actually finish the novel: a detail which, given the convention of this method, the protagonist/narrator could not possess at this stage in the work.

What this passage does is to concentrate attention upon the importance of the interpretative key for which the narrator searches. This early confession of inadequacy is an important part of the persona Fitzgerald chose for the narrator. Unfortunately, it has been his misfortune that such excerpts have been read only with their outer level of meaning and used as a gloss of Fitzgerald's own struggles.

This has also confused another important issue in *The Romantic Egotist*. Although it is clear that Fitzgerald attached great importance to the concept of egotism, his presentation of Stephen Palms as 'the supreme egotist' is generally thought to indicate his own misconceptions. After all, naked egotism is hardly to be thought of as an admirable quality in an individual. The image of Fitzgerald as the 'childlike fellow, very much wrapped up in his dream of himself and his projection of it on paper'[2] has so dominated criticism that it is easy to deduce the author's adolescent vanities behind the following passage. However, within the perspective of 'juvenile indexes' which 'stand in place of a point of view' it would seem that Fitzgerald was approaching the concept of egotism through an ironic presentation.

> 'It shall be,' said I, 'a volume of poetry; about sixty poems; and Theron Carey shall take it to Scribner's.'
> 'No,' I continued after a pause, 'I have neither the time nor the patience to write forty more poems, I will write an autobiography.'
> 'Who'll read it?' commented Private O'Day.
> 'Everyone,' I replied. 'You see I'll write about Princeton and announce myself on the cover as the only man in the army who says he expects to come back from France and drag out a miserable old age.'
> 'But,' objected O'Day. 'You've done nothing. You're only twenty-one; you've never been out of North America or killed a man . . .'
> 'But think,' I interrupted with dignity. 'I am the supreme egotist. Consider how brilliantly self-centred my book will be; also I am informed that the time has come for a long rambling, picaresque novel. I shall ramble and be picaresque. I shall be intellectual and

echo H. G. Wells, and improper like Compton McKenzie. The chief influence upon my humor will be Booth Tarkington; and toward the end of the book, I'll be very, very serious indeed – My form will be very original for it will mingle verse and prose and not be vers libre; and thus interest the new poets. Here is a great field and I am the man to fill it.'

I looked around and discovered that my last burst of egotism had sent O'Day scuttling out of the room. Then I remembered . . . he was a new poet.

In this excerpt irony is used in the service of satire. The exaggerated praise of something which in itself is not admirable is a staple method of satire. Here Palms makes an indirect comment upon contemporary writers by basing his claims upon the fact that he is the 'supreme egotist'. This supremacy is based upon his openness about having egotism as his driving force. The writers who have gained popularity by vaunting their expectations of early death in the First World War are implied to be disguising their self-centredness, as are Wells, McKenzie and Tarkington.

The difficulty posed by this passage lies in the extent of the intended satire. Is it meant to include Palms himself? Does the reference to the scuttling O'Day indicate conscious self-parody? The use of the first person dramatises the conversation but it does not clearly differentiate between the inner and outer story-lines. It is not possible to tell if Palms is meant to be serious in this view or merely flippant. Either way would indicate his position on the journey towards intellectual maturity but there is no reference point by which his sincerity can be measured.

For the reader with a received opinion about Fitzgerald's immaturity, there is no difficulty in explaining a confused narrative: it is accounted for by the fact that Fitzgerald was writing about real life events which he had suffered but not understood. Indeed, some of the material in *The Romantic Egotist* was taken from the form of a diary kept by Fitzgerald and called by him his *Ledger*[3]. A comparison of the fictional use of such material is quite illuminating.

In a *Ledger* entry dated May 1904, Fitzgerald records memories of stories he had heard. One in particular had made a big impression on him. It was about 'a row between big and small animals, the latter at first succesful but the others gaining in

strength and winning'. *The Romantic Egotist* manuscript version
extends this.

> First there was a book that was I think one of the big sensations
> of my life. It was nothing but a nursery book, but it filled me with
> the saddest and most yearning emotion. I have never been able
> to trace it since. It was about a fight that the large animals, like
> the elephant, had with the small animals, like the fox. The small
> animals won the first battle; but the elephants and lions and
> tigers finally overcame them. The author was prejudiced in
> favour of the large animals, but my sentiment was all with the
> small ones. I wonder if even then I had a sense of the wearing-
> down power of big, respectable people, I can almost weep now
> when I think of that poor fox, the leader . . . the fox has somehow
> typified innocence to me ever since.

There is an important difference in tone between this passage and
the opening remarks of 'the supreme egotist'. In this recollection of
the childhood memory, there is no ironic undercutting of the
narrator's position. There is no blatant vanity which would send
O'Day 'scuttling out of the room'. This emotional highlight is
presented without irony. It should, therefore, be easy to locate the
experience in the developing persona of Stephen Palms. It must be
taken as direct evidence of the influences which shaped his
personality.

At the centre of this passage is 'the saddest and most yearning
emotion' which the story can still evoke in the Stephen Palms of
later years. The pathos which the story commands is directly
related to Palms' 'sense of the wearing-down power of big,
respectable people'. This realisation that the powerful will always
defeat the weak, no matter how worthy the latter might be, is the
key factor. Fitzgerald makes a clear link between this emotionally
intense insight and his narrator's feelings for Princeton.

> I think what started my Princeton sympathy was that they
> always just lost the football championship. Yale always seemed
> to nose them out in the last quarter by superior 'stamina' as the
> newspapers called it. It was to me a repetition of the story of the
> foxes and the big animals in the child's book.

Unfortunately, the conceptual link afforded by the narrator's 'sense of the wearing-down power' is ignored because the conventionally favoured biographical approach believes that Fitzgerald comprehended an emotional rather than a conceptual reality.

True to his belief in Fitzgerald's adolescent immaturities, Mizener, for example, picks up the treatment of sport as an illustration of what he calls Fitzgerald's 'capacity for hero-worship' and he tries to chart the way Fitzgerald identified himself with various sportsmen in order to construct 'an heroic image for himself'.[4] Given that framework, the following excerpt is explained as being based upon an adolescent notion of heroism: one which is sentimentally attracted to the glamour of gallant defeat.

I imagined Princeton men as slender and keen and romantic, and the Yale men as brawny and brutal and powerful ... There was a basket-ball game, and the Captain of the losing side was a dark, slender youth of perhaps fourteen, who played with a fierce but facile abandon that tossed his long hair all over his face and sent him everywhere around the floor pushing, dribbling and shooting impossible baskets from all angles. The smell of a gymnasium and the calls of players in a game always bring him back to mind. Oh he was fine, really one of the finest things I ever saw. I couldn't appreciate the idea of a blond Greek athlete, after I saw him – all athletes were dark and devilish and despairing and enthusiastic.

In fact, since this passage immediately follows the explicit link with the animal story, it should be clear that the concept of the 'wearing-down power' is the factor which supplies the perspective for the emotion. The inevitability of defeat on these terms allows even juvenile contests to suggest an heroic perspective. They become examples of the classic struggle between virtu and fortuna. The 'wearing-down power' is thought of as something like a law of nature.

The surviving fragment of *The Romantic Egotist* supports this reading of the use made of such detail. However, the whole work is needed before an estimate of the importance of the concept in the developing point of view of Stephen Palms can be made. Clearly, if it was to be a significant part of the pattern of his experiences, then it is to be expected that there would be a tonal link between all the incidents. If the inevitability of defeat on these terms were indeed the point of view towards which the 'pile of detail' organised under the heading of *The Romantic Egotist* was leading, it would certainly be apparent.

In fact, as a description of the overall tone of the existing chapters, Fitzgerald's later phrase – 'a qualified unhappiness' (*Crack-Up*, p. 55) – serves very well. However, the evidence of five chapters is too slight to bear such a conclusion; nevertheless, it can be thought of as offering useful hints towards a more satisfactory explanation of the sad note than that given by the usual biographical method.

In this respect, the following passage is also helpful.

> I had not yet come to the stage of thinking most people fools; I considered them only as lay-figures. It is because I was this combination of vanity and self-knowledge that I do not write myself an out-and-out stiff lump of conceit, but compromise, by saying 'egotist.' My object was to pass as many people as possible and get to a vague 'top of the world' and I started my pilgrimage with an odd mixture of qualities that led me up and down through triumph and doubt to the brink of pessimism.

This piece follows a detailed self-appraisal of Stephen Palms and it underlines the importance to him of what Fitzgerald called his 'sense of infinite possibilities'. It is clear that Fitzgerald wished to present Palms as being something more than an average person. On the evidence of the passages quoted so far it should also be clear that a major distinguishing feature of his personality is his egocentricity. He claims it as a virtue but he also indicates that he understands how others think about it. This is how the passage continues.

> All that above has been hard to write. I was proud of being conceited then, but now I know how many people hate such expansive introspection . . . Those who do, had better stop now and give the book to a library . . . The rest of it tells how I looked mistily at the world, and how the world gazed stupidly at me.

The main point established in this 'then' and 'now' summary is Palms' development along an inner story line. At this interim stage in his progress he is represented as having reached greater awareness about how his conceit was viewed by others. The impression is of a wiser man who now lacks the ebullience of the young man who paraded his egocentricity for Private O'Day. That in itself is an indication of a sadder state of affairs but Fitzgerald here indicates a basic pattern in Palms' experiences. The pattern begins with an over-confidence which tempts Palms into false positions.

> Dinner passed in a whirl of faces and voices. The old boys ate together, and at our table the conversation was so shy and silent that I felt at home by contrast and asked rather too many questions of the master at the end about the prowess of the football team and the chances this year.
>
> That night I slept in a riot of gorgeous dreams after a happy thinking spell in bed. Here was a field with a fair start, I thought with something to work for. First, I must be a good athlete, and then I must be popular and be one of the big boys who evidently slouched insolently through their sixth form year above all criticism and restraint. Alas! I had forgotten my handicaps, forgotten all kindly advice about laying low and keeping quiet for two weeks.

What is happening here is that the youthful self-confidence, or egocentricity is represented as a state of innocence and, just as surely as the large animals overcame the smaller ones, the world will wear down youthful exuberance. Since the mature Palms is telling his own story, the tone must imply a sad inevitability. He, of course, possesses all the details of the complete story. His point of view, gained after all the disappointments will, necessarily, colour all the incidents. This accounts for the predominantly sad note in the many recollections of childhood. It is present, for example, in the following piece. However, the pathos is generated by reason of the subsuming but implicit point of view that youth's innocent confidence – the way it looks 'mistily at the world' will inevitably be eroded.

> One night when with Nancy Collum from St. Paul, I sat in a swaying motor-boat by the club-house pier, and while the moon beat out golden scales on the water, heard young Byron Kirby propose to Mary Cooper in the motor-boat ahead. It was entirely accidental, but after it had commenced wild horses could not have dragged Nancy and me from the scene. We sat there fascinated. Kirby was an ex-Princeton athlete and Mary Cooper

was the popular debutante of the year. Kirby had a fine sense of form and when at the end of his manly pleading she threw her arms about his neck and hid her face in his coat, Nancy and I unconsciously clung together in delight. It is a bond between us to this day that we heard that proposal. For the next month we mentally tiptoed over oceans of other people's sentiment . . . My enthusiasm knew no bounds, and I was all for becoming engaged to almost anyone immediately.

The interesting feature here is the relationship between, on the one hand the narrator and the reader and, on the other, the narrator and his earlier self. In the latter case there is a distance between the two because the mature narrator's view point has already been formed; he now knows that life is not like this moonlight-and-proposal scene enacted by the season's best girl and the season's best boy. The narrative tone assumes this knowledge in the reader too. The result is that narrator and reader share a patronising smile at youth's sentimentality. Palms' 'enthusiasm' will, it is implied, be modified by experience.

This complex role which is required of the narrator has escaped the attention of Fitzgerald's biographical critics. This is almost certainly because of a predisposition to see his early attempts at writing as his way of learning about himself. It is on this basis that biographical criticism decides that the surviving fragments of the second draft of *The Romantic Egotist*, 'are especially valuable as biographical material'.[5] However, as even a brief indication of the contents of those five chapters show, there is evidence that Fitzgerald possessed at least a rudimentary point of view which served as a principle of selection. Although the evidence is fragmentary, there is sufficient to indicate that the emotional experiences were being organised so as to point up the concept of an inevitable and ubiquitous 'wearing-down power' which operates almost as a law of the universe. That Stephen Palms was intended to come to understand this as a mature 'point of view' is apparent in explicit comment at the opening of the work, and, equally importantly, in the implicit conclusions to be drawn from his various experiences. Overall, the tone of the narration, as befits the one who has learned the sad truth by experience, supports the truth of 'the wearing-down power' concept. Since the evidence of *The Romantic Egotist* suggests the centrality of this concept, it would be very surprising if the novel which finally emerged as the third working of the material was so different in that it was based upon a different point of view.

II

Despite the indications within *The Romantic Egotist* that Fitzgerald had reached at least one level of understanding about his life at Princeton, Mizener claims that the stories written between the summers of 1917 and 1919 were the products of a search for understanding. It is illuminating to place this claim beside a consideration of one story which Fitzgerald wrote at Princeton during that time, bearing in mind some of the details of *The Romantic Egotist*. It is hard to resist the conclusion that rather than representing a 'seeking to understand his life',[6] it represents the fruits of his understanding. That is to say, he did not discover a meaning by studying the story; he was able to write the story because he already possessed an understanding.

The relevant story first appeared in the Nassau Literary Magazine in February, 1917 under the title 'The Spire and the Gargoyle'. The story was clearly an important one for Fitzgerald since it became incorporated into *The Romantic Egotist* and, in a considerably modified form, plays a significant part in *This Side of Paradise*.[7]

The story as published in the Nassau Literary Magazine was made up of three parts. In the first part, the protagonist is identified simply as 'the boy'. He is first seen lying on the damp grass outside the examination room. He fears that he has failed to achieve a passing grade in an examination he has just taken. He considers the possibility of arranging with the young invigilator for an opportunity to make good his likely failure. The instructor refuses these overtures. 'The boy' then sees in his imagination how the Gothic spire of the university symbolises his 'ideal', while the instructor's bespectacled face suggests the image of a gargoyle who holds 'his destiny' in unsympathetic hands.[8] Part 2 deals with an occasion, five years later, when the protagonist – now designated only by the pronoun 'he' – has a chance meeting with the 'gargoyle'. Both of them have suffered the defeat of hope: the instructor left Princeton to teach in a Brooklyn High School for a higher salary; and the young man is still searching 'for something to cling to'.[9] Part 3 sees the protagonist – now called 'the man' –

revisiting Princeton. Coincidentally, the 'gargoyle' is also making a return visit. This time the spire's symbolism is debilitating rather than inspiring and 'the man' cries out 'from a complete overwhelming sense of failure'. He realises that he is outside it all. 'The gargoyle, poor tired little hack, was bound up in the fabric of the whole system much more than he was or ever could be.'[10] The story ends on this note of dejection.

Mizener's interpretation of this story illustrates the distorting power of the biographical approach. Completely without warrant from the actual text he makes the spire symbolise a social rather than an academic ideal. He then continues: 'The point of the story is the absurd irony of a superior person like Fitzgerald finding himself at the mercy of this academic worm.'[11] This distortion occurs because Mizener is attempting to use the literature to explain the life. It is a vital part of his thesis that Fitzgerald had to write in order that he might fully understand his real-life experiences. Consequently, against the whole thrust of Fitzgerald's story and in pursuit of the idea of the dominance of Fitzgerald's ambitions, the spire becomes the symbol 'for the romance of social success'.[12] Interesting as this interpretation might be to a biographical critic, in fact the story illustrates an even more interesting point. In the third section of the story, Fitzgerald places 'the man' back before the towers and spires of Princeton on another 'typical' night 'very like the night' with its intimations of failure of the first section. However, this time the atmosphere is 'somehow less full and less poignant'. The passage then continues: 'Inevitability became a reality and assumed an atmosphere of compelling and wearing down.'[13] This, pace Mizener, is the true 'point of the story'. In this early story Fitzgerald makes explicit the concept which governed the choice and presentation of his material. It is his handling of this concept when he adapted the story for incorporation into *This Side of Paradise* rather than biographical speculations about the way it was derived which should be the concern of the literary critic.

In this respect, the eventual qualification for *This Side of Paradise* of the original story's pessimistic fatalism is of special interest. In the first version of 'The Spire and the Gargoyle', the protagonist's concluding realisation of his own 'complete sense of failure' as compared with his ex-instructor's secure place in the establishment produces a dejection which is allowed no alleviation. 'The man' gets on the train which will return him to New York and the story ends with this sentence. 'Wearily he sank onto a redplush seat, and pressed his hot forehead against the damp window pane.'[14] Here the dampness is an ironic reminder of the way 'the damp grass by the sun-dial'[15] had cooled the boy's eyes and cleared his vision for the perception of the symbolism of the spire. The train is now returning him to New York's 'tepid, stuffy environment' and 'the dingy middle class cloud that hovered on his boarding house'.[16] The 'damp window pane' is a poor substitute for Princeton's dews. Through a competent use of contrast between the 'hot and stuffy'[17] atmosphere of the outer world and the cool 'ideal'[18] of Princeton, the story moves to an effective conclusion involving an ironic image. The boy's self-identification with 'the spirit of spires and towers'[19] gives way to an ironic baptism into a drab material world. This is the deeply pessimistic note on which the story ends.

The crucial error to which biographical speculation is prone is to explain this gloom in terms of Fitzgerald's own sense of failure at Princeton. If that explanation is accepted, then indeed the tragic tone of the story does seem excessive and self-indulgent. But such an explanation also devalues the 'wearing-down' concept which alone explains the sense of tragedy about the story. Even at the moment when the boy feels closest to the spirit of Princeton the 'inevitability' of his failure is implicit in his perception. It is this sense of the boy's helplessness in the face of an inexorable law which heightens the emotion and suggests a tragic dimension. It is clear that, at the time of writing 'The Spire and the Gargoyle' Fitzgerald was working from a very pessimistic point of view. It is also clear that the technique by which this view was presented involved the use of ironic symbolism.

Some idea of the way that pessimistic view was modified for *This Side of Paradise* can be given by considering Fitzgerald's 'view of life' as he expressed it just three months after the publication of *This Side of Paradise*. In reply to a letter from President Hibben of Princeton University which had criticised the portrayal of the University in that work, Fitzgerald first blames his own temperament for producing a 'cynical' picture and then says: 'My view of life, President Hibben, is the view of the Theodore Dreisers and Joseph Conrads – that life is too strong and remorseless for the sons of men.'[20] At this point it is useful to consider the evidence for Fitzgerald's early knowledge of Mencken's work. Although Fitzgerald disclaimed any conscious debt to Mencken in regard to *This*

Side of Paradise,[21] this expression of his 'view of life' reveals a curious affinity to some of Mencken's words.

In an essay on Theodore Dreiser contained in his *Book of Prefaces,* published in 1916, Mencken attempts to show the similarities between 'the general ideas' of Dreiser and 'the fundamental assumptions' of Conrad. He does this by means of a quotation from Hugh Walpole: '"Conrad," says Walpole, "is of the firm and resolute conviction that life is too strong, too clever and too remorseless for the sons of men."'[22] Fitzgerald, of course, could have taken his sentence directly from Walpole, but his departure from Walpole's original text points strongly to Mencken's influence. In order to be more precise about Dreiser's view Mencken added his own comment to Walpole's assertion.

> Substitute the name of Dreiser for that of Conrad, and you will have to change scarcely a word. Perhaps one, to wit, 'clever'. I suspect that Dreiser, writing so of his own creed, would be tempted to make it 'stupid,' or, at all events, 'unintelligible.'[23]

Fitzgerald's own omission of 'clever' in the Hibben letter is, therefore, interesting. It would suggest an earlier acquaintance with what he termed for Hibben a 'cynical' view than that suggested by Edmund Wilson. More to the point, however, is the fact that the description of the strength and remorseless aspect of life is a good definition of the 'wearing-down power' which had been so important in Fitzgerald's early writings. And, indeed, Dreiser's view of the world's dullness is echoed in Palms' attitude when he summarises a large part of *The Romantic Egotist* as showing, 'how I looked mistily at the world, and how the world gazed stupidly at me'.[24] This, in fact, is an important aspect of the 'wearing-down power' as it operates in *The Romantic Egotist.* Fitzgerald gives no hint of a 'clever' strategy behind the remorseless power: the power, if not stupid, seems to be indifferent in its operation.

There is a further important aspect of Fitzgerald's point of view in those early days which can also be associated with Walpole's essay on Conrad. Although it is most likely that Fitzgerald read the Mencken essay which summarises Walpole after he had written *This Side of Paradise,* there is little doubt that he would see his own attitude to life mirrored in that which Walpole attributed to Dreiser.

It is as though, from some high window, looking down, he were able to watch some shore, from whose security men were forever launching little cockleshell boats upon a limitless and angry sea . . . From his height he can follow their fortunes, their brave struggles, their fortitude to the very end. He admires their courage, the simplicity of their faith, but his irony springs from his knowledge of the inevitable end.[25]

This is a good description of Fitzgerald's authorial position in 'The Spire and the Gargoyle'. In that story, the inevitability of the ultimate failure is implicit from the beginning: the reader is aware of this and also, more poignantly, the boy is becoming aware of it too. As Walpole says, it is the suggestion of 'the inevitable end' which produces the irony. And, in the case of *The Romantic Egotist*, all the material tended towards a fatalistic pessimism. It is that pessimism which forms the basis of the point of view towards which the 'juvenile indexes' were pointing. Oddly enough, in view of Wilson's later estimate, the phrase 'ironical pessimism' is quite apt.

In the sense that Fitzgerald had believed in the inevitable disappointment of all optimistic expectations, it would be quite correct to describe his attitude as 'cynical'. It would, however, be misleading to use that term in connection with the point of view which created *This Side of Paradise*. The third rewrite of the material from *The Romantic Egotist* had the advantage of a less limiting viewpoint. Yet it would be wrong to suppose that the early fatalism had been the chief obstacle preventing a successful draft. Of the two critical factors which caused Fitzgerald most difficulty when trying to assemble the material for *The Romantic Egotist*, the 'cynical' viewpoint was the one less likely to prove too much for him: it was his decision to use the first person narrator which, as a method of expressing that philosophy, proved too difficult.

As his comment on the 'juvenile indexes' shows, Fitzgerald elected to use an indirect way of indicating the progress of his central character's perceptions. In the case of 'The Spire and the Gargoyle' his method works very well. In Walpole's image, the omniscient author watches from his 'high window' the brave struggle of his character, and the ultimate failure is implicit from the very beginning. The reader is aware of two levels of perception: the character's and the author's. The irony is increased by the impression that the boy possesses a reluctant knowledge of the inevitable end too. In the more ambitious attempt to create this double level of meaning in *The Romantic Egotist*, Fitzgerald created patterns of action for his central character which would allow the reader to perceive the inevitable final failure but, since he chose a first person narrative, he greatly increased the difficulty of creating an ironic distance between himself and Stephen Palms. This complicated the erection of the vital inner structure. The problem was already big enough because, unlike Huck Finn's unsophisticated innocence, Palms' egocentricity is not readily placed against an authorial scale of values. Huck's innocence provides a measure of society's corruptions: Palms' egocentricity does not start with that advantage and, as the previously quoted excerpts show, Fitzgerald fails to suggest another norm by which Palms' bursts of egocentricity can be measured. The patterning of experience in the outer structure of the narrative goes some way in this direction because it does establish Palms' own sense of hurt in his regular defeats, but, again, unlike Huck Finn, it is necessary for Fitzgerald's character to advance in his level of perception, and, for that, the kind of ironic distancing achieved in 'The Spire and the Gargoyle' is necessary.

III

Fitzgerald's early ability to handle irony so as to suggest a tragic inevitability is shown in another story written during this period. 'Sentiment – and the Use of Rouge' was written within a few months of 'The Spire and the Gargoyle' and published in June of 1917.[26] This story links the behaviour of a contemporary young lady with the realities of service on the battlefields of France in the First World War. However, the central feature is the parallel between Lieutenant Syneforth's actual death in the trenches and his metaphorical death when he suddenly perceives the destruction of his simple faith in older notions of morality. By the end of the story, the inevitability of the victory of 'the grey creed of a new materialistic world',[27] has been realised in the tragic ending. As in the case of 'The Spire and the Gargoyle', the distance between the youthful ideals and harsh realities is suggested by an ironic image. Here it is the linking of rouge and blood. As in 'The Spire and the Gargoyle', the image increases the sense of misery; its effect is not cathartic. The controlling viewpoint was indeed a pessimistic fatalism.

In a story called 'The Pierian Springs and the Last Straw',[28] the irony is more complex and there is subsequently a significant modification in the idea of tragedy. The story concerns the narrator's Uncle George. The manner of presentation suggests that he is rather a figure of fun. The family think of him as dissolute. He 'had been engaged seven times and drank ever so much more than was good for him'. Although he had written several fairly successful novels, according to the narrator, none of them 'were quite good'. Uncle George tells his nephew that a failed romance had provoked the dissolute life style. Like Lieutenant Syneforth, he too had suffered a metaphorical death. 'My life stopped at twenty-one one night in October at sixteen minutes after ten.' After this information they meet the lady who had caused all the trouble. She is now a widow and she treats Uncle George's obvious devotion with great contempt, imagining she can say anything to him. However, she goes too far and in a moment of anger he stamps her wedding ring 'into a beaten button of gold'. Uncle and nephew then leave. That, however, is not the end of the story. Unlike 'The Spire and the Gargoyle' and 'Sentiment – and the Use of Rouge', the story is not one of unqualified misery. In this story, Fitzgerald's ironic point of view moves the emotion into another perspective to indicate an interesting notion of tragedy as experienced on the domestic level of everyday life.

> The story ought to end here. My Uncle George should remain with Mark Anthony and De Musset as a rather tragic semi-genius, ruined by a woman. Unfortunately the play continues into an inartistic sixth act where it topples over and descends like Uncle George himself in one of his more inebriated states, contrary to all the rules of dramatic literature.

The climax of Uncle George's decisive moment is followed by the anti-climax of respectable married life. He married the girl he had loved for so long, and his life style changed. 'Uncle George never drank again, nor did he ever write or in fact do anything except play a middling amount of golf and get comfortably bored with his wife.'[29]

The basic ironic point is suggested in the title's reference to the Pierian Springs. The legend, of course, tells of the place where

Pegasus, the winged horse, refreshed himself at the cool waters of the Hippocrene fountain. It was there that Bellerophon caught and broke the marvellous creature. The context for Uncle George's story is, therefore, the legendary one in which divine refreshment leads to a harnessing and domination. Fitzgerald has heightened the contrast between Pegasus and Uncle George, partly by the familial 'Uncle' – and partly by the implied family disapproval heard so clearly behind the idea that he 'drank ever so much more than was good for him'. However, Uncle George's contemporary domestic tragedy is not laughed away by this comparison: rather is it rendered more powerfully. This is because of the feeling of inevitability which is invoked. Even Pegasus was caught and tamed, so great is the 'wearing-down power'. Uncle George's more mundane capabilities are subject to the same inexorable force. His story testifies to the truth contained in the ancient legend that the source of power is also the means of enchainment.

There are several interesting factors about this story which makes use of an 'inartistic sixth act' and a young lady who inspires obsessive and life-long devotion, but at this point the relevant fact is that as early as 1917 Fitzgerald was creating a story on the basis of a rather sophisticated ironic point of view. Both 'Sentiment – and the Use of Rouge' and 'The Spire and the Gargoyle' end on the kind of tragic note which the narrator of 'The Pierian Springs and the Last Straw' would describe as recognising 'the rules of dramatic literature'. For the story of Uncle George, the narrator insists on a realistic – that is to say an 'inartistic' – setting. This intrusion of real life with its unfortunate habit of 'toppling over' like a drunk has the effect of universalising the central truth of the Pierian myth. It achieves this effect by locating the idea of the common origin of freedom and subjugation within the perspective of modern marriage. The ultimate realisation of Uncle George's fondest hopes is also a kind of death. His only real life had followed his broken romance. That failure had produced successful novels and an extremely eventful social life. In other words, the time of his greatest disappointment had been the spur to his greatest achievement. The narrator leaves no room to doubt that Uncle George would have been better off without the success of his romantic hopes. The story ends with the following sentence. 'You see I claim that if Dante had ever won – but a hypothetical sixth act is just as untechnical as a real one.'[30]

This insistence upon a real-life ending is extremely illuminating.

It reveals that Fitzgerald's point of view is based upon two fundamental opinions which he attributes to the narrator. First, there is the idea that even Dante's literary genius as well as Uncle George's was better served by the frustration of expectation than by success. Secondly, and even more fundamentally, life – as distinct from 'dramatic literature' or other hypotheses – will never allow the first condition to operate within the perspective of conventional literary tragedy. Together, these opinions form a point of view which could reasonably be described in Edmund Wilson's later phrase 'ironical-pessimistic'. It is pessimistic because it believes in the inevitability of failure, and ironical because it inverts conventional standards of success and failure.

This is the sense in which 'life is too strong and remorseless for the sons of men'. This is the point of view towards which the 'wearing-down power' remorselessly and mindlessly tends. It is the knowledge of this which gives the narrator in 'The Pierian Springs and the Last Straw' his ironical position. The important aspect of this point of view lies not in biographical speculations about *how* Fitzgerald had reached this position by late 1916 or early 1917 but rather in the novelistic use to which he put it. In this respect its operation as the organising principle for the third rewrite of the material of *The Romantic Egotist* is quite evident.

In the original version the story concludes with the ironic image of a baptism into the real world of the depressing commercialism of New York. That image had confirmed the impression that this was a tragic fate for the young man. The irony was dramatic irony in that the reader becomes aware of the ultimate failure from the very beginning. In the novel's version, the notion that life will not allow the individual the kind of tragic destiny open to literary figures is strongly in evidence. It is this changed notion regarding the actual circumstances of inevitable failures which most accounts for the changes in the two versions of the story. The change in the symbolism from the ironic baptism to the dripping rains reinforces the point: the dampness is now a pointer to something more fundamental than the reality of depressing New York; it symbolises a remorseless erosion of illusion to the point where the 'Pierian Springs' viewpoint is eventually perceived.

In this sense 'A Damp Symbolic Interlude' is characteristic of *This Side of Paradise*. Each incident in Fitzgerald's 'pile of detail' is organised so as to be an index to that final 'ironical-pessimistic' viewpoint. Each incident has at its core that 'inspiring secret', in

Conradian terms, by which all its details are given meaning. Such was Fitzgerald's attempt and, as such, it created a novel of selection rather than of saturation.

IV

The process can be well illustrated by noting the changes which 'The Spire and the Gargoyle' experienced in becoming assimilated into the novel. The original story as published in the *Nassau Literary Magazine* was some ten pages long. In its final form in the published novel where it appears under the heading 'A Damp Symbolic Interlude' it consists of only two pages. Its influence, however, extends over a far greater area than this implies.

Length apart, the most obvious change for the second version is the removal of the settled gloom of the 'young man'. In the novel, instead of his awareness of 'a complete overwhelming sense of failure', there is only a premonition of a later awareness of inadequacy.

More particularly, the conclusion of the revised version reveals the same kind of awareness of life's pathetic tendencies as that which characterises Uncle George's story. Although the novel's version retains the association of dignity and melancholy beauty with Princeton's Gothic architecture, this young man's solemn moment of insight is punctured by mundane reality.

> 'Oh, God!' he cried suddenly, and started at the sound of his voice in the stillness. The rain dripped on. A minute longer he lay without moving, his hands clinched. Then he sprang to his feet and gave his clothes a tentative pat.
> 'I'm very damn wet!' he said aloud to the sundial.[31]

V

Fitzgerald's decision to drop his attempts to tell the story of *The Romantic Egotist* in the first person was the crucial factor in resolving the narrative difficulties. The complications which followed the attempt to express an ironic philosophy by means of an ironic technique were formidable. When Stephen Palms spoke it was not always possible to appreciate whether a particular level of naïvety was being articulated. The introduction of the omniscient author made it possible for there to be an ironic distance between the protagonist's viewpoint and the author's own. The reader is aware of this and thus the double structure of inner and outer story-lines is much more apparent. In the following passage, for example, Amory's conceit is well expressed without the author making an explicit statement.

> Amory wondered how people could fail to notice that he was a boy marked for glory, and when faces of the throng turned toward him and ambiguous eyes stared into his, he assumed the most romantic of expressions and walked on the air cushions that lie on the asphalts of fourteen.[32]

Unfortunately, Fitzgerald's basically ironic technique imposes a further level of meaning upon that easily appreciated one regarding the distance between author and protagonist. The fundamental irony upon which the whole book is constructed is that Amory is indeed to be thought of as 'a boy marked for glory', *but not in the way Amory at first imagines*.

In this sense, and depending upon the reader's own prejudices against egotism, the gap between author and character in the above passage, might not be very great. Although the narrative tone seems to invite the reader to smile at Amory's misconception, in fact the humour implicit in the authorial stance is derived from the belief that Amory was indeed correct in his sense of a glorious destiny; it was his perception of the basis for this sense which was wrong. In other words Fitzgerald prepares a similar trap for the reader as did Jane Austen with the opening sentence of *Pride and Prejudice*. The reader's own prejudices condition the ways in which the story is read. In Austen's case the issue concerns the idea of money in the marriage chase: in Fitzgerald's case it is the idea of egocentricity in the adventure of life. It has been Fitzgerald's misfortune to have been misread rather more consistently than Austen.

The problem of appreciating the levels of irony has, of course, been compounded by the unwillingness of Fitzgerald's critics to admit the possibility that he was intelligent enough to construct his first published novel upon such a principle. However, a careful study of its construction will show that it has a consistent pattern-ing of action along the outer story line which is so essential if the inner story line is to be seen to reach the final ironic truth first apparent in the story of Uncle George. In addition, the careful organisation of imagery of travel and music points to the existence of a dominating point of view which gives coherence to all the 'pile of detail'.

VI

Essentially, then, Fitzgerald's method in *This Side of Paradise* was to make use of an indirect, that is to say, ironic method of showing his protagonist's inner journey towards his glorious destiny. The key to an appreciation of Amory's progress will be seen to lie in the concept of egocentricity, and, in that respect, the apparent distance between author and character must be treated cautiously. Howev-er, just as in 'The Pierian Springs and the Last Straw' and the early version of 'The Spire and the Gargoyle', the imagery is so arranged as to leave no doubt of the author's intention. In particular, in *This Side of Paradise* the imagery of roads to be travelled is quite unambiguous in its indirect commentary upon Amory's intellec-tual and moral position. The point can be illustrated by further reference to the use made of the spires and gargoyle material.

The first version of that story created opposing symbolism. The spire of Princeton symbolised the boy's 'perception' of an 'ideal', and the script-marker, in related imagery, was a gargoyle which symbolised the 'inevitability' of Amory's failure. In *This Side of Paradise* the original title is made to cover the whole of section two of the first book. This deals with Amory's first experiences of and reactions to Princeton and takes him up to his romantic affair with Isabelle, 'the crest of his young egotism'.[33] The novel's version of the story drops the script-marker and with him goes his role as an important symbol of fate.

So why did Fitzgerald retain the idea of the opposition inherent in the title 'Spires and Gargoyles'? The answer is that Amory and the other undergraduates are the gargoyles in this version. Throughout this section of the novel, Princeton as an ideal is powerfully present. The undergraduates themselves are transient figures who play out their little games and then disappear.

However, as far as Amory is concerned, his gargoyle-like role is reinforced by imagery which reveals his lack of progress towards his destiny. The idea of drifting and dreaming is carefully present in this section of the novel. For example, his reaction to Princeton's architecture shows a lack of purpose: 'the spirit of spires and towers made him dreamily acquiescent.'[34] And although earlier in this section, Amory's ambitions force him to say that unlike Kerry he 'can't drift', that is exactly what he comes to do. By the careful use of this kind of imagery Fitzgerald clearly indicates the emptiness of Amory's life at Princeton.

> Amory thought of sophomore spring as the happiest time of his life. His ideas were in tune with life as he found it; he wanted no more than to drift and dream and enjoy a dozen new-found friendships through the April afternoons.[35]

This method of showing Amory's lost purpose results in a series of what might be called negative experiences. These are, in the imagery of travel, designed to show how far Amory has strayed from the true path of his development.

The various activities which make Amory's college life seem happy include his posing as a literary intellectual, his success with the Triangle Club, his romance with Isabelle and his satisfaction at gaining election to Cottage Club. In fact the true guide to the value of these successes is the growing boredom and ennui which induces Amory to neglect his work and spend the hot and lazy days and the dreamy evenings of June simply talking and not worrying about exams. Fitzgerald supplies a serious moral perspective for this drifting and dreaming by extending the idea of travel. The horrific climax is, of course, the death of Dick Humbird in a car crash. Fitzgerald's presentation of the events leading up to this climax should leave no doubt about the way the undergraduates' boorish behaviour is to be measured. The incident begins in a seaside escapade which involves the stealing of a meal and it continues in a bad joke concerning the humiliation of a girl picked up on the boardwalk. The vocabulary which describes Amory's reaction to that piece of unpleasantness is interesting in the light of what follows. 'Amory was content to sit and watch the by-play, thinking what a light touch Kerry had, and how he could transform the barest incident into a thing of curve and contour.'[36] The adventure continues through unfunny jokes of further stealings from restaurants and a cinema until rides are hitched back to Princeton.

Fitzgerald has Amory sense the unsatisfactory nature of this kind of happiness. 'It's just that I feel so sad these wonderful nights. I sort of feel they're never coming again, and I'm not really getting all I could out of them.'[37] Even his love affair with Isabelle is shown to be part of his pose; indulged in because it was a part of the personality he was trying to project. At this time he is still convinced that Princeton is teaching him an important social lesson. On a late-night bicycle ride out of Princeton he tells Tom, 'Princeton invariably gives the thoughtful man a social sense.'[38] But Fitzgerald inserts a reminder of the transiency of undergraduate experience when he has Amory notice the noon-time gatherings of the alumni. 'Amory looked long at one house which bore the legend "Sixty-nine." There a few gray-haired men sat and talked quietly while the classes swept by in a panorama of life.'[39] Such a description makes it hard to avoid the conclusion that Fitzgerald is making a moral comment upon Amory's lack of purposive movement. The whole framework of this second section, dominated as it is by the symbolism of spires and gargoyles and images of drifting and dreaming, clearly suggests this conclusion. However, the point is unavoidable in the climax of the car crash. The incident occurs in the episode called 'Under the Arc-Light' and, indeed, the stark light of reality glares upon Amory.

True to symbolism of journeying, it is quite fitting that Amory should have been in the car which was following Humbird: the car which lost its way. Humbird, who had been one of the chief influences on that seaside incident 'of curve and contour', lost control of the car at what Ferrenby calls 'this damn curve' and now lies in ugly reality. A 'heavy white mass' which irresistibly recalls the idea of a gargoyle, is all that remains of the charm and personality of Humbird. In this context of heavy symbolism, the last sentence of the section is itself a comment upon the kind of waste which the lives of gargoyles represent. 'Amory stepped outside the door and shivered slightly at the late night wind – a wind that stirred a broken fender on the mass of bent metal to a plaintive, tinny sound.'[40]

The effectiveness of this important episode in Amory's moral development derives mainly from Fitzgerald's use of imagery; in particular in the bringing together of three main images, each of which is designed to show how far Amory's behaviour is removed from an idea of correct development. The three combine powerfully to make a climax. First, casting their influence over the whole series of Princeton incidents are the towers and spires of the university: a silent reminder of the ugliness, 'transiency and unimportance of the campus figures'.[41] Second, within the basic image of travel, the mental and moral torpor which is the effect of drifting and dreaming is made horrifyingly apparent by Humbird's 'grotesque and squalid' corpse. Thirdly, and most subtly, the 'plaintive' note of the broken fender fits most appropriately into a careful structure of musical associations within the novel by means of which Fitzgerald suggests a true perception of reality.

The importance of the musical associations is seen quite early in the novel. Amory is presented as being occasionally aware of the true note. It is the sound he hears on his first night at Princeton.

> The early moon had drenched the arches with pale blue, and, weaving over the night, in and out of the gossamer rifts of moon, swept a song, a song with more than a hint of sadness, infinitely transient, infinitely regretful.[42]

Even during the time of his closest involvement with the unpleasant 'fun' in the beach episode, the evening sea at Asbury gives Amory the sense of an underlying 'infinitely sorrowful' music.[43] In contrast to this sad music, Fitzgerald places the contemporary sounds of the undergraduates at the cinema as they stamp, whistle and sing to a song called 'By the Sea'.

> Oh-h-h-h-h
> She works in a Jam Factoree
> And – that-may-be-all-right
> But you can't-fool-me
> For I know-DAMN-WELL
> That she DON'T-make-jam-all-night!
> Oh-h-h-h![44]

Similarly, the activities of the Triangle Club as it struggles to get a typical musical comedy into production – 'Ha-Ha Hortense' – are placed in a perspective which suggests moral triviality in the same degree as musical triviality which is itself measured by its distance from the underlying 'infinitely sorrowful' music of humanity. It is this use of musical associations which gives depth of meaning to the 'tinny-sound' which signals the end of one particular road for Amory and forms the basis for his first 'bouleversement'.[45] Throughout the whole novel, Fitzgerald makes consistent use of this kind of musical imagery. However, the basic image of travel is always present, clearly indicating Amory's wavering sense of purpose. Fitzgerald expresses the change which Humbird's death started in Amory in these terms. Amory is brought back from his drifting. 'Amory was enjoying college immensely again. The sense of going forward in a direct, determined line had come back.'[46] However, before Amory can achieve this strong sense of purpose he has to undergo a further horror. This, of course, involves the apparition of the devil.

In order fully to appreciate Fitzgerald's purpose in introducing the devil episodes, it is necessary to be clear about the fact that his basic method of showing Amory's moral position was to place him at the negative end of images, thus illustrating the wide gap between ideal and actuality. Amory's progress therefore, is to be charted through a series of negative experiences. The cumulative effect of his weak behaviour – ugly 'fun', wrong roads taken, wrong notes heard – is seen in a crisis at which time Amory is forced to reconsider his position. In this respect it is most important to recall that Amory always has a sense of his own great potential.

Of course, the reader might feel that the youthful belief in the capacity for 'infinite expansion for good or evil'[47] is part of youth's illusion of Self; nevertheless, Fitzgerald makes this a key factor in Amory's progress. It is that which allows him to go forward immediately after the death of Humbird. It is that sense of his own glorious destiny which makes credible the movement, albeit through negative experiences, towards a path which will (most nearly) match his sense of true Self. This notion of progress requires Fitzgerald to suggest the inner reality before outlining the details of a correspondingly adequate behaviour in the real world. Consequently, by illustrating the kinds of attitudes which Amory had to reject, Fitzgerald aimed to clear the way for Amory to be equipped with the essential inner knowledge which would guide him through the outer world of actuality. This method of working can be seen clearly in the way Fitzgerald builds up to the devil climax after the death of Humbird.

The key point at the centre of the appearance of the devil is what

Fitzgerald calls in the letter from Monsignor Darcy the 'woman proposition'. It would seem that of all the experiences which distract Amory from his true path, his involvement with the opposite sex is the most dangerous. However, once again, the saving grace is something at the centre of his true self which allows him moments of perception. Darcy calls it the 'half-miraculous sixth sense by which you detect evil'[48] and it is no accident that has Fitzgerald relate this 'woman proposition' to notions of evil. It is no accident because it is one of the book's most persistent themes. It is that 'sixth sense' which operates in the early encounter with Myra in the incident entitled 'A Kiss for Amory'. As early as this in the book Fitzgerald is illustrating Amory's instinctive awareness of the wrong paths. Amory's 'disgust, loathing for the whole incident',[49] i.e. the kiss with Myra, might seem at first to be excessive but Fitzgerald is demonstrating a principle: Amory cannot easily ignore the promptings of his inner self; if he succumbs to temptation and follows the wrong path, then, inevitably, the reckoning will be extremely uncomfortable. His attitude to Myra was dictated by vanity and curiosity: clearly she represents a turning away from his true purpose.

If Amory's reaction to Myra's kiss seems excessive, an incident which takes place a little later involving a similar adolescent idea of romance seems, at first glance, to be presented in a tone of indulgent humour in that the attitude is only to be expected in adolescence. The episode concerns the 'Incident of the Wonderful Girl' in the play 'The Little Millionaire'. As in the incident in *The Romantic Egotist* where Byron Kirby proposes to Mary Cooper,[50] here the narrative tone seems to imply a smile of indulgence at youth's dreams of moonlight and romance. However, in this book, the careful structure of imagery which symbolises a turning aside from the true development, offers clear evidence that the incident is to be seen as marking a decline in Amory. Even in this event of apparently harmless pleasure, Fitzgerald's use of music in association with contemporary sounds and sights fixes the scene in the perspective which anticipates the appearance of the devil. In particular, a sentence like the following is a clear indication that Amory has been seduced by a false tune.

When they walked down the aisle of the theatre, greeted by the nervous twanging and discord of untuned violins and the

sensuous, heavy fragrance of paint and powder, he moved in a
sphere of epicurean delight.

Clearly, 'the languorous magic melody' of the wonderful tune
sung by the tenor:

> Oh – you – wonderful girl,
> What a wonderful girl you are –
> . . .
> All – your – wonderful words
> Thrill me through –

is more closely related to the undergraduate song about the girl
who worked in the 'Jam Factoree' than the 'infinitely sorrowful'
music of which Amory is sometimes aware. Just as clearly, the
association of the popular music with 'the sensuous, heavy fragrance of paint and powder' suggests that the senses are drugged,
that the attraction is for something bogus. 'The last scene was laid
on a roof-garden, and the 'cellos sighed to the musical moon, while
light adventure and facile froth-like comedy flitted back and forth
in the calcium.'[51]
Such a description might just fit into the category of indulgent
mockery of Amory's youthful notions of life and romance were it
not for the fact that it is part of a careful patterning of negative
experiences. Amory has succumbed to the debilitating attractions
of the artificial. Fitzgerald expresses Amory's faulty perception by
concentrating upon the triviality of the glamour.

> They wandered on, mixing in the Broadway crowd, dreaming on
> the music that eddied out of the cafés. New faces flashed on and
> off like myriad lights, pale or rouged faces, tired, yet sustained
> by a weary excitement. Amory watched them in fascination.[52]

After this, Amory's state of mind is indicated by his mood of
'dreamy content', his thoughts are dominated by the patently
unreal ideas generated by his New York experiences. Significantly,
Fitzgerald signals the divergence from the true by emphasising the
kind of music which accompanies the dreaming.

> Many nights he lay there dreaming awake of secret cafés in Mont
> Martre, where ivory women delved in romantic mysteries with

diplomats and soldiers of fortune, while orchestras played Hungarian waltzes and the air was thick and exotic with intrigue and moonlight and adventure.[53]

It is this mood, this kind of perception, which takes Amory to Princeton. In that state of mind, although dimly aware that the true note of moonlight beauty is a sad one and that the true 'symbol of [his] perception' is a spire of Princeton University, he is seduced by the false attractions of the superficial. Faithful to these bogus notions he attempts to fit Isabelle into the dream world.

The romance with Isabelle is presented in explicit terms of game-playing but more importantly the narrative technique establishes a clear link between the Myra episode and the appearance of the devil. The 'romantic scene' with Isabelle actually takes place in the same little den in the Minnehaha Club where he kissed Myra. With Isabelle the scene parallels the scene from 'The Little Millionaire' in that a tenor is singing a popular song.

> Give me your hand –
> I'll understand
> We're off to slumberland.[54]

And the mood is, therefore, akin to his dream moods of 'moonlight and adventure'. Love, of course, is not involved. Neither of them cares deeply for the other. The kiss is prevented by the sudden entrance of others. 'Lips half parted, she turned her head to him in the dark. Suddenly the ring of voices, the sound of running footsteps surged toward them.'[55] The romance has to be continued by correspondence. On Amory's part this involves 'an eternal monotone' of self-delusion which manifests itself in letters full of moonlight and popular music.[56] However, the feature which makes the link with the later devil episode is the reference to 'the sound of running footsteps'. It is this which is later expanded to become the most frightening aspect of Amory's nightmare vision.

The devil's appearance marks a crisis point in the series of negative experiences which have carried the implicit message that Amory has been following the wrong ways, listening to the wrong music. As Fitzgerald used the concept, the devil is the visual manifestation of the 'half-miraculous sixth sense' by which Amory is able to 'detect evil'.[57] In preparation for the event, Fitzgerald gathers together 'a typical crowd' for a typical party of Amory's

New York set. In this he builds on the foundation of the moral decline made apparent in the 'Incident of the Wonderful Girl'. From the beginning of the party the terminology indicates a Bachanalian evening. They 'burst into the café like Dionysian revellers' and immediately begin ordering drinks. Fitzgerald then makes the point that most of this type of revelry is 'harmless' and Amory's party was intended to be of the kind which is indulged in really for its effect only. However, he indicates the danger of such harmless fun: 'about one-fourth continued on into the dimmer hours and gathered strange dust from strange places'.[58]

Once again, as in the unfunny clowning at the seaside, the moral point about a thin dividing line between the acceptable and the unacceptable is being made but in this case the context is very clearly that of good and evil. In this respect the use of the image of 'strange dust' to indicate the almost imperceptible accretion of moral taints is noteworthy. It is a very effective way of indicating the belief that corruption can begin without the individual being aware of its presence. In the context of Amory's experience it is important to note that this belief is used to indicate an evil which is actively engaged to entrap the unwary. Although Amory's party intends to indulge in innocent fun, they run the risk of becoming tainted with evil.

> But strange things are prepared even in the dead of night, and the unusual, which lurks least in the café, home of the prosaic and inevitable, was preparing to spoil for him the waning romance of Broadway.[59]

Later, in Phoebe's flat, Amory is the only one who sees the man from the café now transformed into an inhuman form reclining on the divan. Amory's horror is concentrated on the feet: 'They were unutterably terrible.'[60] In Amory's flight from this horror the impression is given that those feet make the sound of footsteps.

> Ten, fifteen steps away sounded the footsteps. They were like a slow dripping, with just the slightest insistence in their fall. Amory's shadow lay, perhaps, ten feet ahead of him, and soft shoes was presumably that far behind.

This reminder of the constant threat of evil personified into the notion of pursuit by a devil not only gives added meaning to the scene with Myra but is extended to give a powerful illustration of the result of prolonged, if unappreciated exposure to evil. 'Suddenly he realized that the footsteps were not behind, had never been behind, they were ahead and he was not eluding but following ... following.'[61]

This realisation in these terms fully exploits the imagery of travel and is a very effective image with which to sum up Amory's moral position at this stage in his career at Princeton. The point is made even more powerfully at the true climax of this episode when Amory is made to realise just how wrong he has been. In the final vision of horror Fitzgerald expresses Amory's moral position in terminology which makes use of the lines of meaning, already established by musical association and gargoyle symbolism.

> Then something clanged like a low gong struck at a distance, and before his eyes a face flashed over the two feet, a face pale and distorted with a sort of infinite evil that twisted it like flame in the wind; *but he knew, for the half instant that the gong tanged and hummed, that it was the face of Dick Humbird.*[62]

The realisation frees him from his immobility in the alley which is 'narrow and dark and smelling of old rottenness', and he now sees the way out. 'He started on a steady run for the light that showed the street at the other end.'[63]

In these terms, then, Fitzgerald makes plain the serious consequences which follow Amory's 'purposeless and inconsecutive' behaviour during his first months at Princeton. By a consistent use of imagery relating to travel, spires and gargoyles and with musical references occurring at strategic moments, Amory's career is presented as a stumbling movement along the road towards a dimly realised high destiny during which time he is at the mercy of every temptation along the way, guided only by instinct. The plain result of Fitzgerald's concentration on what is right or wrong for Amory is the fixing of the context as the issue of good or evil. Amory's seduction from the correct path of true development is consistently represented as a surrender to evil; the difference being one of degree only. Thus, addiction to trivial temptations such as his ambitions in Princeton's 'glittering caste system'[64] or the Triangle Club are shown as rather minor matters while his collaboration in undergraduate pranks is more serious. Fitzgerald then shows that the cumulative effect of such sidetracking is that

Amory is brought to the point of no return. It is then that the 'half-miraculous sixth sense' comes to his aid and he has a clear perception of evil. In this way Amory's career takes on the kind of interest which is inherent in a morality play. Amory's progress is not unlike the pilgrimage of Everyman except that the only helpful companion Amory has is his sixth sense; in that he appears to be specially blessed.

After Amory has recognised the devil he sees his way much more clearly. 'He had a sense of reality such as material things could never give him.'[65] In particular, he is now wary of the close association of female attraction and evil.

> As he walked into the barber-shop, intending to get a head massage, the smell of the powders and tonics brought back Axia's sidelong, suggestive smile, and he left hurriedly.

Then on the return train journey to Princeton he experiences further revulsion. 'The presence of a painted woman across the aisle filled him with a fresh burst of sickness.'[66]

At this point Fitzgerald returns to his earlier story, 'The Spire and the Gargoyle' to use some words from the last sentence. In the first version of the story the ending had contained the ironic image of a baptism into misery. In this case Amory – confirmed in the rightness of his instinct – is returning by train with clearer perceptions of the path to tread. The towers of Princeton are not now silent symbols of reproach to the aberrant gargoyle: now he greets them with relief. 'He nearly cried aloud with joy when the towers of Princeton loomed up beside him and the yellow squares of light filtered through the blue rain.'[67] Clearly, this return to Princeton is meant to be seen as a return to the right paths after the various negative experiences which have threatened to overwhelm him. In this respect, one of the epigraphs which preface the novel is applicable: 'Experience is the name so many people give to their mistakes.' Amory has progressed through a series of mistakes and failures in perception.

After his brush with the devil, Amory has a new sense of purpose. 'Amory was enjoying college immensely again. The sense of going forward in a direct, determined line had come back.'[68] But he still lacks a full knowledge of the way forward. He becomes quite dependent upon Burne Holiday, and Fitzgerald's expression clearly indicates a lack of purpose. 'Burne stood vaguely for a land

Amory hoped he was *drifting* toward.'[69] (My emphasis.) However, he does realise the danger of a possible mistake in judgement. 'Yet he sighed . . . here were other possible clay feet.'[70]

At this point Fitzgerald introduces another example of feminine attraction. In this case the young lady is entirely good. Once again Fitzgerald establishes the context of good and evil. '"Oh, Clara!" Amory said; "what a devil you could have been if the Lord had just bent your soul a little the other way!"'[71]

Amory's mistake this time is not to fall in love with evil but rather to pretend that he has fallen in love with good. In his imagination he creates a beautiful but artificial world which is quite removed from the real world he inhabits; a world growing increasingly aware of the ugliness of the First World War. The contrast is made clear by the fact that the following passage is immediately countered by details of the way war is intruding upon the Princeton scene.

> But that night seemed a night of stars and singing and Clara's bright soul still gleamed on the ways they had trod. *'Golden, golden is the air – '* he chanted to the little pools of water . . . *'Golden is the air, golden notes from golden mandolins, golden frets of golden violins.'*[72]

Although this dream world is at the other end of the scale of values in which the ugly sounds of broken fender were sounded it is just as far away from the infinitely sorrowful music of which Amory is occasionally aware. About this time in Amory's career Fitzgerald says he 'talked and dreamed'.[73] This, then, is another mistake in perception.

Book 1 ends as Amory leaves Princeton for army service. At this point, Fitzgerald's method of indicating Amory's level of development by means of association with key images is so much a part of a pattern that he is able to use this essentially indirect method to form a fitting finale to a major period of Amory's learning process. Characteristically, music plays an important part. In this instance Fitzgerald uses it to show how Amory attempts to come to terms with war and particularly with literary responses to war. He reacts strongly against his lecturer's suggestion that Swinburne's poem 'A Song in the Time of Order' could have been the real title of Tennyson's 'Locksley Hall'. Amory's own thoughts on the disruptions of the war have been conditioned partly by his own feelings:

'Germany stood for everything repugnant to him; for materialism and the direction of tremendous licentious force'[74] and he is affected by Burne's firm belief in pacifism; Burne can say: 'It seems a path spread before me.'[75] No such clear view of the way forward is available to Amory: he has yet to discover a sense of purpose; mostly he 'talked and dreamed'.[76]

He does reject Tennyson's poetry as inadequate but is unable to produce a song of his own, and his 'dissatisfaction with his lack of enthusiasm'[77] leads him to the attempt to see the contemporary world chaos in the perspective of world history, and the important first section of the novel ends with Amory and Tom consciously associating themselves with history. In a close which deliberately picks up hints from 'A Damp Symbolic Interlude' Fitzgerald again sounds the sad note which seems to symbolise man's true history and he suggests that if it were ever possible to capture 'the essence of an hour' then the true vision would contain a paradox because it would encompass 'the splendour and the sadness of the world'.[78]

Amory carries into Book 2 a sense of the sadness of the world but he arrives at this through his romance with Rosalind and, once again, Fitzgerald shows how this relationship represents a misdirection. Although Amory thinks of it as providing his second 'complete bouleversement', by means of which he 'was hurrying into line with his generation', Fitzgerald is careful to point out that the relationship moves from a spell into a trance. 'All life was transmitted into terms of their love, all experience, all desires, all ambitions, were nullified – their senses of humor crawled into corners to sleep.' Although Amory has the impression when he walks the evening streets that there is 'pageantry and carnival of rich dusk and dim streets' and that he has 'stepped into the sensuous vibrant walks of life', the vocabulary which Fitzgerald employs strongly recalls that other occasion involving the devil's footsteps.

He moved in a half-dream through the crowd as if expecting to meet Rosalind hurrying toward him with eager feet from every corner . . . How the unforgettable faces of dusk would blend to her, the myriad footsteps, a thousand overtures, would blend to her footsteps; and there would be more drunkenness than wine in the softness of her eyes on his. Even his dreams now were faint violins drifting like summer sounds upon the summer air.[79]

There are so many associations with past misdirections here that it should be impossible for the reader to think that Amory is following the correct path. His new perception of beauty must be seen in this light.

At one point Amory and Rosalind reflect in a bitter sweet mood on the transience of love and beauty, the paradox of sadness within happiness and the agony of sacrifice. At the time this seems rather like *fin de siècle* decadent posing but it is also an unwitting prophecy of the way their affair will end. Rosalind, in fact, makes the sacrifice of Amory's love because she realises that they have been merely drifting 'so like a dream'[80] and that it cannot continue. She will marry Dawson Ryder for the good and practical reason that he will allow her to stay a little girl much longer than Amory could.

> I like sunshine and pretty things and cheerfulness – and I dread responsibility. I don't want to think about pots and kitchens and brooms. I want to worry whether my legs will get slick and brown when I swim in the summer.[81]

Amory gets over the agony of the loss of Rosalind by means of a three weeks' drunken spree which is only stopped with the coming of prohibition. Although Fitzgerald shows that Amory really was in love with Rosalind he also indicates a crucial weakness at the heart of the relationship: the key to this is the issue of sentimentality.

Amory thinks of himself as a romantic and in a definition which is lifted almost verbatim from 'Sentiment – and the Use of Rouge' he claims that 'a sentimental person thinks things will last – a romantic person hopes against hope that they won't. Sentiment is emotional.'[82] The interesting difference from the earlier definition is the addition of 'against hope' which has the effect of suggesting the basic concept of the later ability of 'the first-rate intelligence' of balancing opposing ideas while retaining 'the ability to function'.[83] The point of the statement in *This Side of Paradise* is that by Amory's own definition he is a sentimental rather than a romantic person. He is the one who wants to perpetuate their emotional 'paradise of rose and flame'.[84] And although Rosalind wants to perpetuate her youth, she also has the practical sense to see that Amory's financial state will not accomplish that. At one point in his drunkenness he cries in misery for their past bitter sweet love and then luxuriates 'in an ecstasy of sentiment' before returning to his drinking.[85] Even five months after their break-up he is still affected by the Rosalind-induced sentimentality and Fitzgerald offers a measure for this state of Amory's development in the characteristic way of associative imagery. Once again the idea of a musical note is central. In this case the use of the unusual onomatopoeic 'tanging' is crucial because it so obviously recalls the way the gong 'tanged' when the Devil appeared with the face of Dick Humbird.

> *There was a tanging in the midnight air – silence was dead and sound not yet awoken – Life cracked like ice! – one brilliant note and there, radiant and pale, you stood ... and spring had broken.*[86]

In this way the sentimentalist struggles 'to immortalize the poignancy of that time'.[87] The lack of perception which has taken him down another false path is well symbolised in his inability to differentiate between the true sad note and the note of sentimental poignancy which is the keynote of his love affair with Rosalind. In addition, the wintry imagery of Amory's purple prose furthers the impression of the essential emptiness of the affair.

However, it is not only the associative imagery which indicates the true perspective that remains hidden from Amory, though it becomes increasingly apparent to the reader. At this point Fitzgerald makes explicit the divergence from what might be called the correct moral norm for Amory by reintroducing the influence of Monsignor Darcy. In a letter to Amory, Darcy gives his explanation of Amory's predicament. Darcy's view is not only entirely consistent with the thematic purpose of the imagery, it goes straight to the point of Amory's present difficulty in identifying himself as a sentimentalist or a romantic. There is a technical difficulty in this but that it exists at all is further evidence for the fact, already discernible in the structure of negative experiences, that Fitzgerald preferred to tell his story in an indirect, that is to say, an ironic way.

Although Monsignor Darcy seems to be presented as a rather amusing anachronism, he has the important role of expressing those insights which Amory has to discover through painful experience. Because of his early devotion to Amory's mother and because he seems to take Amory's posing seriously, it is easy to underestimate his importance.

Fitzgerald's method of presentation seems to invite the reader to smile at this character. 'When he came into a room clad in his full purple regalia from thatch to toe, he resembled a Turner sunset, and attracted both admiration and attention.' However, it is probably the fact of his early association with the capricious Mrs Blaine together with his immediate and uncritical acceptance of young Amory that most implies Darcy's inadequacy. It is not immediately apparent that this priest who 'could dazzle an embassy ball'[88] is the one character in the novel who sees Amory's career in the correct perspective. In fact by encouraging Amory in his social poses – 'being Irish . . . should, by all means, be one of his principle biasses'[89] – Darcy seems to be afflicted with the same unappealing egocentricity which Amory exhibits from the beginning. In this lies a fundamental irony, for the whole structure of the novel indicates that the egocentricity which proves to be the source of Amory's humiliating failures is also his one priceless asset. Although at first it might seem that there is a seemingly irrelevant intrusion of religious terminology in the context of undergraduate pranks, Fitzgerald's construction is seen to be based upon the concept of evil; it is that concept which, for example, dominates the action in the 'Spires and Gargoyles' section of the novel. There, it is clearly the concept of evil which produces the standard by which Amory's behaviour can be seen as a decline into moral corruption. All this testifies to the relevance of Darcy's religious perspective, and in this respect, his explanation of the 'half miraculous sixth sense' is crucial.

Increasingly, it becomes apparent that this is very close to what Amory thinks of as his egotism. At first Amory made the error of confusing egotism with vanity. Darcy saw this clearly and helped Amory on to the next hurdle.[90] Unfortunately, Amory missed the key warning: 'You are unsentimental, almost incapable of affection.'[91] The sentimental love affair with Rosalind is another negative experience which proves the truth of Darcy's assessment. After this affair, Darcy's next appraisal would have provided a way for Amory to avoid another painful experience, but, as his purple prose attempt to immortalise his broken affair shows, he is still dominated by the emotion. And in his own terms – 'sentiment is emotional' – he is luxuriating in sentimentality. Although he claims to be a romantic, in the perspective provided by Monsignor Darcy, one vital ingredient is missing. 'You make a great mistake if you think you can be romantic without religion.'[92] However, just as before, Amory is unable to see the truth of the statement; he has to have it brought home to him by means of a negative experience. This, of course, is the lesson to be learned from his affair with Eleanor.

The use of negative experiences to express Amory's progress in 'the adventure of life',[93] is completely consistent with the basic irony of the novel. Amory's egocentricity is both the cause of his humiliating failures and the means by which he will survive them.

As an unqualified concept, egotism will surely indicate vanity and a self-satisfaction which is unlikely to be thought admirable. This is certainly the way Amory's first appreciation of his gift takes him but to dismiss the egocentricity as mere vanity would be to make the same mistake as Amory and also to underestimate the important role played by Monsignor Darcy. Gradually, through the negative experiences and with the clues of the imagery of travel and music to assist the process, the religious perspective is asserted. By this means the egocentricity is seen to be 'the mystical element'[94] shared by Darcy and Amory. It is nothing less than 'the half-realized fear of God in [Amory's] heart', which Darcy had earlier pointed out in a letter.[95] This is the true nature of Amory's strong sense of individuality which he instinctively strives to preserve. Unfortunately, until he has a full appreciation of the nature of his egocentricity, he is peculiarly susceptible to misdirections. In particular, until he can make the link between his instinct and religion, he will fail to be the romantic which he claims to be.

This is the clear point which lies behind the episode concerning the love affair with Eleanor. In this section of the novel Fitzgerald continues the use of the terminology of travel and, to a lesser extent, music, to combine with notions of pagan languor but more particularly with religious vocabulary. The effect clearly suggests the negative aspects of the affair. Amory has not yet made the connection between his egocentricity and 'the mystical element' but the affair with Eleanor will be 'the last time that evil crept close to Amory under the mask of beauty'.[96]

Lacking the religious element, Amory remains locked in his sentimentality and is in the great danger which Darcy had warned against. 'Beware of losing yourself in the personality of another being, man or woman.'[97] That is why Eleanor's attractions represent the devil; a point made very clear in the frequent use of that word. The loss of identity is further indicated by the variety of poses Amory assumes. He begins as Don Juan but he also acts the part of Rupert Brooke for much of the time. To some extent he is also Edgar Allen Poe and Swinburne and Shelley, yet, because he is 'in a trance', he is not aware that he is role-playing. 'He didn't at all feel like a character in a play.'[98] The language of indolence reveals the true nature of the experience

> Often they swam and as Amory floated lazily in the water he shut his mind to all thoughts except those of hazy soap-bubble lands where the sun splattered through wind-drunk trees. How could any one possibly think or worry, or do anything except splash and dive and loll there on the edge of time while the flower months failed. Let the days move over – sadness and memory and pain recurred outside, and here, once more, before he went on to meet them he wanted to drift and be young.[99]

Once again Amory is sentimentally trying to make 'things ... last'.[100] Even Eleanor recognises the trait. 'I thought so, Juan, I feared so – you're sentimental.'[101]

Fitzgerald illustrates the essential emptiness of the experience by suggesting the silence and loneliness which characterise even their moments of beauty.

> One night they walked while the moon rose and poured a great burden of glory over the garden until it seemed fairyland with Amory and Eleanor, dim phantasmal shapes, expressing eternal beauty and curious elfin love moods.[102]

In this scene of 'eternal beauty' the only sound heard is the unusual scratch of a match. The lack of substance is emphasised and Amory feels the sensation is oddly familiar. He senses the patterning of his negative experiences. 'The night and the scarred trees were like scenery in a play, and to be there with Eleanor, shadowy and unreal, seemed somehow oddly familiar.'[103]

Fitzgerald shows that Amory's 'sixth sense' is again at work and the incident of the ride which ends in the horse's death leap over a cliff is placed firmly in a religious context. Once again the loneliness and eerie silence characterises their relationship. This time the sense that they are both headed down a false trail is given further point by Eleanor's hubristic challenge: 'If there's a God let him strike me – strike me!'[104] This angers Amory and his reaction causes Eleanor to race to the brink of the cliff before throwing herself from the horse which plunges to death. Fitzgerald ends the

episode with imagery of cold beauty and a clear indication that
Amory has survived another negative experience.

> The stars were long gone and there were left only the little
> sighing gusts of wind and the silences between ... but naked
> souls are poor things ever, and soon he turned homeward and
> let new lights come in with the sun.[105]

Fittingly enough, Fitzgerald calls the section which deals with the
affair with Eleanor 'Young Irony'. In fact the affair provides an
interesting comment on the negative aspects of an experience. At
one point Amory reflects upon the irony which he sees in any
attempt by a poet to immortalise his lady's beauty.

> The irony of it is that if he had cared *more* for the poem than for
> the lady the sonnet would be only obvious, imitative rhetoric
> and no one would ever have read it after twenty years.[106]

The implication for Amory is clear. Although the affair represented
a wrong turning, his complete involvement in it has brought him
nearer to an understanding of his essential Self. In the terms of the
analogy of Shakespeare's sonnet, if he had been more selfishly
concerned to come to terms with his lingering egocentricity rather
than imagining himself in love with Eleanor, he would have been
proportionately less aware of his own true nature. Or to use
another image from this episode, if he had not adopted so many
poses he would have been less likely to know the real Amory.
These are the implications for the developing Amory. The two
poems which end the episode underline this point by means of
musical imagery. Eleanor and Amory had created an imaginary
world which was completely removed from the real one. Fitzgerald's presentation of this leaves no doubt that their play-acting
produced the impression of a splendour which was artificial and
therefore doomed. Their instinctive knowledge of this cast an air of
sadness over everything; not only the splendour but also the
sadness was artificial. This is why their poems typify the affair in
the language of whispers and fading songs. Amory has yet to see
'the splendour and the sadness of the world'.

Although it is not immediately apparent to Amory, Fitzgerald
has so ordered the novel that his protagonist has experienced the
ironic truth that selfish interests can be furthered by unselfish

actions. Paradoxically, by losing himself in various poses under the power of Eleanor's personality, he is nearer to a complete understanding of himself. The next lesson which Fitzgerald has him learn has to do with the notion of selfishness as it relates to the concept of egocentricity.

Fitzgerald now presents Amory as being listless and disillusioned. He is not yet in possession of an understanding of his experiences. 'He was in an eddy again, a deep, lethargic gulf, without desire to work or write, love or dissipate.'[107] In this mood Amory is presented with the embarrassing problem of Alec Connage and the girl he brings to his hotel room in defiance of the Mann Act. The scene in which Amory decides upon the act of offering himself to the hotel detective in place of Alec recalls earlier incidents concerning the Devil's appearance. However, on this occasion it is God who is invoked twice, not the devil. In addition, although there is the unmistakeable sign of evil –

> over and around the figure crouched on the bed there hung an aura, gossamer as a moonbeam, tainted as stale, weak wine, yet a horror, diffusively brooding already over the three of them . . .

Fitzgerald also has Amory sense another presence: 'over by the window among the stirring curtains stood something else, featureless and indistinguishable, yet strangely familiar.' These presences hover and listen while Amory considers the consequences of sacrifice. He rejects the way of another Princeton man who had made a similar sacrifice 'in a gust of sentiment'[108] and in the clear knowledge that when 'the emotional wave' had passed, 'Alec would secretly hate him for having done so much for him', he accepts the 'responsibility' which has come to him in the same manner as 'a great elective office' is offered. Fitzgerald expresses the moment of decision in the following way. *'Weep not for me but for thy children.* That – thought Amory – would be somehow the way God would talk to me.'

Immediately Amory has made this connection with religion he is aware of a joy and he recovers a sense of purposive action.

> Amory felt a sudden surge of joy and then like a face in a motion-picture the aura over the bed faded out; the dynamic shadow by the window, that was as near as he could name it, remained for the fraction of a moment and then the breeze seemed to lift it swiftly out of the room.[109]

There is an element of the old Morality plays here in that the second presence is later identified with Monsignor Darcy who had died shortly before this incident. The impression is of the Good and the Bad Angels hovering anxiously awaiting the Soul's decision. This is surely intended. It is the culmination of Darcy's role. Amory has been led to the point where he is able to appreciate an important fact about himself. His egocentricity, which first revealed itself as vanity, identified him as one of the 'certain people' whose true destiny is to sacrifice Self for the sake of others. Fitzgerald has placed this notion of Amory's true Self within a religious context so the Christian paradox stands behind him at this point. In this case, the idea of service to another providing 'perfect freedom', is used to show how the sacrifice of Self brings not freedom but a 'responsibility' and 'an infinite risk'. In other words, a greater awareness of the true Self and the way one can 'influence people in almost every way, even for evil'.[110] This was the kind of instinct Fitzgerald gave Amory in the early 'Code of the Young Egotist'. But so much will depend upon the spirit in which sacrifice is made. It must be done with a full appreciation of the truth; he must know

> that sacrifice was no purchase of freedom. It was like a great elective office, it was like an inheritance of power – to certain people at certain times an essential luxury, carrying with it not a guarantee but a responsibility, not a security but an infinite risk.[111]

This, then, is an important moment of insight towards which Amory's instincts have carried him. It is, of course, an ironic climax because his intuitions had led him to dream of a much more splendid summit. In his sixth-form year at St. Regis' he thought of the promised land in the pagan terms of Pan and Arcady. In the old swing he lifted himself high

> until he got the effect of swinging into the wide air, into a fairyland of piping satyrs and nymphs with the faces of fair-haired girls he passed in the streets of Eastchester. As the swing reached its highest point, Arcady really lay just over the brow of a certain hill, where the brown road dwindled out of sight in a golden dot.[112]

This image of the beautiful land just over the horizon is echoed in the sentimental notions of Isabelle's 'moonlight and pale starlight'[113] world, the Rosalind inspired 'paradise of rose and flame',[114] and the 'hazy soap-bubble lands'[115] to which Eleanor turns Amory's thoughts. The same image lies behind Amory's notions of success following a fruitful exploitation of Princeton's 'glittering caste system'.[116] However, all these dreams of happiness are clearly represented as mistaken. Fitzgerald accomplishes that by establishing the ideas of the wrong road and the wrong musical note as judged by another, more authoritative standard. That standard he fixes firmly in a religious context of good and evil. This context is not only established by the careful use of imagery, Monsignor Darcy is also used to make the religious explanation quite explicit. The actions of the novel, in particular the climax of Amory's understanding of sacrifice, are designed to illustrate that these serious terms of reference are indeed the correct ones.

The manner of Fitzgerald's presentation of Amory's actions then, always makes clear the gap between the dream world and the real one. However, it must not be thought that Amory's sense of a splendid destiny is to be entirely dismissed as being simply part of youth's optimism; an optimism which will inevitably be modified by time and bitter experience. This would be to devalue the 'sixth sense' and, clearly, the use made of Darcy precludes that. Amory's intimations of a vague, but glorious destiny are wrong in detail but right in principle. His belief in his own special election is seen to have been well founded, but not in the way he had surmised. The key to Arcady was indeed located within his egocentric Self but he has to learn how to sacrifice that Self in an act of detached unselfishness before he can possess it. Fitzgerald's careful association of this act with a fundamental Christian paradox shows plainly that he intended to suggest a similar ironic truth.

Nor does the irony stop there. Instead of the beautiful magical world of imagined Arcady, Amory steps into a new awareness of New York's ugliness. His perception of the subway scene and the crowds on the wet streets is governed by a sense of 'detachment'[117] which has carried over from his act of sacrifice. It would seem that this ugliness is the real Arcady. However, once again, and quite typically, even at the pivotal point in his development Amory has not quite grasped the whole truth. His act of self sacrifice was not merely disinterested; it was patronisingly so. His own definition of sacrifice describes it as 'arrogant' as well as 'impersonal'. 'Sacrifice should be eternally supercilious.'[118] It is this attitude which he takes into the dirty New York streets. It results in a Sweeny-type of vision. 'It was an atmosphere wherein birth and marriage and death were loathsome, secret things.' Against this background Fitzgerald now has Amory equate ugliness with poverty.

> 'I detest poor people,' thought Amory suddenly. 'I hate them for being poor. Poverty may have been beautiful once, but it's rotten now. It's the ugliest thing in the world. It's essentially cleaner to be corrupt and rich than it is to be innocent and poor.'[119]

This mood of disillusionment extends over a review of his own life with all his disappointments to the fore. He remembers all those figures who had inspired him with a sense of their ideals.

> The pageantry of his disillusion took shape in a world-old procession of Prophets, Athenians, Martyrs, Saints, Scientists, Don Juans, Jesuits, Puritans, Fausts, Poets, Pacifists . . . each had tried to express the glory of life and the tremendous significance of man.

Now they are lumped together and dismissed in the conclusion that 'man in his hunger for faith will feed his mind with the nearest and most convenient food'. Similarly, 'Women – of whom he had expected so much' are dismissed. Their only contribution had been 'a sick heart and a page of puzzled words'.[120] In this mood he even doubts the value of Monsignor Darcy.

This, then, seems to be the real-life Arcady. It is no magical world of beauty. There is no clear path through it. Fitzgerald introduces a new image which extends the previous imagery of travel and exactly captures Amory's disillusionment.

> Progress was a labyrinth . . . people plunging blindly in and then rushing wildly back, shouting that they had found it . . . the invisible king – the *élan vital* – the principle of evolution . . . writing a book, starting a war, founding a school.

Nothing, it seems has any meaning. Crucially, Amory's own instinct is not to plunge into the labyrinth but to start egocentrically, with himself.

He was his own best example – sitting in the rain, a human creature of sex and pride, foiled by chance and his own temperament of the balm of love and children, preserved to help in building up the living consciousness of the race.

This summary and, in particular the cynical evocation of the resolutely confident Stephen Dedalus, indicates the true nadir of Amory's spirits. 'In self-reproach and loneliness and disillusion he came to the entrance of the labyrinth.'[121]

Once again, it is Monsignor Darcy who indicates the correct way forward. At the Monsignor's funeral, despite his cynicism, Amory is aware that the crowds of 'people with daft, staring faces'[122] are truly grieving. It is this which supplies the sense of direction which takes him out of the labyrinth. His crucial mistake in the matter of self-sacrifice is wiped out.

Of Amory's attempted sacrifice had been born merely the full realization of his disillusion, but of Monsignor's funeral was born the romantic self who was to enter the labyrinth with him. He found something that he wanted, had always wanted and always would want – not to be admired, as he had feared; not to be loved, as he had made himself believe; but to be necessary to people, to be indispensable.[123]

The great mistake which Darcy had pointed out is finally fully rectified: Amory has discovered his 'romantic self' because he has seen it in the correct religious perspective. What he had overlooked in his 'attempted sacrifice' was the injunction: 'Weep not for me but for thy children.'[124] Instead of an appreciation of this self-abnegation, Amory had moved to the idea of the arrogance of sacrifice: that was in fact another manifestation of the mis-apprehension of egocentricity; it led Amory directly to his scorn of 'poor people'. Now, again thanks to Darcy, he has recovered a sense of value. He now feels the need to be of service to others. 'Amory felt an immense desire to give people a sense of security.'[125]

Immediately after this confirmation of purpose Fitzgerald has Amory return to Princeton. That in itself is a symbolic action and the whole episode fully exploits earlier images in order to show Amory's new awareness. The opening paragraph, for example, takes on deeper meanings as it recalls all the other uses to which images of travel and music have been put.

> On the day that Amory started on his walk to Princeton the sky was a colorless vault, cool, high and barren of the threat of rain. It was a gray day, that least fleshy of all weathers; a day of dreams and far hopes and clear visions. It was a day easily associated with those abstract truths and purities that dissolve in the sunshine or fade out in mocking laughter by the light of the moon. The trees and clouds were carved in classical severity; the sounds of the country-side had harmonized to a monotone, metallic as a trumpet, breathless as the Grecian urn.[126]

The scene is clearly set for a test of Amory's new desire to put service to others before his old egocentric Self. He gets his opportunity when he is given a lift. Fitzgerald makes the intended echo of a previous trip by car from New York to Princeton quite obvious in that the owner of the car is the father of Ferrenby who was with Humbird on the night of the crash. On this occasion, although it is the first time in his life that he has argued Socialism, Amory speaks passionately against the idea that money is 'the only stimulus that brings out the best that's in a man'.[127] He suggests that 'honor' would be a better incentive. In this he sees an escape from the materialism which he typifies as 'an enclosed treadmill that hasn't any windows'.[128] This concern for the enforced drudgery for the mass of men is in great contrast to the earlier Amory's selfish concerns. The link with the earlier escapades of the undergraduates is made even more pointed when it is realised that on the earlier occasion the younger Ferrenby had turned the conversation around to money. '"Anybody got any money?" suggested Ferrenby, turning around from the front seat.'[129]

At the heart of Amory's new-found espousal of Socialism is the desire to improve the lot of others, to hasten reform so that it will fit 'the needs of civilization'. He has talked himself into a new set of values.

> Even if, deep in my heart, I thought we were all blind atoms in a world as limited as a stroke of a pendulum, I and my sort would struggle against tradition; try, at least, to displace old cants with new ones.

This important commitment to the need to struggle forwards is accompanied by a rather rueful admission. 'I've thought I was right about life at various times, but faith is difficult.'[130]

The belief in the importance of struggle is to be seen against the background of disillusionment with tradition. The key factor is an awareness of the way selfishness can be transcended and the way opened for a 'poise and a balance' which will preserve optimism in the face of disillusion.

This selfishness is not only part of me. It is the most living part.

It is by somehow transcending rather than by avoiding that selfishness that I can bring poise and balance into my life.[131]

At this point the inner story of Amory's moral development reaches its conclusion. His early egocentric sense of his eventual translation to an Arcadian world of beauty and success has preserved him through vanity-induced mistakes where he failed as a sportsman, as an academic, as a lover, as a personality, through the ensuing period of dejection to this moment where he realises the true nature of selfishness: it can be used in the service of others, even though he has 'not one drop of the milk of human kindness' within himself. He has discovered that a life devoted to others 'may be the best possible expression of myself'.[132] This is, in fact what he had felt God would say to him. 'Weep not for me but for thy children.'

The concern for others is shown in Amory's concern for the way in which 'chosen youth' will continue to be deluded by the past. In a deliberate echo of the earlier moment in 'Spires and Gargoyles', Fitzgerald takes Amory back to the sights and sounds of Princeton after midnight. Now the symbolism of knowledge is given a different gloss. The impression of traditional knowledge is countered by Amory's certain knowledge that in reality the chosen youth will be 'fed romantically on the mistakes and half-forgotten dreams of dead statesmen and poets'. With his new insight he thinks of the future undergraduates 'shouting the old cries, learning old creeds' destined to discover for themselves that it was all a delusion; they will 'find all Gods dead, all wars fought, all faiths in man shaken'.[133]

However, Amory's 'poise and balance' allows him to come to terms with disillusionment: it is the inevitable corollory of optimistic hope which itself derives from that special sense of individual election: the hallmark of egocentricity. Without that special sense of a vague but glorious destiny there would have been no vanity. Without that vanity there would have been fewer humiliating failures. Without those failures there would have been a less intense dejection. Without that dejection there would not have been the eventual realisation of the way selfishness can be trans- cended. Without the ensuing 'poise and balance' the way towards true development in the real world would have remained closed. The deep irony is that without egotism there would not have been the struggle but an easy acceptance of 'drifting and dreaming'; a life of pagan self-indulgence. The book ends with a confirmation of Amory's determination to continue the struggle. 'One thing I know. If living isn't a seeking for the grail it may be a damned amusing game.'[134]

Shortly before the end of the novel Fitzgerald has Amory's mind turn towards the idea of the Catholic Church. Although Amory thinks of it as being 'seemingly the only assimilative, traditionary bulwark against the decay of morals', he decides that he cannot, for the present, accept it. For the moment, it seems, and with a full knowledge that his new ideas about Socialism could be another mistake, he will allow his new notion of Self to point the way forward. 'He wanted to keep the tree without ornaments, realize fully the direction and momentum of this new start.'[135] The interesting feature of this new direction is that it has been indicated to Amory chiefly by the operation of a religious sense. The construction of the whole book is very clearly based upon Darcy's religious explanation of 'the mystical element' which he and Amory have. Yet, by the end of the book, Amory assimilates his changed notion of Self, not into a religious belief, but into a hesitant and half-worked theory of Socialism.

In the following passage Fitzgerald outlines the new under- standing and in the lack of compassion which is indicated suggests a possible reason for the decision to leave the question of Catholicism for later consideration.

This selfishness is not only part of me. It is the most living part.

It is by somehow transcending rather than by avoiding that selfishness that I can bring poise and balance into my life.

There is no virtue of unselfishness that I cannot use. I can make sacrifices, be charitable, give to a friend, endure for a friend, lay down my life for a friend – all because these things may be the best possible expression of myself; yet I have not one drop of the milk of human kindness.[136]

Fitzgerald ends the novel with another deliberate echo of the moment earlier in 'Spires and Gargoyles' when Amory had interpreted the symbolism of the Gothic peaks as 'warehouses of dead ages'.[137] In this closing moment Amory now sees that he was wrong. The knowledge was, in reality, only 'the mistakes and half-forgotten dreams of dead statesmen and poets'. His newly won 'poise and balance' allows him to survey objectively the continual cycle for 'chosen youth': the enthusiastic grasping of illusion followed by inevitable disillusion.

Here was a new generation, shouting the old cries, learning the old creeds, through a revery of long days and nights; destined finally to go out into that dirty gray turmoil to follow love and pride; a new generation dedicated more than the last to the fear of poverty and the worship of success; grown up to find all Gods dead, all wars fought, all faiths in man shaken.[138]

If he had ended his novel here, Fitzgerald could have been accused of cynicism. But what he had dramatised is the way towards a 'poise and balance' despite the inevitability of the defeat of youth's hopes. The key to this lies in a concept of Self whereby selfishness can be transcended. Although the young Amory's overweening vanity was the cause of much of his unhappiness, ironically it was the cause of his salvation because when he reached the depths of his despair at 'the entrance of the labyrinth', he naturally 'started all inquiries with himself'.[139] The way was thus opened, finally, for his discovery of his 'romantic self'. This involved him not in being admired, loved or even feared by others, but of service to them. In this idea of service to others is located Monsignor Darcy's explanation that is was impossible for Amory to be the romantic he so much wished to be without religion. Darcy was the ideal model. 'People felt safe when he was near.' This desire 'to give people a sense of security',[140] represents the transcending of Self: it is a selfless dedication based upon a selfish need. In that sense Amory can stretch his arms towards the sky and in the last sentence of the novel claim: 'I know myself ... but that is all.'[141]

The crucial fact about Amory's 'poise and balance' which goes

right to the heart of Fitzgerald's organising principle is the determination to continue 'the struggle'.[142] Although the novel dramatises a pattern of inevitable failures – a pattern which is seen as an
inescapable fact of life – it makes the ironical point that the struggle
itself 'may be a damned amusing game'.[143] The point is so central
to the work that it determined the actual title. In Rupert Brooke's
poem 'Tiare Tahiti' the problem faced by the lover is that, although
Paradise seems to offer endless bliss and no pain, a great deal of
human joy would be lost.

> Oh, Heaven's Heaven! but we'll be missing
> the palms, and sunlight, and the south;
> And there's an end, I think, of kissing,
> When our mouths are one with Mouth

So, although 'the wise' assure him of eternal delight when Paradise
has been reached, his advice to Mamua is that they should take
advantage of all the pleasures available to them on earth; that is,
'well *this* side of Paradise'.

It might be that at the time of his efforts over the material for *The
Romantic Egotist*, Fitzgerald was not fully in possession of the point
of view which would make intellectual sense of the 'pile of detail'
concerning Stephen Palms. However, *This Side of Paradise* is firmly
based upon a coherent intellectual foundation: it was that which
determined the choice and presentation of all the material. All the
details of Amory Blaine's outer story are careful indexes to an inner
development which culminates in a philosophy of qualified pessimism. Amory's bouleversements lead him to the mature insights
of an ironic perception: although life offers only disillusionments,
the struggle to find happiness should be undertaken. An intriguing
point about this issue is not only was Fitzgerald intellectually and
artistically capable of such literature some time around the year
1919 – aged, perhaps twenty-three – but that the basic elements of
his mature work, both content and technique, are to be found in
This Side of Paradise.

3

The Beautiful and Damned

The key factor which had guided Amory Blaine on his stumbling path toward maturity was the sixth sense by means of which he was able to detect evil. That saving grace was located in a special concept of self-election. Ironically, although his self-esteem might appear to be preposterous, Amory's intuitive sense of election was the vital means by which his true Self was able to preserve the essence of his dream in the face of the world's ineluctable attrition. By following its promptings, a kind of Arcady was reached: apparently, the only one available to mortals; it is the state in which a viable balance between hope and inevitable disappointment is held.

Exactly the same base of seriousness informs *The Beautiful and Damned*. As most critics have noted, the novel does indeed deal with the theme of life's meaninglessness, but far from proceeding from Fitzgerald's own alleged lack of intellectual comprehension, the meaninglessness came directly from the same conceptualising power which created *This Side of Paradise*. When this link is recognised, there can be no question of a confused presentation of the material blamed upon the author's emotional participation in the pages of his own fiction.

The only issue which could stand in the way of an appreciation of Fitzgerald's intentions in his second novel is presented by his predilection for an oblique method of presentation. However, since he had used that technique in his first novel, he could have been expected to use it again for *The Beautiful and Damned*. As in *This Side of Paradise*, the interest in *The Beautiful and Damned* focuses upon the inner development of the central character. Fitzgerald achieves this for Anthony Patch in essentially the same way as he did for Amory Blaine: he indicates a disparity between the author's and the character's perception of events. As in the first novel, the clearest indication of this disparity is to be seen in the way the imagery is continually suggesting a deeper meaning. Both novels use imagery of travel and of music in this normative fashion but *The Beautiful and Damned* gives an important place to imagery which is associated with either warmth or coldness. However, in this second novel, the ironic complexity of the triangular relationship no longer obtains. There is no ironic trick practised upon the reader. One is not tempted to dismiss a concept – such as egotism – only to discover later that it was much nearer the truth than at first imagined. The irony is much simpler than that. It is, basically, dramatic irony in that the reader is expected to appreciate the true norm quite early in the work and to measure all the events from the point of view of that code.

In both novels the idea of the individual's inescapable need to find the right correlation between inner Self and outer public activity is paramount. Indeed, as Amory Blaine's movement through a pattern of symbolic experience shows, the failure to follow the correct path or discern the correct note registers a divergence from a moral norm which is so clearly related to a scale of evil that at one point the Devil himself appears. In *This Side of Paradise* the moral norm absolutely requires steady movement towards the final enlightenment: mere drifting and dreaming is in that sense unnatural. Fortunately for Amory, although like Anthony in that he too is unaware of a role in the outer real world of society which will adequately match his inner, private Self, he has, underlying all his doubts, the fundamental belief that he is 'a fortunate youth, capable of infinite expansion'.[1] It is this sense of infinite possibilities which Anthony lacks. Since Fitzgerald has shown how that concept of Self was intimately related to a special religious sense, it is clear how seriously he regarded the plight of an individual who lacked the 'mystical element'. Without the sixth sense by which he might detect evil, the less gifted individual, such as Anthony, is much more vulnerable to evil: that is, there is a greater likelihood of his being damned.

Right from the beginning of *The Beautiful and Damned*, Fitzgerald indicates a crucial difference between Amory and Anthony in this vital concept of the Self. Compare the following passage with Amory's notion of his special election.

he considered that he would one day accomplish some quiet subtle thing that *the elect* would deem worthy and, passing on, would join the dimmer stars in a nebulous, indeterminate heaven half-way between death and immortality.[2] (my emphasis)

This role of lesser luminary finds support in imagery of travel. The following excerpt captures Anthony's lack of an intuitive guide: but, crucially, he is seen to be lacking hope: 'It seemed a tragedy to want nothing – and yet he wanted something, something. He knew in flashes what it was – some path of hope to lead him toward what he thought was an imminent and ominous old age.'[3] In this way *The Beautiful and Damned* gives the same metaphorical importance to images of travel as does *This Side of Paradise* but in the second novel that earlier sense of Amory's slow progression which existed despite the periods of drifting and dreaming is replaced by images which highlight the emptiness and lack of colour which characterise aimlessness. Thus Anthony's spiritual ennui which hampers that morally vital movement towards the union of inner and outer worlds is well signified in his reluctance to travel. 'Travel, which had once charmed him, seemed, at length, unendurable, a business of color without substance, a phantom chase after his own dream's shadow.'[4] His vague dream is that, without any effort on his part, something might enter his life and bring some sense of purpose: 'some purpose yet to be born would find him work to do'.[5]

At this point it is helpful to recall the technique Fitzgerald used in *This Side of Paradise* to show how Beauty together with the desire to be loved constituted the greatest threat to Amory's moral progress. In the first novel this perception of the inseparable link between Beauty and Evil formed 'the second step'[6] which brought Amory to the final maturity. On two important occasions, even he with his sixth sense had almost been subverted from his true purpose by the temptations of Beauty. In the second novel, Anthony, lacking the sixth sense, is completely overwhelmed by Beauty and is therefore damned.

The two occasions when Amory was most seriously distracted from his path of true moral progress occurred when he fancied that he was in love with beautiful girls. Although the imagery which accompanies scenes which recount Amory's reactions to attractive girls is always expressing for the reader the unnaturalness – even the underlying horror – of the attraction, Fitzgerald delays Amory's own flash of insight into this reality. Not until his mistaken perceptions have led him through a succession of negative experiences and he is at the nadir of 'self-reproach and loneliness and disillusion' is Amory allowed to discover the key to the 'labyrinth'.[7] Significantly, Fitzgerald's expression of this insight makes explicit the two fundamental misconceptions which are the consequences of a failure to recognise the moral obligations which bind the elect. The wish to be admired and to be loved signify a selfish concern with tokens of the outer world's preoccupation with trivialities and, as the episode with the Devil most clearly indicates, that complete reversal of the true notion of purposive movement has to be seen in the conventional religious perspective of good in pursuit of evil. Thus, for Amory's moment of insight, Fitzgerald makes clear that the misconception has been removed: instead of looking for a movement from outside towards Self, the true movement must be away from Self outwards to others.

> He found something that he wanted, had always wanted and always would want – not to be admired, as he had feared; not to be loved, as he had made himself believe; but to be necessary to people, to be indispensable.[8]

After achieving this perception, the world no longer appears to Amory as 'a damned muddle . . . a football game . . . the referee gotten rid of'.[9] He now has a sense of purpose. He demonstrates this by rejecting an epigram which had occupied his former listless mind. 'Very few things matter and nothing matters very much.'[10] He recovers a sense of hope and is able to find proof of its existence even in a graveyard. 'He wondered that graves ever made people consider life in vain. Somehow he could find nothing hopeless in having lived.'[11]

It is this ability to throw off the old misconceptions and move to a position whereby the Self can withstand the constant 'wearing down' process which is life that most clearly illustrates the difference between Amory Blaine and Anthony Patch. The vital feature is the concept of Self. As Fitzgerald makes clear on the opening page of *The Beautiful and Damned*, Anthony is not one of the elect. He lacks Amory's optimistic sense of his own potential which, though it certainly brought an increase in disappointment for Amory, eventually brought him to an appreciation of his true role.

The difference is apparent early in the work where Anthony is seen to have no ambitions or hopes, apart from wanting to continue in a life of epicurean luxury and eventually to inherit his grandfather's millions. Fitzgerald does allow him a faint intuition of 'a sense of waste' in this kind of life, but it is only faint and it is shut out as 'absurd' in Anthony's 'justification of his manner of living'. That justification is 'of course, The Meaninglessness of Life'.[12] The same weak flash of intuition occasionally makes him see how empty his life is without hope. However, these flashes do not suggest hope; they merely emphasise its absence. Although Amory's progress through life was marked by painful negative experiences, his sense that he was a candidate for a great elective office, that he was heir to an inheritance of power is vindicated by his eventual realisation of the ironic truth about life. For Anthony, who is not one of the elect, there is only the gradually weakening sense that he is treading the wrong path. Unlike Amory, he is incapable of the final insight into reality which will create the correct perspective. Significantly, Fitzgerald's expression of the mature Anthony's moral dilemma highlights the ennervating effect of a life lived under the code of 'The Meaninglessness of Life'. 'Anthony Patch had ceased to be an individual of mental adventure, of curiosity, and had become an individual of bias and prejudice, with a longing to be emotionally undisturbed.'[13] He has become what Amory Blaine described as 'the spiritually married man'. This is the crucial difference which characterises the non-elect.

If the elect do in fact follow their instinctively correct path they become mental adventurers of the kind described by Amory; the kind of men who have a notion of man's true progress.

> there are these two sorts of brains. One sort takes human nature as it finds it, uses its timidity, its weakness, and its strength for its own ends. Opposed is the man who, being spiritually unmarried, continually seeks for new systems that will control or counteract human nature. His problem is harder. It is not life that's complicated, it's the struggle to guide and control life. That is his struggle. He is a part of progress – the spiritually married man is not.[14]

It is clear that Fitzgerald wished to present Anthony as the kind of 'spiritually married man' defined in this way. Amory on the other hand is able to win through to a belief that 'the struggle to guide and control life' was 'worth while', but Anthony has the 'spiritually married' man's convenient attitude that 'to struggle was to believe, to believe was to limit'.[15]

Once this link with *This Side of Paradise* is recognised, it is clear that an idea of marriage is used to complement the basic image of the Self's search for its ideal union with outer reality. In this respect marriage offered Fitzgerald a useful symbol by which he could dramatise the individual's early misconception about wanting to be loved in the special context of the fatal link between Beauty and Evil.

From the very beginning of *The Beautiful and Damned* Fitzgerald makes clear that Anthony is profoundly affected by beauty. Once again, as in *This Side of Paradise*, the actual representation of this attraction implies a moral significance.

A good example of the way in which he achieves this correlation can be seen in the way in which Anthony's delight in his bathroom is expressed. It is 'the heart and core of the apartment'. Presiding over it are images of physical beauty.

> Framed around the walls were photographs of four celebrated thespian beauties of the day: Julia Sanderson as 'The Sunshine Girl,' Ina Claire as 'The Quaker Girl,' Billie Burke as 'The Mind-the-Paint Girl,' and Hazel Dawn as 'The Pink Lady.' . . .
> It was his pride, this bathroom. He felt that if he had a love he would have hung her picture just facing the tub so that, lost in the soothing steamings of the hot water, he might lie and look up at her and muse warmly and sensuously on her beauty.[16]

This description recalls the 'hazy soap-bubble lands' which were part of Amory's misconception of his love affair with Eleanor. Like that usage, the terminology aims to suggest a dreamy indolence, 'a drowsy content' which is far removed from the idea of 'the struggle to guide and control'. The process of establishing this scene as a symbol of Anthony's faulty perception is continued by another device used in the first novel: a snatch of a popular song strongly implies superficiality.

> 'To . . . you . . . beaut-if-ul lady,'

He was singing as he turned on the tap.

> 'I raise . . . my . . . eyes;
> To . . . you . . . beaut-if-ul la-a-dy
> My . . . heart . . . cries - - -'[17]

That this superficiality is meant to indicate a susceptibility to errors in perception is made clear by the succeeding action. Fitzgerald has Anthony wander out of the bathroom still whistling the 'weird uncertain melody' only to be stopped in his tracks by an illusion of living beauty. Through the window he can see a beautiful girl. In fact his 'emotion' approaches 'adoration'. Unfortunately, when next he looks at the girl his perception is more accurate. 'She was fat, full thirty-five, utterly undistinguished.' So he returns to his bathroom haven with its reassuring images of beauty and while continuing his song to a nebulous 'beaut-if-ul la-a-dy' he devotes his attention to his own physical appearance. 'Then with a last soothing brush that left an iridescent surface of sheer gloss he left his bathroom and his apartment and walked down Fifth Avenue to the Ritz-Carlton.'[18] Significantly, this glittering image echoes an unusual image which appears in the novel's opening paragraph. In that first image Fitzgerald had used the idea of the essential ugliness of surface glitter to describe Anthony's recurrent impression of his true Self. The image is of 'a shameful and obscene thinness glistening on the surface of the world like oil on a clean pond'.[19] The strength of this image serves to emphasise the moral consequence of an adherence to the superficially attractive. It is the constant function of the imagery and the pattern of symbolic experience within the novel to suggest that the true meaning of all the action is to be found in the moral perspective which sees that beauty and evil are inseparably linked.

The Beautiful and Damned and This Side of Paradise illustrate various degrees of moral decline implicit in apparently trivial aesthetic enthusiasms. Thus, Anthony's delight in his bathroom and Amory's youthful dream of a musical-comedy type of life in New York, although minor deviations, are, nevertheless, to be seen as examples of the ways in which an individual's evaluative sense is progressively worsened. However, in both works Fitzgerald shows clearly that he believed the chief agent in this aspect of the world's 'wearing down' power was Beauty in the form of an attractive female. Since it is clear that the same belief in the link between beauty and evil influences both novels, it is vital to appreciate the ways in which the literary technique is employed to testify to the truth of the perception.

In the first instance it should be recognised that the strategy of the marriage chase is a natural expression of the image of the individual's journey to reality and, as such, has been used by many writers. In fact, Fitzgerald's use of this idea can be seen to utilise important aspects which are found in other works deriving from the same base. In this respect the Eleanor and Amory episode in *This Side of Paradise* offers useful hints about the general framework which Fitzgerald aimed to erect.

It will be recalled that 'Eleanor was ... the last time that evil crept close to Amory under the mask of beauty.'[20] The negative force of this affair is, thus, made explicit. The terminology of evil and the hubris which leads to an almost fatal incident corroborate this moral estimate. There is, however, one further aspect of Fitzgerald's presentation of Eleanor which, by casting her clearly in the role of Demon Lover, comes very close to acknowledging the literary strategy upon which the episode is based. This involves the use made of Poe's poem 'Ulalume'.

Eleanor had overheard Amory reciting the poem to the cornfields in Ramilly County and at their first meeting almost the first thing she says to him is: 'you can recite "Ulalume" and I'll be Psyche, your soul.'[21] Although Fitzgerald is here making an important ironic point, the interesting feature concerns the fact that Poe's poem deals with the way that an image of feminine beauty deludes man into believing that he has found his true guiding light. 'Ulalume' is, in fact, Poe's version of the Self's pursuit of the Ideal. Since Shelley's treatment of the same idea in his 'Epipsychidion' is probably the highest example of the strategy, it is helpful to term it the psyche-epipsyche format. Of course, in Shelley's 'Epipsychidion' the psyche does achieve the ideal union with his soulmate, whereas in 'Ulalume' there is only disappointment. Fitzgerald's irony concerns Eleanor's assumption of the role of Psyche, the Soul of Poe's narrator, because it was she who distrusted appearances and warned of danger. In the novel Eleanor, far from warning Amory of danger, actually takes him to the brink of death.

Further examination of Fitzgerald's use of 'Ulalume' is helpful for the insight it offers into the way he fitted his attitude to beauty and evil into the psyche-epipsyche type of pattern. In particular it will be seen that in the way in which 'beauty of outward form' becomes 'the object of [Anthony's] quest,' an attitude to beauty which is at least as old as Plato's *Symposium* is suggested.[22] In fact, in Plato's expression of the way in which beauty is in harmony with the divine, there is a clear parallel with that true perception which Amory finally achieves. Although the title of Chapter 2 of *The Beautiful and Damned* is used ironically, the very reference to

'Symposium' corroborates the suggestion of a conceptual link with Plato.

The narrator in Poe's 'Ulalume' fails to detect the evil intentions of Astarte, the horned moon. Psyche is fearful and her beautiful wings sink until they trail 'in the dust'. The narrator is misled by Astarte's 'nebulous lustre' and the 'love in her luminous eyes'. The cold light which she reflects creates the illusion of the unity of Hope and Beauty.

> Let us bathe in this crystalline light!
> Its Sibyllic splendor is beaming
> With Hope and in Beauty to-night.[23]

The illusion is dispelled when this 'sinfully scintillant' beauty leads him to the door of the tomb of his lost love. Clearly, by having Eleanor claim the role of Psyche, Fitzgerald achieved a deliberate ironic juxtaposition; Eleanor is more nearly Astarte. He ends the episode by having the imagery stress the emptiness and ultimate sterility of moonlight when compared with the sun, and Amory's next phase of journeying is suggested by the new dawn.

> Their poses were strewn about the pale dawn like broken glass. The stars were long gone and there were left only the little sighing gusts of wind and the silences between ... but naked souls are poor things ever, and soon he turned homeward and let new lights come in with the sun.[24]

Throughout the episode Fitzgerald uses Poe's terminology: Eleanor is related to the 'crystalline light' of the moon and Fitzgerald uses notions of its infertile 'nebulous lustre' to complement imagery of directionless movement and vocabulary of devilish temptation. Like the narrator in 'Ulalume', Amory is temporarily bewitched by Astarte. In that state the cold light gives the illusion of Arcady. 'The moon rose and poured a great burden of glory over the garden until it seemed fairyland with Amory and Eleanor, dim phantasmal shapes, expressing eternal beauty and curious elfin love moods.'[25] Fitzgerald had earlier used the same kind of moon imagery to show an essentially similar illusion when Amory had sensed that Myra was his epipsyche. The use of Poe's 'crystalline' is interesting, as with other words, like, for example 'nebulous' it suggests a kinship of ideas.

Overhead the sky was half crystaline [sic], half misty, and the
night around was chill and vibrant with rich tension . . .
   'Pale moons like that one . . . make people mysterieuse. You
look like a young witch.'[26]

And at the end of the novel, Amory's symbolic gesture of acceptance is directed to 'the crystalline, radiant sky'.[27] But on that final
occasion there is no question that Amory is deluded by his earlier
need 'to be admired . . . to be loved'.[28]

In *The Beautiful and Damned* the same kind of version of the
psyche-epipsyche strategy is the dominating feature of the
Anthony/Gloria relationship. However, instead of a link with the
moon, Gloria is ironically associated with the sun: ironically
because she is invariably represented as being cold like ice.

The first time she appears the paradox is made apparent. She is
described as being 'dazzling – alight', and her hair is 'gay against
the winter color of the room'. But almost her first words are: 'I'm a
solid block of ice.'[29] Anthony continually mistakes her radiance for
the fructifying radiance which is the sun's property. Fitzgerald's
careful control of imagery continually makes the point that
Anthony is following an illusion. On the occasion of the first kiss,
for example, an image of a false spring combines with the already
established false note of the 'rag-picker' music to signal the
Astarte-like enchantment.

> The night was alive with thaw; it was so nearly warm that a
> breeze drifting low along the sidewalk brought to Anthony a
> vision of an unhoped-for hyacinthine spring. Above in the blue
> oblong of sky, around them in the caress of the drifting air, the
> illusion of a new season carried relief from the stiff and breathed-
> over atmosphere they had left, and for a hushed moment the
> traffic sounds and the murmur of water flowing in the gutters
> seemed an illusive and rarefied prolongation of that music to
> which they had lately danced.[30]

On this occasion her coolness is related to the moon. 'She turned
her face up to him, pale under the wisps and patches of light that
trailed in like moonshine through a foliage . . . No love was there
. . . Her beauty was cool as this damp breeze.'[31]

This impression of Gloria's physical coldness is constantly
presented. Shortly after the kiss Anthony calls on her. It is 'a bleak

two o'clock' on a freezing Tuesday.[32] They walk but she complains of the cold and so they go to her apartment. She allows him to kiss her again but after a kiss 'that was neither a game nor a tribute' she rebukes him. 'Anthony sank down beside her and closed his hand over hers. It was lifeless and unresponsive.' After a 'chilling silence' he leaves and the imagery of the encroaching cold is a clear indication of their relationship. 'Good-by, you ass!' she says to 'the death-bound fire'. The symbolism of this advancing cold is continued in the description which clearly illustrates Anthony's misconceptions about the true nature of Gloria's radiance.

> Not only for that night but for the days and weeks that followed his books were to be but furniture and his friends only people who lived and walked in a nebulous outer world from which he was trying to escape – that world was cold and full of bleak wind, and for a little while he had seen into a warm house where fires shone.[33]

The irony makes the misconception absolutely clear.

This is the basic function of the imagery: it continually illustrates Anthony's faulty perceptions. In this crucial area of his attitude to Gloria's beauty, the psyche-epipsyche strategy is a very effective device. It establishes a framework of reference so that the reader should be in no doubt about Anthony's increasing divergence from the correct path. In the following passage for example, there should be no question of any kind of wavering in Fitzgerald's purpose. Anthony's desperately built hope has been founded on the insubstantial basis of Gloria's sterile radiance. The attentive reader knows that in these moments of reflection on the night of the bridal dinner Anthony is very wrong in his optimistic assessment.

> through his wide-open windows came sound, evanescent and summery, alive with remote anticipation. He was thinking that the young years behind him, hollow and colorful, had been lived in facile and vacillating cynicism upon the recorded emotions of men long dust. And there was something beyond that; he knew now. There was the union of his soul with Gloria's, whose radiant fire and freshness was the living material of which the dead beauty of books was made.[34]

However, Fitzgerald drives the point home very strongly and, in so doing, widens the issue into one of universal proportions. As in *This Side of Paradise*, he utilises a musical image: the 'evanescent' sound which Anthony's present state of love brings to his senses becomes the sound which 'a thousand lovers' were making; 'crying little fragments of it into the air'. It links love with hope and beauty and happiness.

> All the city was playing with this sound out there in the blue summer dark, throwing it up and calling it back, promising that, in a little while, life would be beautiful as a story, promising happiness – and by that promise giving it. It gave love hope in its own survival. It could do no more.[35]

Not only is Anthony mistaken in taking his whole purpose and meaning from 'the union of his soul' (psyche) with Gloria's (epipsyche), so are the thousand others who build a hope for happiness upon the appearance of beauty. For life is not beautiful 'as a story'. Uncle George's story with its 'inartistic sixth act' illustrates that fact. Nor should happiness be taken to be the goal of life: 'truth is the end of life [and] happiness is a mode of it'.[36] And Fitzgerald illustrates the continuity of his thought by recalling the ironic explanation of Amory's search for Arcadian happiness: the promise that we can reach it is the closest we can come to Arcady. To drive this point home still further Fitzgerald now has Anthony hear the true characteristic sound of life. It is a jarring noise. It is 'low, incessant and whining' but it gradually grows louder and becomes 'hysterical'. It falls again to 'the low rumble of a man's voice' and then reaches 'almost the quality of a scream'. Anthony is disturbed by 'some animal quality' in the sound. It arouses 'his old aversion and horror toward all the business of life'. Fitzgerald then gives Anthony a moment of terrible insight. 'Life was that sound out there, that ghastly reiterated female sound'.[37] It is this truth which Anthony's life-style attempts to avoid. His bathroom with its images of remote beauty and air of luxurious indolence is a significant symbol of his wish to retain detached from the ugliness of real life.

This kind of insight for Anthony is quite rare. Usually the imagery which Fitzgerald employs works to establish a distance between Anthony's perceptions and actual reality. It is the biographical critic's insistence on a subjective confusion which creates the difficulty in appreciating the essentially negative aspects of Anthony's experiences.

A good example of Fitzgerald's characteristic method of establishing Anthony's distance from reality occurs in the scene in the section of Chapter 2, of Book 1, called 'Admiration'. This takes place in the 'brummagem' cabaret called the 'Marathon' – a cheap and shoddy imitation of 'the great cafes'. Fitzgerald's presentation of this scene seems to offer the opportunity for the double vision explanation of the critic who sees evidence of the author being allured by the things he attempts to criticise. However, as the complete structure of the imagery shows, this scene takes its place in a process by which Anthony's reaction dramatises the consequences of a fundamental misjudgement about the nature and true worth of beauty.

Anthony is clearly concerned that Gloria will feel out of place in the 'Marathon'. But she says she loves it. At this point 'a gorgeous sentiment' produces for Anthony a vision of Arcadian splendour.

> and they two, it seemed to him, were alone and infinitely remote, quiet. Surely the freshness of her cheeks was a gossamer projection from a land of delicate and undiscovered shades; her hand gleaming on the stained table-cloth was a shell from some far and wildly virginal sea.

But reality attempts to crowd in.

> Then the illusion snapped like a nest of threads; the room grouped itself around him, voices, faces, movement; the garish shimmer of the lights overhead became real, became portentous; breath began, the slow respiration that she and he took in time with this docile hundred, the rise and fall of bosoms, the eternal meaningless play and interplay and tossing and reiterating of word and phrase – all these wrenched his senses open to the suffocating pressure of life.

And then, to his amazement, Gloria murmurs: 'I belong here . . . I'm like these people.' Her 'entrancement' which seems to prove her statement is signified by 'the year's mellowest fox-trot'.

> Something - - - goes
> Ring-a-ting-a-ling-a-ling
> Right in-your ear - - -

After disputing the point with her, Anthony feels the need to preserve her image. 'Anthony for the moment wanted fiercely to paint her, to set her down *now*, as she was, as, as with each relentless second she could never be again.' If the perspective for this unreal wish to preserve Gloria's beauty is not immediately apparent, the fact that Fitzgerald follows it with a reversal of a definition which had been an important part of Amory's experiences ought to establish the point: 'only the romanticist preserves the things worth preserving'. And if this does not sufficiently indicate Anthony's misconception, based upon beauty as an ideal, then his 'understanding' which closes this section should make it absolutely clear.

> The sheath that held her soul had assumed significance – that was all. She was a sun, radiant, growing, gathering light and storing it – then after an eternity pouring it forth in a glance, the fragment of a sentence, to that part of him that cherished all beauty and all illusion.[38]

It should be apparent that references to Gloria as 'a sun' contribute greatly to the reader's sense of the distance between how Anthony sees things and how things really are. The process begins very early in the book and so disproves Wilson's claim that Fitzgerald 'seems never to have planned' his stories.[39] It will be recalled that in Anthony's bathroom, between the photographs of 'The Mind-the-Paint Girl' and 'The Pink Lady' there hung a print. This print represented 'a great stretch of snow presided over by a cold and formidable sun – this, claimed Anthony, symbolized the cold shower'.[40] In fact, this 'cold and formidable sun' is a symbol of Gloria. At first, under the delusion that Gloria radiates warmth, Anthony is very happy. However, Fitzgerald's imagery insistently points up the unreality of the emotion.

> the busses were thronged with congenial kings and the shops full of fine soft things for the summer, the rare summer, the gay promising summer that seemed for love what the winter was for money. Life was singing for his supper on the corner! Life was handing round cocktails in the street! Old women there were in that crowd who felt that they could have run and won a hundred-yard dash![41]

This 'promise that, in a little while, life would be beautiful' is another evasion of that note of essential reality contained in the city's night-time sounds. What Anthony does not know is that it is only the promise of happiness which brings happiness. A more accurate expression of Gloria's effect on Anthony occurs at the beginning of Chapter 2, Book 2 in an image which continues the idea of the sun. 'Gloria had lulled Anthony's mind to sleep. She, who seemed of all women the wisest and the finest, hung like a brilliant curtain across his doorways, shutting out the light of the sun.'[42] The story of their marriage is well symbolised in imagery of lassitude, apathy and lethargy indicative of an increasing boredom with their aimless existence. This is particularly apparent in Chapter 2 of Book 2 which Fitzgerald calls 'Symposium'.

The obvious association with Plato's famous dialogue on the nature of love signals Fitzgerald's ironic intention. At this mid-point in the novel, after establishing the two levels of perception – Anthony's and the author's – the imagery of sunshine, which had indirectly illustrated Anthony's mistaken sense of purpose, is complemented by a similarly oblique technique. A small group of characters who collectively and individually typify faulty perception illustrate that their misconceptions derive from their complete misunderstanding about the nature of love. In dramatising these misconceptions within the framework of an ironic parallel with Plato's *Symposium*, Fitzgerald achieves a positive perspective for his characters. By elevating their cynical opinions and apathetic behaviour to the status of a philosophical debate, the ludicrous inadequacy by which they reason their way to a sense of life's meaninglessness is highlighted.

This concentration upon contemporary misconceptions about the true nature of love takes place upon the same level of meaning as that which had earlier insisted upon the 'inartistic sixth act' for Uncle George. In that story too, Fitzgerald had indicated that a dedication to a false ideal could only end badly. However, the lack of meaning which characterises the successful realisation of such an ideal does not prove that life is meaningless: it proves that life lived on the basis of a false ideal will prove meaningless. The perspective of Plato's great dialogue ensures that the woeful inadequacies of the debaters is satirised and not the concept of love itself. It is fitting that this 'Symposium' should come at the centre of the book because in it is encapsulated the key proposition: love is indeed the vital factor which gives life meaning and a failure to perceive its true nature renders everything meaningless.

In *This Side of Paradise* Fitzgerald had used the idea of a journey to reality to show how a moral compulsion drives a person like Amory Blaine to find the ideal complement in the outer world for his inner Self. Because Fitzgerald's framework for Amory's story is so evidently moral, Amory's progress can accurately be described as illustrating Diotima's proposition that 'love is desire for the perpetual possession of the good'.[43] As she points out to Socrates the desire can express itself in many ways: 'The generic concept embraces every desire for good and for happiness; that is precisely what almighty and all-ensnaring love is.'[44]

Fitzgerald takes Amory through varieties of this desire – the chief one being the notion of finding a soul-mate – in order to show that his motivation had been merely self-love. His misconception of this fundamental issue predetermines his false ideals and inevitable failures. Not until he learns to transcend Self is he able to achieve happiness and a sense of purpose in a firm grasp of reality. This code of reality which is the reference point for all Amory's negative experiences leans quite heavily upon the contribution of Socrates to the debate on love. His, of course, is the prevailing voice in the *Symposium*. In Fitzgerald's version of the debate in *The Beautiful and Damned*, Maury Noble replaces Socrates. His cynicism dominates the 'Symposium'. At the end of this section, he, like Socrates, has put his companions to sleep. Socrates had been arguing about the writing of comedy and tragedy but Maury had given the cynical explanation of the way in which the Bible came to be written. Maury is preconditioned to see no point in either action or ideas. Significantly enough, in view of Fitzgerald's proven interest in thematic imagery, the setting for Maury's cynical philosophy involves the grotesque effects of pre-dawn star light. 'Maury had climbed to the roof of the shed, where he sat dangling his feet over the edge, outlined as a shadowy and fantastic gargoyle against the now brilliant sky.'[45] He tells how he learned to reject the illusion of wisdom represented by religion, professors and poets. He also rejected the illusion of beauty and inevitably reached the position of boredom. After this he had pinned his hopes on reaching eventual happiness simply by the accumulation of experiences, but that too was proved wrong. He then began to be aware that he was being used 'for some inscrutable purpose' as though there were 'some ultimate goal' towards which he could feel himself impelled. However, he had the feeling 'that there was no ultimate goal for man'. At this point Fitzgerald has Gloria interrupt to summarise the understanding which Maury has slowly deduced. 'There's only one lesson to be learned from life . . . That there's no lesson to be learned from life.'[46]

This is 'the fundamental sophistication' with which Gloria 'first looked at the world' and the one which Maury had 'struggled to attain'. This perception indicates the essential difference between Maury and Amory Blaine. Amory came to realise that Arcady was a state of mind which reconciled hope with the knowledge of likely failure; this gave him the necessary balance with which to go forward to meet his future. Maury's is a philosophy of defeat because it posits a meaningless universe. Thus, gargoyle-like, he perches on the station roof and sees a future of no hope.

> Only Maury Noble remained awake, seated upon the station roof, his eyes wide open and fixed with fatigued intensity upon the distant nucleus of morning. He was wondering at the unreality of ideas, at the fading radiance of existence, and at the little absorptions that were creeping avidly into his life, like rats into a ruined house.[47]

In basically the same way, the nine sections of Fitzgerald's 'Symposium' – which loosely correspond to the nine parts of Plato's dialogue – testify to the same melancholy conclusion of life's boring pointlessness. Central to them all is an expression of Self in terms of self-gratification. In this there is a continual reversal of Plato's claims for love. The opening episode, for example, which tells of the intrusion of violence into the marriage when Anthony physically prevents Gloria from boarding the train, is an obvious contrast to Agathon's claim that 'violence never touches Love'. Indeed, the increasing round of drinking which, for one thing, results in their signing of a new lease for the house they did not want and could not afford, is a constant denial of Agathon's declaration that 'Love is richly endowed with self-control.'[48] Overall, the evidence of the behaviour in each section of the 'Symposium' continually makes the point that although, like Plato's *Symposium*, love is acknowledged to be the prime motivator, a very different concept of love is involved. Given the deliberate perspective of Plato's masterpiece, it is impossible to imagine that anything but satire is intended for these modern debaters of the nature of love.

Fitzgerald's method provides an efficient means of suggesting the correct moral framework for the 'inartistic sixth act' of Anthony's and Gloria's marriage. Although the imagery of sunshine and warmth becomes less frequent, it still exists to illustrate how 'a measure of brightness faded from the world'.[49] In this it combines with the implicit sense of an inexorable process by which their illusion of happiness will eventually be worn away. After the incident on the railway station, for example, Fitzgerald says of Gloria that 'she was aware even then that she would forget in time and that it is in the manner of life seldom to strike but always to wear away'.[50] However, in an incident – called 'Nietzschean' – involving Gloria's pregnancy, the moral consequences of the misunderstanding of love are made most apparent. Because Fitzgerald strongly implies Plato's examination of the subject, Gloria's attitude to the effect which pregnancy will have on her body is given special meaning. It will be recalled that Diotima had told Socrates: 'The object of love . . . is not, as you think, beauty . . . Its object is to procreate and bring forth in beauty.'[51] Gloria's decision not to have the child is seen to derive from a very different notion of beauty and a concept of Self which owes more to self-interest than self-sacrifice. In this sense it suggests that, of the two kinds of love as defined by both Pausanias and Eryximachus, Gloria's notion of love comes closer to being inordinate or 'vicious' rather than to 'virtuous' love. Eryximachus' explanation of the way love is in harmony with the seasons of the year is particularly interesting in this connection.

> When the elements . . . hot and cold and dry and wet, are bound together in love which is orderly, and combined harmoniously in due proportions, man and the other animals and plants thrive and are healthy and take no harm. But when inordinate love gets the upper hand in the matter of the seasons, it causes widespread destruction and injury.[52]

Fitzgerald's treatment of love is always sensitive to atmospheric conditions. This is particularly observable when, as in the Amory and Eleanor episode, he wishes to dramatise the disharmony which their relationship signifies. At the moment when Gloria is trying to decide about the baby he again adds a thematic background of light and dark.

She lay upon the long lounge down-stairs. Day was slipping warmly out of the window . . .

'All I think of ever is that I love you,' she wailed. 'I value my body because you think it's beautiful. And this body of mine – of yours – to have it grow ugly and shapeless? It's simply intolerable . . .'

'And then afterward I might have wide hips and be pale, with all my freshness gone and no radiance in my hair.' - - -

Her sobs lapsed. She drew down a merciful silence from the twilight which filled the room. 'Turn on the lights,' she pleaded. 'These days seem so short – June seemed – to – have – longer days when I was a little girl.'

She ends by referring to a concept of Self which, by reason of the context described, clearly suggest a crucial failure of perception. 'I'm being true to me, you know.'[53]

Fitzgerald shows that the consequence of this kind of appreciation of what Maury Noble calls 'the tremendous importance of myself to me, and the necessity of acknowledging that importance to myself',[54] is an increasing weariness and lack of purpose. The following passage captures the unnatural detachment of this state in imagery which suggests the disharmony referred to by Plato. Anthony and Bloeckman have been waiting for Gloria to liven up their conversation. Momentarily she brings them 'atmosphere and an increase in vitality'. But that soon disappears.

As the conversation continued in stilted commas, Anthony wondered that to him and Bloeckman both this girl had once been the most stimulating, the most tonic personality they had ever known – and now the three sat like overoiled machines, without conflict, without fear, without elation, heavily enamelled little figures secure beyond enjoyment in a world where death and war, dull emotion and noble savagery were covering a continent with the smoke of terror.

In a moment he would call Tana and they would pour into themselves a gay and delicate poison which would restore them momentarily to the pleasurable excitement of childhood, when every face in a crowd had carried its suggestion of splendid and significant transactions taking place somewhere to some magnificent and illimitable purpose ... Life was no more than this summer afternoon; a faint wind stirring the lace collar of Gloria's dress; the slow baking drowsiness of the veranda . . . Intolerably unmoved they all seemed, removed from any romantic imminency of action. Even Gloria's beauty needed wild emotions, needed poignancy, needed death.[55]

This is the state of boredom to which Maury Noble refers. The lack of vitality which can only be remedied by the 'gay and delicate poison' now typifies the Patches' life-style. It is impossible to imagine that Fitzgerald was in any way recommending any part of this joyless existence, or that he considered it to be heroic.

The overall technique of the 'Symposium' section, then involves continuing the documentation of the Patches' moral decline mainly by the device of an ironic comparison with Plato's dialogue on the nature of love. The language of languor and aimlessness and the familiar images of sunlight and warmth also assist the process. However, if there is any doubt about the moral norm of the work, that should be dispelled when it is realised that Fitzgerald also uses the same kind of suggestion of the appearance of the supernatural as he uses in *This Side of Paradise*.

The incident occurs in the section called 'In Darkness' and is introduced by associating ideas of a disturbing unpleasantness with a new arrival at the house. His name is Hull. He wears 'weird-looking clothes' and, most disturbingly, Gloria can see his toes through his white shoes. This is a clear echo of the strange presence who appeared before Amory in Phoebe's flat. Although Maury claims to have 'known him all [his] life', Anthony says: 'The devil you have!' The technique of associating moral and climatic states is again used and, in a familiar use of contemporary song, the true state of affairs is made explicit.

It had been a tropical day, and even into late twilight the heat-waves emanating from the dry road were quivering faintly like undulating panes of isinglass. The sky was cloudless, but far beyond the woods in the direction of the Sound a faint and persistent rolling had commenced . . .

Maury began a song, which they accomplished in harmony during the first course. It had two lines and was sung to a popular air called Daisy Dear. The lines were:

'The - - pan-ic - - has - - come - -over us,
So *ha-a-as* - - the moral de*cline*!'

Maury soon reminds them of an unfunny practical joke he played
in a Turkish bath in Boston. This, clearly, parallels the undergraduate pranks at Asbury in *This Side of Paradise* and, like that earlier
occasion, indicates the worsening of standards. This moral reference is continued by another attempt at the two-line song. However, and significantly, the words 'the moral decline' are drowned
out by 'a drum of thunder from outside'. Gloria's sense of unease
increases and she puts down her drink because 'the first taste
nauseated her'.[56]

There then follows a grotesque scene which involves drunken
singing and dancing; even Tana their servant is drunk. The storm
has 'come up amazingly' by this time. Gloria leaves them.

> She had said good night but no one had heard or heeded her. It
> seemed for an instant as though something had looked down
> over the head of the banister, but she could not have gone back
> into the living room – better madness than the madness of that
> clamor

She lies on her bed for more than two hours.

> She was in a state half-way between sleeping and waking, with
> neither condition predominant ... and she was harassed by a
> desire to rid herself of a weight pressing down upon her breast.
> She felt that if she could cry the weight would be lifted

The sound of the rain reminds her of her childhood.

> It was like days when the rain came out of yellow skies that
> melted just before twilight and shot one radiant shaft of sunlight
> diagonally down the heavens into the damp green trees. So cool,
> so clear and clean – and her mother there at the centre of the
> world, at the centre of the rain, safe and dry and strong.[57]

This image of security within the innocent world of a child's
perception is in marked contrast to the 'slow baking drowsiness'
and stultifying warmth which characterises the summer in 'the
gray house'. In this recollection the sun really is 'radiant' and the
dews are refreshing whereas the present storm outside, indicative
of an inner turbulence, seems unnaturally menacing. This impress-

ion is continued by the action because a threatening presence comes to her door and stands, swaying slightly, watching her: 'this figure, swaying, swaying in the doorway, an indiscernible and subtly menacing terror, a personality filthy under its varnish, like smallpox spots under a layer of powder'.

The figure is Hull but in Gloria's perception of him he seems associated with 'the thing'. 'She must go from this house where the thing hovered that pressed upon her bosom, or else made itself into stray, swaying figures in the gloom.' Anthony, too 'was part of this weight, part of this evil house and the sombre darkness that was growing up about it'.[58]

It is quite clear that this incident, like the similar one in *This Side of Paradise* is meant to symbolise the increasing vulnerability to evil which follows an adherence to the wrong standards. The build-up to the incidents is very much the same in both novels: they both stress repeated drinking sprees and recount bad jokes played on innocents; they both make use of a hot stuffy atmosphere from which the victim of the experience longs to escape to find relief in some refreshing dampness; and both exploit Fitzgerald's impression of horror which is concentrated upon feet. In this last respect, Amory's experience stresses the sound of footsteps which first seem to pursue and then to lead. They are said to sound 'like a slow dripping'.[59] Gloria's experience is also heightened by the steady dripping noise of the rain. It would seem that Fitzgerald intended an irony by this in that a reassuring sound from her childhood has now become associated with 'the thing'. However, he did not sufficiently link the dripping with the footsteps as he did in the first novel and so there is some loss of effect.

There is, however, a more interesting difference between the two episodes. In the first novel Fitzgerald's presentation of the strange presence is such that it does have an objective existence. It is for example, seen by Tom as well as Amory. It cannot, therefore, be thought of as a drink-induced hallucination. Fitzgerald asks the reader to accept that a turning aside from the path of correct moral development can produce the actual physical presence of evil. In the second novel, Gloria's experience can be explained as completely subjective. The reader is not asked to believe that a devil actually appeared. The visitation could have a psychological explanation. Yet this does not distract from the symbolic force of the incident. The cumulative effect of certain actions, even if undertaken with no consciously evil intent, can produce a vivid reaction which eventually erupts into the conscious mind.

Gloria's panic-assisted escape takes her to the railway station and it is there that Maury Noble outlines his philosophy which Gloria is able to summarise as her own. And that is exactly the point which the haunting experience has symbolised. A life lived according to that code of meaninglessness when even self-gratifying pleasures are mechanical and bring no joy is indeed damned. By establishing the Patches' behaviour in descriptions of Bachanals, of 'dank staleness of wine and cigarettes' as their way of seeking 'the moment's happiness as fervently and persistently as possible'[60] within the overall context of an older dialogue on the nature of love, Fitzgerald leaves no doubt that he wishes to make the strong point that they have fatally misunderstood this key to life. Without a proper appreciation of love, life is meaningless.

'So this is love!'[61] begins Anthony when he is jealously preparing a speech for Gloria. Clearly, on the terms of Plato's *Symposium*, it is not. The fact that it leads to Maury's dead-end philosophy damns it. It has failed to create hope and it has failed because, in Diotima's words, it is the result of identifying 'Love with the beloved object instead of with what feels love.'[62] This mistake led Anthony to fix all his hopes of happiness upon the beauty of Gloria. He had failed to perceive what Amory finally came to realise, that 'beauty must be relative or, itself a harmony, it would make only a discord'.[63]

Although *The Beautiful and Damned* prefers the imagery of sunlight over musical imagery, the same belief lies at the centre of Anthony's story. After the insights of 'Symposium' the rest of the story can only be of further decline. Increasingly the Patches' deteriorate; gradually their moral deterioration is matched by their physical appearances. Their love, being insecurely based on a selfishness, can inspire them with no hope save the one of inheriting Grandfather Patch's money and no guiding principle other than that of self-gratification. Their lives illustrate in a painfully negative way the truth of the statement which Plato gave to Phaedrus. 'The principle which ought to guide the whole life of those who intend to live nobly cannot be implanted either by family or by position or by wealth or by anything else so effectively as by love.'[64]

It is indeed difficult to understand how, so conspicuously lacking this key, the story of Anthony and Gloria can ever be thought of as suggesting an heroic perspective. In addition, since the first two novels are both derived from a consistent ironic point

of view which centres upon the concepts of self and love, it is
surprising that a belief in Fitzgerald's inability either to plan his
stories or to think on a conceptual level ever gained any credence
at all. An objective study of the content and technique of the first
two novels reveals not only a careful organisation based upon a
coherent ironic point of view but also evidence that these early
works should be viewed as being much closer to *The Great Gatsby*
and *Tender is the Night* than any double vision theory has so far
allowed.

4

The Great Gatsby

The Great Gatsby, Fitzgerald's third novel, was published in April 1925, three years after the appearance of *The Beautiful and Damned*. Almost from the beginning it has been highly acclaimed and today it is probably the novel which most critics regard as Fitzgerald's masterpiece. But the fact that this reputation has been built upon the foundation of biographical explanations of his talent should cause some disquiet. As long as it is believed that Fitzgerald was an emotional rather than a conceptual thinker, as long as it is believed that the key element in his artistic development was his struggle to understand his emotional memories, then his first two novels will be undervalued and the true artistry of *The Great Gatsby* will remain hidden. Crucially, if the ironies in the first two novels are not seen in Fitzgerald's intended perspective, then his special view of the tragic – the very heart of Gatsby's story – will remain hidden in an alleged mystery: how to explain a dramatic leap from the immaturities of *The Beautiful and Damned* to the 'deeper understanding' revealed in *The Great Gatsby*.[1]

Conventionally, the sense of the tragic in Fitzgerald's fiction has been linked to the pathetic details of the real-life story. Because it has come to be widely believed that 'he often wrote with a desire to relieve and to cope with his sense of hurt,'[2] suggestions of a tragic sense are invariably related to the life-cycle. Professor Mizener certainly helped to establish this tendency. His use of the now famous 'taking things hard' comment from Fitzgerald's Notebooks seems to confirm the notion that otherwise inexplicable tragic notions playing around rather everyday events have a simple explanation: the fictional events can normally be traced to failures and humiliations suffered by Fitzgerald in the real world.[3]

Henry Dan Piper's *Critical Portrait* of Fitzgerald leans heavily upon the idea of a subjectively derived sense of the tragic. In his version of the literary manifestations of Fitzgerald's alleged intellectual immaturities, Piper shows an allegiance to the Wilsonian dictum by claiming that only after *The Beautiful and Damned* did

Fitzgerald begin to sense 'the tragic ambiguities imbedded in ordinary, everyday American bourgeois experience'. However, for Piper, *The Great Gatsby* failed to achieve full artistic maturity mainly because its author, allegedly, could not distance himself sufficiently from those experiences so that he could control the ironies.[4] Hence, according to Piper, the attempt to achieve a tragic perspective for Gatsby's story lacks consistency.

Mizener's criticism of *The Great Gatsby* is based upon the same belief in a lack of detachment. He sees a confusing fundamental opposition in the novel. On the one hand Fitzgerald has created the impression of the underlying corruption of Daisy's world, and on the other, the strong impression of Gatsby's 'heroic' and 'essential incorruptibility'. This leads to imbalance because, according to Mizener, Fitzgerald was drawn too much to Gatsby: he was personally committed to his character's 'romantic attitude'.[5]

The estimate of Norman Podhoretz, although less sympathetic, follows the basic assumptions of Mizener. In addition, like Piper, he makes it clear that he believes that in writing *The Great Gatsby* Fitzgerald was embarked on a voyage of self-discovery.

> If in the character of Gatsby Fitzgerald expressed a deeper understanding of his own predicament than he had ever achieved before, the shadowy abstractness with which Gatsby is drawn also indicates that there were severe limits to this new self-awareness . . . it is as though he could only go as far as he did in confronting himself by shrinking deliberately from the ultimate act of self-confrontation toward which the writing of this novel was pulling him.[6]

The determination to see important themes in Fitzgerald's work as evidence of an immature solipsism inevitably means that his actual ironic-pessimistic view of life which sees life constantly toppling over into 'an inartistic sixth act' will never be given its correct weight at the centre of his tragic vision.

A useful indication of the misreading which can follow such a neglect of Fitzgerald's concept of tragedy can be given by means of a close examination of the way Piper discusses what he takes to be an artistic weakness in *The Great Gatsby*. He claims that at a certain point in the story only a knowledge of autobiographical details can give the passage meaning. The relevant passage comes toward the end of Chapter 6. According to Piper, Fitzgerald's chief difficulty here concerned the way he might give details of Gatsby's past. He claims that Fitzgerald had originally intended to use 'a long monologue' early in Chapter 8 but he was too much afflicted by a familiar problem. 'But at this point in his first draft Fitzgerald so identified himself with his hero that he had difficulty controlling his prose; the result was a long, soggy autobiographical confession as bad as the poorer parts of "The Romantic Egotist".'[7]

The interesting feature of Piper's explanation is the evidence which he offers as proof of Fitzgerald's inability to distance himself from his fiction. Piper's major point concerns an experience from Gatsby's belief that if he could return to 'a certain starting place' and rethink the event slowly then he might be able 'to recover something, some idea of himself perhaps, that had gone into loving Daisy'.[8] This is the relevant passage.

One autumn night, five years before, they had been walking down the street when the leaves were falling, and they came to a place where there were no trees and the sidewalk was white with moonlight. They stopped here and turned toward each other. Now it was a cool night with that mysterious excitement in it which comes at the two changes of the year. The quiet lights in the houses were humming out into the darkness and there was a stir and bustle among the stars. Out of the corner of his eye Gatsby saw that the blocks of the sidewalks really formed a ladder and mounted to a secret place above the trees – he could climb to it, if he climbed alone, and once there he could suck on the pap of life, gulp down the incomparable milk of wonder.[9]

Piper's criticism centres upon the last sentence of this passage. Believing as he does in the applicability of the subjectivity/ objectivity interpretation, he concludes that Fitzgerald's own confusions created a condensed version which is inexplicable without certain details from the earlier 'soggy' draft.

Here the words 'if he climbed alone' make sense only if they are put back into the context of the original passage. There is nothing explicit in the final version of the novel to indicate that Gatsby felt shackled by his first affair with Daisy or that he wanted to escape from her. Fitzgerald momentarily confused Gatsby's feeling toward Daisy with his own growing concern over Zelda[10]

This kind of criticism of this important passage from *The Great Gatsby* completely misses the point that Fitzgerald is here outlining the central issue which for him stamps Gatsby's story as tragic. Piper's approach simply cannot accommodate even the possibility that Fitzgerald knew precisely what he was doing in this passage. In fact, far from signalling a confusion in comprehension, the Gatsby/Daisy relationship is a carefully controlled and perfectly adequate objective correlative for Fitzgerald's idea of modern tragedy. Moreover, since the same point of view had been the shaping intelligence behind the first two novels, *The Great Gatsby* should not be thought of as a startling advance in Fitzgerald's abilities. If *This Side of Paradise* can be read freed from biographical speculations it will be seen to provide a sound basis for an appreciation of this central issue of the tragic.

The specific factor which effectively prevents Piper from recognising the tragic dimension of *This Side of Paradise* is its irony. The idea that Fitzgerald's first novel could be ironic in both content and technique is completely incompatible with the received opinion about his early intellectual abilities. Consequently, since it could not possibly be expected, the controlling irony is not discerned. Criticism, therefore, proceeds in a self-fulfilling fashion. Only an approach which concentrates upon the work itself rather than upon assumptions about the author's personality will break the logical circularity of the biographical method. *This Side of Paradise* operates on several levels of meaning. Two are fairly obvious: Amory's level of perception, and another level which continually implies the negation of Amory's insights. The significant factor about this form of dual narrative is that the distance between the two levels of perception is an ironic one expressed by the non-explicit use of thematic imagery and symbolic action. This preference for an implicit means of expression is an important pointer for the succeeding works. The use of an ironic technique however, was wholly dependent upon an ironic vision and it is Piper's failure to detect that prime feature which caused him to deduce a technical weakness in Fitzgerald's treatment of the Gatsby/Daisy relationship.

To appreciate the full ironic philosophy which informs *This Side of Paradise* it is necessary to realise that the novel actually establishes three planes of meaning. Although it might at first appear that the ironic gap between Amory Blaine's perceptions and the true meaning of his experiences is closed when he achieves the pessimistic insight that life is simply a sequence of struggles from illusion to illusion, this insight is only the first part of the final vision. The full ironic perspective is to be found in the fact that Fitzgerald has Amory see that 'the struggle was worthwhile'.[11] Amory's experiences illustrate the paradox that the struggle to reach an illusory happiness, although destined to fail on one level, will provide the highest form of happiness available on this side of Paradise. It is the expectation of happiness alone which creates happiness. Thus Amory's egotistical confidence was more securely based than at first seemed possible. The third level of meaning, then, the true norm of the novel, offers an ironic modification of the sad fact that life will continually offer a series of disappointments.

Although the ironic vindication of Amory's intuitions is the major factor in the final vision, it is heavily dependent upon that first idea of the inevitability of disappointment. It was that idea which characterised *The Romantic Egotist* where it appears explicitly in the notion of an apparently 'wearing down power'. Drawn into a hopeless struggle against this force are the innocent who bravely believe that they can win against the odds. These brave innocents are typified by the fox of the nursery book story and the gallant Princeton athlete who defied the might of Yale. For Fitzgerald this area of conflict was a form of epic action. Respect for the stand of the innocent is established by the contrast between the inevitability of their failure and the intensity of their illusion that they would succeed. However, the inevitable defeat of the brave innocents is only the first part of Fitzgerald's concept of modern tragedy. He also shows how, in an important way, the losers can gain a great deal by their defeat.[12]

As early as 1917, as the short story 'The Pierian Springs and the Last Straw' illustrates,[13] Fitzgerald was constructing his fictions on the basis of an ironic vision. In that story Fitzgerald shows that in contrast to the comfortable and uncreative mediocrity which followed Uncle George's long-hoped for marriage, the earlier apparent failure when the lady first refused him was actually the basis of his artistic success. As in Amory's case, Fitzgerald's emphasis upon the superiority of hope over attainment vindicates the early illusions: happiness based upon false hopes is still happiness. The irony in Uncle George's story is reinforced by an implicit comparison with the marvellous horse Pegasus who found shackles where he took his magical refreshment. Life's inexorable movement towards an 'inartistic sixth act' which exposes the frailty of the illusions ensures that the shackles of reality are always waiting. Thus, like Amory Blaine, Uncle George's nearest approach to Paradise was the illusion that he knew how to get there.

The short story illustrates several important characteristics of Fitzgerald's irony which could help to resolve the problem which Piper has set himself with the *Gatsby* passage. The most significant characteristic is the choice of the concept of love to illustrate an ironical-tragic view. In all his novels Fitzgerald's treatment of man's most fundamental illusion – that he is destined to achieve happiness – is centred upon the illusion that it is love which will transport him to a magical world of eternal happiness. Amory Blaine survives this illusion as it presents itself to him through the beautiful masks of Isabelle, Rosalind and Eleanor. Anthony Patch is less fortunate: like Uncle George, he marries his dream girl and has to live with the inevitable disillusionment. The fate of these characters should provide definite hints about the way Fitzgerald thinks about Gatsby's predicament.

In *This Side of Paradise*, although the three major love affairs carry the main burden of illustration, the pattern begins to be established as early as the episode concerning Myra St. Claire.[14] In that episode Fitzgerald presents the key elements which distinguish two levels of meaning: on the one hand there is Amory's sense that happiness is just one symbolic gesture away; and on the other hand there is his instinctive revulsion when he actually achieves the kiss.

Although the full meaning of this incident of the kiss can only be appreciated when the third level of meaning has been discerned, it is quite clear that Fitzgerald intends it to be seen as what he had earlier called a juvenile index to the final point of view. In this respect it offers direct assistance towards understanding of the *Gatsby* passage. The following excerpt which sets the scene for Amory's kiss has much in common with the one singled out by Piper.

> Overhead the sky was half crystalline, half misty, and the night around was chill and vibrant with rich tension. From the Country Club steps the road stretched away, dark creases on the white blanket; huge heaps of snow lining the sides like the tracks of giant moles. They lingered for a moment on the steps, and watched the white holiday moon.[15]

As in the *Gatsby* passage, Fitzgerald creates an atmosphere of 'mysterious excitement'. The same sense of 'rich tension' vibrates through both paragraphs. It is generated by the impression that a magical happiness is within reach. In these tense but calm moonlight moments, both Amory and Gatsby sense a great potential. The imagery suggests a oneness with the wider natural world. Amory's dominant idea of a road to Arcady is prefigured here and the same image of a magical pathway is contained in Gatsby's vision of the ladder which leads to 'a secret place'. Such is the power of illusion. Both passages concentrate upon the high peak of expectation at the moment before ambition is realised and the disillusioning process begins. In Amory's case, because this incident occurs early in the novel before the pattern of imagery which forms the second plane of meaning has been established, this juvenile index towards the final ironical-tragic point of view is not immediately understandable. Amory's instinctive revulsion to the kiss can appear to be excessive. However, in Gatsby's case, his own reported impressions convey a sense of his dilemma more fully. It is clear that Fitzgerald wishes to suggest Gatsby's intuitive understanding that a commitment to Daisy will effectively prevent his access to Arcady.

The paragraph immediately following the one chosen by Piper actually expresses Gatsby's awareness that Daisy represents a serious limitation of his potential. Unfortunately for Piper, Fitzgerald uses the non-explicit device of imagery to express Gatsby's intuition. However, since the first two novels provide sufficient evidence of Fitzgerald's predilection for that form of expression, such a preference might reasonably be expected to appear in his third novel. In any case, Gatsby's sense of limitation is perfectly clear in the following paragraph, although the image which suggests Gatsby's god-like potential might seem rather unusual and perhaps excessive; it is clearly derived from the same point of view which produced the ironic image of Pegasus who found shackles where he took his refreshment and which also created Amory's experiences with various masks of beauty.

His heart beat faster and faster as Daisy's white face came up to his own. He knew that when he kissed this girl, and forever wed his unutterable visions to her perishable breath, his mind would never romp again like the mind of God. So he waited, listening for a moment longer to the tuning-fork that had been struck upon a star. Then he kissed her. At his lips' touch she blossomed for him like a flower and the incarnation was complete.[16]

This memorable image invests the kiss with an enormous import-ance. It is unlikely that it is merely the product of Fitzgerald's personal confusion. It is much more likely that it was drawn from the ironical-tragic point of view which created *This Side of Paradise* and the story of Uncle George.

Although it is indeed inspired by the same point of view, there is a crucial point of difference between the way Fitzgerald employed the imagery in the passage singled out by Piper and the way he used it in the first two novels. In the first two works, imagery is the principal means by which the second level of meaning is estab-lished: it forms that level which continually calls into question the perceptions of the protagonists. In *This Side of Paradise* metaphors of travel and music work to suggest that Amory is following the wrong road, listening to the wrong musical note. In *The Beautiful and Damned* Anthony's mistake is implied by a structure of imagery which represents Gloria as a sterile radiance rather than a fructify-ing warmth. However, as the *Gatsby* passage shows, there is no ironic distance between Gatsby's perception and the standard represented by the imagery. Indeed, from the manner of the narration it would seem that Gatsby himself produced these images when he recounted the incident for Carraway. The fun-damental point which this method establishes is that Gatsby was in no doubt that by choosing Daisy he was giving up a tremendous power. The importance of this fact cannot be overemphasised. It is directly related to the central issue of the whole novel and, as such, Piper's failure to understand its relevance is particularly dis-turbing.

The key factor which Piper has failed to detect is that important first part of Fitzgerald's philosophy: the idea of the tragic. Since Piper missed this aspect in the first two novels it was, therefore, much more unlikely that he would see it in the third because *The Great Gatsby* actually extends the concept. The extension comes in the very area which Piper focuses upon for his major criticism of the novel. Although Piper is unaware of it, Fitzgerald makes it quite clear that Gatsby chooses to be shackled to Daisy, to be incarnate, to cut himself off from the inspiration of a celestial note. From the boundless freedom of a wider universe he turns to the narrower world where mortal beauty is the inspirational factor. Uncle George's story can supply the perspective for this kind of change. He had imagined that his tragedy was that he had failed to win his girl for his wife. Fitzgerald shows that the greater tragedy came later when Uncle George actually married the lady. The 'inartistic sixth act' cruelly exposed the fact that he was happier when he was living under the influence of his illusion. It was the loss of the illusion which produced the real tragedy. It is this basic idea of tragedy which *The Great Gatsby* extends, for, unlike Uncle George and unlike Amory Blaine, Gatsby is shown to be conscious of the limitations he is accepting in making his commitment to Daisy.

There is an irony here, which would be amusing were it not so indicative of a widespread misunderstanding, for, in support of his idea of Fitzgerald's immaturity, Piper turns to Fitzgerald's own comment in which he offers direct help with this vital part of his philosophy. In the following comment Fitzgerald shows that the basis of Gatsby's story is the same as Uncle George's, in that *The Great Gatsby* is about 'the loss of those illusions that give such color to the world that you don't care whether things are true or false so long as they partake of the magical glory'.[17] Although *This Side of Paradise* and *The Beautiful and Damned* were also about 'the loss of those illusions', in neither case were the protagonists aware of delusion at the time of their significant experiences. In Anthony's case he never realised he had been deluded and in Amory's case it was not until the end of the novel that he was able to come to terms with disillusionment. In making Gatsby aware of the loss Fitzgerald added an extra poignancy to the tragic dimension. The tragic dimension to the heroic struggles of those who oppose the 'wearing down power' comes when the essential innocence which caused them to begin their efforts in the first place is lost and they see their visions were merely illusions.

In this way Fitzgerald developed the idea of a double vision: an idea which biographical critics like Piper consistently misapply. Although the idea was not made explicit until February 1936 in 'The Crack-Up' essay it is implicit in *This Side of Paradise*. It is the key to Amory Blaine's final position. Although he comes to know that all past happiness was based upon illusion, still he determines that 'the struggle was worth while'. His determination to continue the struggle, although he knows he will fail, characterises him as one of those beings earlier defined as 'being spiritually unmarried'.

These men attempt the impossible in their 'struggle to guide and control life'. They are opposed to the immense influence wielded by the 'spiritually married' men who have the 'direct power' – derived from wealth – which makes them 'the keepers of the world's intellectual conscience'.[18] Gatsby's predicament is simply an extension of this idea.

The perspective of the 'spiritually unmarried man' allows the full extent of Gatsby's tragic struggle to be seen. Fitzgerald presents him as a man of tremendous potential who directs his energies towards an idea of happiness represented first by Dan Cody's yacht and then by Daisy Fay. However, unlike the protagonists in the first two novels, Gatsby is given insight into the real meaning of his actions and this has the effect of increasing the sense of tragedy. According to the later notion of 'the test of a first-rate intelligence' this 'spiritually unmarried man' was just that. He had 'the ability to hold two opposed ideas in the mind at the same time, and still retain the ability to function'.[19] It is this which lies behind the passage which causes Piper so much trouble. Only the determination to refuse to believe that Fitzgerald was intellectually capable of this level of thought early in his career will continue to misinterpret such passages.

'The Crack-Up' essay begins with a statement which rephrases the idea of the 'wearing-down power' contained in *The Romantic Egotist*. Like that first expression it contains the essence of the prime fact which is the setting for tragedy – the inevitability of unhappiness. But the essay illustrates the same ironic philosophy which vindicated Amory Blaine's struggle and it does so by illustrating – as does *This Side of Paradise* – that the greatest happiness comes in the expectation of happiness. So, accepting that, 'Of course all life is a process of breaking down',[20] the illusion of imminent happiness produced in Fitzgerald 'such an ecstasy that I could not share it even with the person dearest to me'.[21] This emphasis upon the power of illusion should not be underestimated but Fitzgerald points out that in this respect he was unusual. 'I think that my happiness, or talent for self-delusion or what you will, was an exception.'[22] It is in this respect that Gatsby too is to be thought of as unusual. It signifies a greater degree of innocence than the average: an innocence which is made even more remarkable by the intimations of the eventual defeat of happiness. This is the complication which Piper's criticism isolates but cannot explain.

One important aspect of Fitzgerald's extension of his basic idea of modern tragedy is to be seen in the way Gatsby's story takes on an epic quality. The ironical-tragic philosophy supplies a meaning which functions on the level of an historical national truth. However, there are other more obvious details consequent upon Gatsby's instincts and these should be considered first.

In the first instance, the important role played by Nick Carraway should be noted. The change to a first-person narrative is a key element in a literary structure which provided Fitzgerald with an admirable form for the expression of his philosophy. In the first two novels – given the overwhelmingly biographical approach of the critics – the omniscient author technique has sometimes obscured the ironical point of view. In *This Side of Paradise* for example, the imagery of travel and music is seemingly invested with an authority which makes it difficult to appreciate that it too must be questioned in order that a third level of meaning can be reached. Amory's instincts must be seen to have been nearer the truth than the imagery appears to allow. *The Great Gatsby* functions without that structure of imagery which, in the first two novels, seems consistently to set an implicit ironic comment against the perceptions of the protagonists.

In the two major areas in which the imagery in *The Great Gatsby* operates, no ironic intention is present: it establishes Carraway's equal disapproval, both of Gatsby's social world of vulgar wealth and the Buchanans' less ostentatious material vulgarity; and it makes clear Gatsby's remoteness from both these worlds. In each area the personality of the narrator is vital. From the beginning of the work Carraway draws attention to the fact that conduct is an accurate expression of an inner code but he also warns against the tendency to make quick moral assessments. He even goes so far as to suggest a moral perspective for Gatsby 'who represented everything for which I have an unaffected scorn', because he says that 'Gatsby turned out all right at the end'.[23] The focus, therefore, is upon the kind of moral code which can resolve the apparent paradox. The use of a scrupulously honest and morally aware participating narrator introduces the right kind of hesitancy consistent with someone who is re-enacting his original confusion, albeit with the tone of his narrative naturally tinged with his mature assessment.

Carraway's first experience of Gatsby's parties offers a good example of the way that the narrator's strong moral sense works on the people who surround Gatsby but fails when it comes to Gatsby himself. In Chapter 3 Carraway's disapproval of the expensively contrived festivities is quite apparent. There is no difficulty in detecting the essential emptiness and unnatural aspect of the activities described.

> The bar is in full swing, and floating rounds of cocktails permeate the garden outside, until the air is alive with chatter and laughter, and casual innuendo and introductions forgotten on the spot, and enthusiastic meetings between women who never knew each other's names.
>
> The lights grow brighter as the earth lurches away from the sun, and now the orchestra is playing yellow cocktail music, and the opera of voices pitches a key higher. Laughter is easier minute by minute, spilled with prodigality, tipped out at a cheerful word. The groups change more swiftly, swell with new arrivals, dissolve and form in the same breath; already there are wanderers, confident girls who weave here and there among the stouter and more stable, become for a sharp, joyous moment the center of a group, and then, excited with triumph, glide on through the sea-change of faces and voices and color under the constantly changing light.[24]

In this implicit criticism of part of the 'universe of ineffable gaudiness' which Gatsby created, the sea imagery which expresses the constant and mindless fluidity of the party's movement, suggests a non-human perspective: the continual forming and dissolving of groups is as purposeless as the movements of fish-shoals. The impression is of a scene viewed through a long-shot lens. However, the major element which works to establish this sense of distance is the introduction of a cosmic scale to these festivities. This occurs in the deliberate periphrasis for the coming of darkness – 'as the earth lurches away from the sun'. The unnaturalness of the increased abandon which night-time brings is suggested in the idea of 'yellow cocktail music', louder voices and faster movements. The unreality of the situation is continued a little later in the episode by speculations about Gatsby's past but more particularly by the incredulity of Owl Eyes that the books in Gatsby's library were 'absolutely real'.[25]

As the party develops, Carraway's descriptions of its various component parts become more marked by his pointed disapproval.

In the following passage the effect is achieved in the main by key adjectival and adverbial qualifications but the last sentence again emphasises the cosmic scale by implying how the unrealities of 'vulgar, and meretricious beauty' impinge upon the natural world.

> There was dancing now on the canvas in the garden; old men pushing young girls backward in eternal graceless circles, superior couples holding each other tortuously, fashionably, and keeping in the corners – and a great number of single girls dancing individualistically or relieving the orchestra for a moment of the burden of the banjo or the traps. By midnight the hilarity had increased. A celebrated tenor had sung in Italian, and a notorious contralto had sung in jazz, and between the numbers people were doing 'stunts' all over the garden, while happy, vacuous bursts of laughter rose toward the summer sky. A pair of stage twins, who turned out to be the girls in yellow, did a baby act in costume, and champagne was served in glasses bigger than finger-bowls. The moon had risen higher, and floating in the Sound was a triangle of silver scales, trembling a little to the stiff, tinny drip of the banjoes on the lawn.[26]

That last description of the sound of the banjoes in conjunction with the moonlight has the effect of symbolising the distance which exists between the activities of the partygoers and the natural world.

It is against this background of Carraway's evident distaste that Fitzgerald introduces Gatsby. As the author of all this mirthless festivity, Gatsby should become the focus for Carraway's criticism. In fact although Carraway senses that Gatsby's 'elaborate formality of speech' hides 'an elegant young roughneck',[27] Carraway also stresses that Gatsby had 'nothing sinister about him', and actually seems to stand apart from the party activities. 'I wondered if the fact that he was not drinking helped to set him off from his guests, for it seemed to me that he grew more correct as the fraternal hilarity increased.'[28] This impression is continued through the drunken bickering and the confusion which follows the minor car smash. In fact Fitzgerald makes Gatsby's isolation absolutely clear by means of the tableau which closes the party.

> The caterwauling horns had reached a crescendo and I turned away and cut across the lawn toward home. I glanced back once.

A wafer of a moon was shining over Gatsby's house, making the night fine as before, and surviving the laughter and the sound of his still glowing garden. A sudden emptiness seemed to flow now from the windows and the great doors, endowing with complete isolation the figure of the host, who stood on the porch, his hand up in a formal gesture of farewell.[29]

The isolation of Gatsby is an important factor in the structure of the novel. By this kind of description Fitzgerald creates the strong impression that there is indeed something about Gatsby which sets him apart from others. At this point in the story, Carraway's subjective impression places Gatsby somewhere between two worlds: one of a natural calm and quietness; the other of an artificial rowdiness associated with moral laxity. As in a similar scene at the close of Chapter 1, the description locates Gatsby more nearly to the world of nature than it does to the world of society gaiety. In the above scene, like the fine night, he too survives the human cacophony. In the earlier scene Gatsby's 'curious' gesture of apparent supplication to the 'dark water' of the Sound distances him from the Buchanans' world (which has 'confused and a little disgusted'[30] Carraway) in the same way that his 'formal gesture' here distances him from his own noisy party. In both instances Gatsby is placed closer to the natural world than he is to the human. In the context of Carraway's implicit moral sense these impressions of Gatsby suggest a symbolism which is not immediately understandable. The two scenes produce powerful images which do not fit within the pattern of Carraway's explicit disapproval. The effect is to invest Gatsby's isolation with a degree of mystery which will make credible Carraway's desire to understand it.

This is exactly what Fitzgerald requires. Gatsby's predicament has been illustrated rather than merely described and an enigma is suggested. The impression is given that his actions are the expression of a morality which is different from either the materialistic hedonism of the partygoers or the socially superior materialism of the Buchanans' 'rather distinguished secret society'.[31] Just as importantly, Carraway's own rather stern provincial morality seems an inappropriate measure for Gatsby's conduct. The need to find the key which will unlock the enigma is heightened by the various speculations about Gatsby's unknown past. Had he been a German spy? Had he killed a man? Was he involved in corrupt business deals? Even Carraway feels that the man's origins might explain his behaviour.

> I would have accepted without question the information that Gatsby sprang from the swamps of Louisiana or from the lower East Side of New York. That was comprehensible. But young men didn't – at least in my provincial inexperience I believed they didn't – drift coolly out of nowhere and buy a palace on Long Island Sound.[32]

Carraway's opening remarks have prepared the way for a narrative which seeks all the time to place human behaviour on a moral scale. Although he warns of the need 'to reserve all judgements'[33] his own narrative contains clear, if usually implicit, judgements about events and characters. Once again, as in the first two novels, the imagery is largely instrumental in establishing an indirect level of meaning. In the first of the two major areas where it is to be found, that is in the expression of Carraway's equal disapproval of Gatsby's vulgar social world and the Buchanans' 'secret society', it so typifies the inhabitants of those two worlds as to accentuate and morally enhance that second major area – Gatsby's detachment. It does this by characterising the conduct of most of the other characters as either purposeless or mindlessly selfish. Thus, in the descriptions of the first party, imagery of movement, sound and light reveal a fundamental lack of purpose: this assumes a moral dimension, for such behaviour indicates a moral code founded only upon a fashionable idea of pleasure.

In the same way the imagery which is associated with the Buchanans also expresses a moral judgement. Tom Buchanan is typified by imagery which suggests physical dominance. His awareness of his physical superiority matches his position and his sense of financial and social superiority. The deadening effect of this cruel power is well represented in the first scene in which Carraway meets Daisy. The scene is set by a description of the liveliness of the Buchanans' extensive lawn. The metaphor is of a runner who starts at the beach, runs 'for a quarter of a mile' and loses momentum as he approaches the house. There 'standing with his legs apart on the front porch' is the dominating figure of Tom Buchanan.[34]

In the following description, the image which implies Buchanan's control over nature is extended to include Daisy and Jordan

Baker. The image of a fluttering movement which is so susceptible to control extends the impression of the power which Buchanan holds over his possessions. It also suggests the unnatural aspect of possessions within this environment.

> We walked through a high hallway into a bright rosy-colored space, fragilely bound into the house by French windows at either end. The windows were ajar and gleaming white against the fresh grass outside that seemed to grow a little way into the house. A breeze blew through the room, blew curtains in at one end and out the other like pale flags, twisting them up toward the frosted wedding-cake of the ceiling, and then rippled over the wine-coloured rug, making a shadow on it as wind does on the sea.
>
> The only completely stationary object in the room was an enormous couch on which two young women were buoyed up as though upon an anchored balloon. They were both in white, and their dresses were rippling and fluttering as if they had just been blown back in after a short flight around the house. I must have stood for a few moments listening to the whip and snap of the curtains and the groan of a picture on the wall. Then there was a boom as Tom Buchanan shut the rear windows and the caught wind died out about the room, and the curtains and the rugs and the two young women ballooned slowly to the floor.[35]

Daisy's first words to Carraway continue the image of enforced stillness and take on the quality of a moral judgement of herself. She says: 'I'm p-paralyzed with happiness.'[36]

It is against this background of an unnatural calmness that Carraway hears of Tom's infidelity. The knowledge makes him wish to take some kind of action. However, no sense of urgency penetrates Daisy's languid boredom. She describes herself as being 'pretty cynical about everything'.[37] Then, in a speech in which she attempts to justify her bitter cynicism, she actually reveals that the emotion is simply an act.

> 'You see I think everything's terrible anyhow,' she went on in a convinced way. 'Everybody thinks so – the most advanced people. And I *know*. I've been everywhere and seen everything and done everything.' Her eyes flashed around her in a defiant way, rather like Tom's, and she laughed with thrilling scorn. 'Sophisticated – God, I'm sophisticated!'

Carraway makes clear the revealing point: Daisy is not really stirred by any depth of feeling. She is an empty and bored person who is happy to remain in her very privileged position.

> The instant her voice broke off, ceasing to compel my attention, my belief, I felt the basic insincerity of what she had said. It made me uneasy, as though the whole evening had been a trick of some sort to exact a contributory emotion from me. I waited, and sure enough, in a moment she looked at me with an absolute smirk on her lovely face, as if she had asserted her membership in a rather distinguished secret society to which she and Tom belonged.[38]

The special characteristic of this 'society' is a failure of emotion, an inability to feel anything strongly enough to take action over a moral principle. It is this which disgusts Carraway. 'It seemed to me that the thing for Daisy to do was to rush out of the house, child in arms – but apparently there were no such intentions in her head.'[39]

Carraway also shows that the same kind of moral inertia lies behind Tom's infidelity. 'The fact that he "had some woman in New York" was really less surprising than that he had been depressed by a book.'[40] Thus, as in the description of the activities of the first party, the conduct of the Buchanans reveals an emptiness, an inability to feel which, when measured against Carraway's own instincts of moral rectitude – 'I'm a bond man'[41] he claims, meaning more than his profession – suggests that such insensitivity is an important factor in the progress towards the novel's code of morality. In this sense, such descriptions are useful 'indexes' to the final point of view.

Chapter 1 ends with Carraway's first glimpse of Gatsby. Still under the influence of his insights into the 'remotely rich' world of the Buchanans, Carraway at first sees Gatsby as he first saw Tom firmly planted on the front porch surveying his possessions. 'Something in his leisurely movements and the secure position of his feet upon the lawn suggested that it was Mr. Gatsby himself, come out to determine what share was his of our local heavens.'[42] Although Carraway does not realise it, that rather cynical assessment is badly placed because Gatsby does not have Tom's aggressive sense of ownership. The difference is apparent in their different gestures. Tom's 'broad flat hand' makes a sweep that encompasses 'a sunken Italian garden, a half acre of deep, pungent roses, and a snub-nosed motor-boat'.[43] Gatsby stretches out his arms 'toward the dark water'[44] not his possessions. His whole interest is focused upon the 'single green light'[45] at the end of Daisy's dock. As in the later scene at the end of the first party, Gatsby is associated with the natural world and his distance from the Buchanans and his own guests takes on a moral significance. Although the picture lacks important details at this point, it is clear that, whereas the others exhibit an almost mechanical behaviour, Gatsby is motivated by a sense of purpose which is so strong as to reveal itself in the trembling gesture he makes towards the green light.

The importance of the imagery in establishing a general poverty of emotion can be seen clearly in Chapter 2. The chief factor which establishes the sordid aspect of Tom's affair with Myrtle Wilson is its lack of passion. It seems peculiarly pointless: as though Tom were simply following some pattern of expected behaviour. Fittingly, the image which introduces this empty relationship exploits the sterility and unnaturalness of the 'valley of ashes'. In this landscape reality is counterfeited by a true nothingness.

> This is a valley of ashes – a fantastic farm where ashes grow like wheat into ridges and hills and grotesque gardens; where ashes take the forms of houses and chimneys and rising smoke and, finally, with a transcendent effort, of ash-gray men who move dimly and already crumbling through the powdery air.[46]

This dead world is presided over by the faceless, bespectacled eyes of the Doctor T. J. Eckleburg advertisement. The nightmare phenomenon that a barren valley can suggest reality is matched by imagery which highlights a sense of the unnatural in the episode at Myrtle's apartment. The most obvious aspect of this is the way various incongruities blur reality. As in the valley of ashes, there is absolutely nothing substantial behind the impression of solidity. A bogus domesticity is being followed. Myrtle seems to be led by her image of society style and Tom, since he gives no indication of anything other, simply by lust.

The descriptions continually draw attention to the differences between appearance and reality. Even before the whisky produces its distorting effect, Carraway so senses the 'almost pastoral' feeling in the sun on Fifth Avenue that he 'wouldn't have been surprised to see a great flock of white sheep turn the corner'. That incongruity is continued by the description of the furniture in the crowded apartment. Carraway continually stumbles 'over scenes of ladies swinging in the gardens of Versailles'. There is also a picture which looks at first to be 'a hen sitting on a blurred rock' but might be the picture of 'a stout old lady'. Although the 'cheerful sun' is in evidence outside the apartment, it merely serves to emphasise the grotesque human behaviour within. Although Carraway thinks it could have been the setting for a pastoral scene, this particular New York Sunday afternoon is dominated by the selfish concerns of Tom's acquaintances. 'The late afternoon sky bloomed in the window for a moment like the blue honey of the Mediterranean – then the shrill voice of Mrs. McKee called me back into the room.'[47] Nothing blooms in this environment where drunken confusion passes as the normal social activity. The sterility matches that of the valley of ashes where human activity is only dimly perceived through an 'impenetrable cloud' of ash. In the cigarette smoke and alcoholic haze of Myrtle's apartment. 'People disappeared, reappeared, made plans to go somewhere, and then lost each other, searched for each other, found each other a few feet away.'[48]

The episode reaches a climax in an act of controlled violence when Tom restrains Myrtle from using Daisy's name. 'Making a short deft movement, Tom Buchanan broke her nose with his open hand.' Even the violence is peculiarly passionless and it is immediately accepted and assimilated in an attempt to maintain the impression of urban *savoir faire*. McKee comes out of his drunken doze and observes the scene as his wife and Catherine attempt to restore order –

> scolding and consoling as they stumbled here and there among the crowded furniture with articles of aid, and the despairing figure on the couch, bleeding fluently, and trying to spread a copy of *Town Tattle* over the tapestry scenes of Versailles.[49]

This is a fine image for Myrtle's devotion to materialism. Carraway's depiction of her concentrates entirely upon the details of her taste which her status as Tom's mistress allows her to indulge. From the moment she arrives in New York to this point, Fitzgerald indicates Myrtle's delight in the kind of material possessions denied her by her married life back in the valley of ashes. It is clear she aspires to a life-style derived from ideas given by magazines like *Town Tattle*. Fitzgerald's descriptions of the typical possessions leave no doubt of Carraway's disapproval. In addition to the 'tapestried furniture' and the 'elaborate afternoon dress' – and, of course, the 'Airedale' puppy – Myrtle is set on buying 'one of those cute little ash-trays where you touch a spring, and a wreath with a black silk bow for mother's grave'.[50] However, it is not merely an aesthetic difference which causes the disapproval: Carraway's concern is focused upon the original idea rather than the expression of that idea.

Tom and Myrtle's apartment was prefigured there 'where ashes take the form of houses' and people. Myrtle's materialism and Tom's lust form the central emptiness which, like the ash, simulates reality. The emptiness is apparent in the joylessness of the whole episode. The pathetic picture of Myrtle, 'bleeding fluently' and trying to save her fake furniture from damage, well illustrates where her chief pleasures are to be found. Tom's insistence that Carraway meets his 'girl' when seen against the events of that meeting strongly suggests that he thinks of her as another of his possessions.

The emptiness at the heart of Tom's illicit relationship matches the condition of his legal union with Daisy. The imagery of the first chapter clearly indicates Daisy's willing acquiescence in the paralysis which the membership of the 'rather distinguished secret society' demands of her. If Tom's conduct is determined by his innate sense of physical, social and fiscal elitism, hers is derived from that 'secret society's' conventions of discreet behaviour. In each case the impression is given of a joyless acceptance of an apparently inevitable role. Daisy and Myrtle accept Tom's physical dominance because union with him represents the security which, in their different ways, they need. Tom takes Daisy and Myrtle as he took Demaine's house, as possessions necessary to a man of his stature. The conduct of these three characters is an accurate expression of their inner promptings and, given the dominance of images of power, paralysis and sterility, there is no doubt that Carraway's narrative carries an implicit moral disapproval.

The same disapproval is also apparent in Chapter 3 where it is in fact emphasised by explicit criticism of the activities of the drunken guests at Gatsby's house. Their joyless gaieties correspond to the behaviour at Myrtle's apartment suggesting that they too are driven by a received opinion about the way to have a good time. In this episode too, Fitzgerald's descriptions of the various activities leave the strong impression of a kind of willed unnaturalness: the determination to have a good time is in contrast to the calm beauty of the fine night. In the same way the 'cheerful sun'[51] which promises a classical pastoral is a silent reproach to Myrtle's guests.

Thus, although the use of a first-person narrator requires that all the characters are presented from the limited viewpoint of a participator, Carraway's undoubted interest in the inner conditions which motivate action ensures a concentration upon morals rather than manners. The first three chapters set up a pattern of analysis. Varieties of conduct are presented not as indicators of gradations on a social scale but as expressions of an inner moral code. In this way practically all the characters are seen to be motivated by a mindless selfishness served by an insensitivity and insincerity: two attributes which become advantages rather than disadvantages in their materialistic world. Jordan Baker illustrates the technique. Carraway is drawn to her and is puzzled by her. He knows he is not in love with her but feels 'a sort of tender curiosity' towards her. The crucial explanatory information concerns her moral code: 'She was incurably dishonest. She wasn't able to endure being at a disadvantage.'[52]

All Carraway's observations of conduct in the first three chapters are made with this kind of interest in the private inner values which motivate the characters. Despite his warning to the reader about the need to reserve judgements, it is clear that he has made up his mind. It is clear from the imagery which strongly suggests a moral emptiness at the heart of conduct. Only Gatsby is exempt from this criticism and not only does Fitzgerald have Carraway make that explicit in the introductory remarks, but he also has the imagery illustrate Gatsby's essential difference. Although Gatsby makes only a brief appearance in Chapter 3 after a fleeting one at the end of Chapter 1, these appearances produce two powerful and puzzling visual images. In this respect Fitzgerald exploits the convention of the participating narrator by having Carraway re-enact his initial difficulty in probing the springs of Gatsby's conduct. However, the narrative also exploits that other advantage of the method: the advantage of hindsight; Carraway does, after all, know the end of the story. Thus he can declare that 'Gatsby turned out all right at the end'.[53] This concentrates attention upon that hidden code which lifts Gatsby above that dimension of moral disapproval which Carraway uses for all the others.

Carraway's only justification of his opening remark about Gatsby turning out all right at the end is that he possessed 'some heightened sensitivity to the promise of life'. This is related to his 'extraordinary gift for hope, a romantic readiness'[54] which Carraway feels could be unique. In this important statement Carraway generalises about a crucial characteristic of Gatsby's which Fitzgerald illustrates in Chapter 6 where the information about the way James Gatz responded to the opportunity offered by Dan Cody is given. At that youthful time life appeared to promise that beauty and glamour could be attained if the right kind of determined effort were made. 'So he invented just the sort of Jay Gatsby that a seventeen-year-old boy would be likely to invent, and to this conception he was faithful to the end.'[55] At this point the link with Amory Blaine should be apparent and the continuity in Fitzgerald's thought remarked. The key element in Gatsby's character is essentially the same as Amory's egotism. It is the amazingly confident (and apparently misplaced) 'instinct towards his future glory'.[56]

Like the young Amory, James Gatz was finely tuned to detect opportunities in the outer, public world which adequately matched the powerful inner sense of self-election. This sensitive receptivity to chances of making the correct correlation is finely caught in the image of Gatsby as a seismograph. In *This Side of Paradise*, Amory's self-confidence seems to be called into question by imagery which continually suggests he is wrong in his various attempts to grasp happiness. Only at the end is there an ironic vindication of his illusions of imminent happiness. In Gatsby's case that qualifying role of imagery is replaced by the uncompromising attitude of Carraway's provincial morality. His assessment of the young man's commitment is that he had enrolled himself in 'the service of a vast, vulgar and meretricious beauty'.[57]

The following passage not only illustrates the power of vision, it also makes clear how inadequate Carraway feels this dream of beauty was.

The most grotesque and fantastic conceits haunted him in his bed at night. A universe of ineffable gaudiness spun itself out in his brain while the clock ticked on the wash-stand and the moon soaked with wet light his tangled clothes upon the floor.[58]

This criticism of the central character's perceptions differs from the way that *This Side of Paradise* forms its second plane of meaning because Carraway's subjective assessments do not carry the same weight of authority as does the imagery of an ominscient author. It is therefore easier in *The Great Gatsby* to reach the final ironic third level of meaning which requires that the other two be modified. In fact Fitzgerald specifically prepares for this by having Carraway warn about reserving judgements and by presenting Gatsby as a moral paradox: someone who appears to be so wrong and yet turns out all right. The key is indeed his 'heightened sensitivity to the promises of life'. That, in the light of his early commitment to gaudy dreams is another way of indicating his susceptibility to illusion and it is on this basis that Fitzgerald constructed his story.

Carraway's description of Gatsby's commitment to a dream of the 'universe of ineffable gaudiness' comes after Jordan had supplied him with that telling piece of information that 'Gatsby bought that house so that Daisy would be just across the bay.' This explains Gatsby's gestures on those earlier puzzling occasions. 'Then it had not been merely the stars to which he had aspired on that June night. He came alive to me, delivered suddenly from the womb of his purposeless splendor.'[59] But this newly appreciated purpose is given a framework of implicit judgement. Carraway's description carries an implicit criticism of Gatsby's choice. It leaves no doubt that wealth was a crucial element in the attraction. The 'excitement in her voice'[60] which intrigues Carraway as well as other men is diagnosed by Gatsby. 'Her voice is full of money,'[61] he tells Carraway. The early impression of Daisy is of a languid boredom which amounts to a paralysis; an inability to feel any emotion except, perhaps, self-pity. Beside this, Gatsby's tremendous energy suggests an ill-matched pair. Carraway's description of the occasion when the two met at his house emphasises Gatsby's vitality. 'He literally glowed; without a word or a gesture of exultation a new well-being radiated from him.'[62] Carraway's knowledge of Daisy produces misgivings which influence his subjective reading of Gatsby's mind now that Gatsby seems to be at the point of the realisation of his long-cherished hope.

As I went over to say good-by I saw that the expression of bewilderment had come back into Gatsby's face, as though a faint doubt had occurred to him as to the quality of his present happiness. Almost five years! There must have been moments

even that afternoon when Daisy tumbled short of his dreams –
not through her own fault, but because of the colossal vitality of
his illusion. It had gone beyond her, beyond everything. He had
thrown himself into it with a creative passion, adding to it all the
time, decking it out with every bright feather that drifted his
way.[63]

This guess of Carraway's is followed almost immediately by the
details of Gatsby's first encounter with Dan Cody. This increases
the strength of the impression that Gatsby has badly deluded
himself. His first mistake was to form the illusion that Cody's yacht
'represented all the beauty and glamour in the world'.[64] His second
mistake, like Rickie's in Forster's *The Longest Journey*, was to
imagine that all the world's beauty hung on a single peg, and that
was Daisy.

It is against this background that Carraway's presentation of
Gatsby's recollection of 'a certain starting place' (which so misleads
Piper) is given. Even at this point Carraway fails to understand the
crucial issue but it is here that the honesty which is part of his fairly
rigid provincial morality is most helpful. After the striking
metaphor which indicates Gatsby's sense of what he voluntarily
relinquished in committing himself to Daisy, Carraway adds:

> Through all he said, even through his appalling sentimentality, I
> was reminded of something – an elusive rhythm, a fragment of
> lost words, that I had heard somewhere a long time ago. For a
> moment a phrase tried to take shape in my mouth and my lips
> parted like a dumb man's, as though there was more struggling
> upon them than a wisp of startled air. But they made no sound,
> and what I had almost remembered was uncommunicable
> forever.[65]

Fitzgerald had used this technique in *This Side of Paradise*, notably
in the incident at Atlantic City involving Alec Connage and the girl
in the hotel bedroom. On that occasion Amory's intuition supplied
him with a wisdom denied his conscious mind and he was able to
take action and sacrifice his reputation for the sake of his friend's.
Here, Carraway's sense of an elusive memory suggests an earlier
moment, possibly in childhood, at which time he would more
easily have understood Gatsby's 'appalling sentimentality'.
Although this illustrates Carraway's sense of Gatsby's immaturity,

it also increases the impression of his isolation and does so in such a way as to suggest that the explanation exists on a dimension which can only be reached by a return to the outgrown understandings of earlier times.

Carraway's narrative makes it clear that Gatsby remained faithful to the end to ideas formed when he was seventeen. It is also clear that at this stage in their relationship Carraway feels that Gatsby was mistaken in his perceptions. The essence of Gatsby's dream was an idea of beauty and glamour which was rooted in wealth. This was why he was attracted to Daisy: she was the epitome of all that his adolescent sensitivity had marked out as desirable 'and Gatsby was overwhelmingly aware of the youth and mystery that wealth imprisons and preserves, of the freshness of many clothes, and of Daisy, gleaming like silver, safe and proud above the hot struggles of the poor'.[66] This insight is given ironic corroboration in that first impression of Daisy where she and Jordan appear to have been floating around the hot room. There, the imagery of Tom's dominance and the idea of Daisy's paralysis illustrates the irony of Gatsby's sense of the power of wealth to imprison and preserve. The imagery of flight is well suited to indicate Carraway's impression of Gatsby's fundamental mistake. It indicates the insubstantial foundation on which he erected his idea of reality – a belief in 'the unreality of reality, a promise that the rock of the world was founded securely on a fairy's wing'.[67]

Yet, for all his obvious disapproval, Carraway's narrative suggests a sympathy for Gatsby. This seems to be due in part to the fact that Gatsby is clearly on his own and driven by a dream which is so far removed from reality that it could not possibly be realised. His illusions are no match for 'the hard malice'[68] of that 'secret society' which is obviously based upon a different view of reality. However, the moral condition of that more powerful society is characterised by imagery of sterility and paralysis and its actions seem only to produce an unnatural and false gaiety. Gatsby, on the other hand, has a vitality and potential for intense happiness which clearly attracts Carraway despite his misgivings. Thus, when he rode in Gatsby's car, although he is by nature 'slow-thinking and full of interior rules that act as brakes on [his] desires',[69] he enjoys the journey for the sense of excited pleasure that it creates. Significantly, the imagery suggests flight. Through the valley of ashes they speed, catching only a glimpse of Mrs Wilson.

With fenders spread like wings we scattered light through half Astoria . . .

Over the great bridge, with the sunlight through the girders making a constant flicker upon the moving cars, with the city rising up across the river in white heaps and sugar lumps all built with a wish out of non-olfactory money. The city seen from the Queensboro Bridge is always the city seen for the first time, in its first wild promise of all the mystery and the beauty in the world . . . 'Anything can happen now that we've slid over this bridge,' I thought; 'anything at all . . .'

Even Gatsby could happen, without any particular wonder.[70]

The fact that Carraway is caught up by this kind of expectant wonder is important.

Carraway's next journey along this route produces a very different impression: it lacks the pleasurable excitement which attended the illusion of the city's 'wild promise of all the mystery and beauty in the world'. The parallel journey comes at Daisy's request on the occasion of the gathering at her house on a day dominated by the enervating heat of one of the last days of summer. On that day the true nature of Daisy's remoteness is again stressed by the extension of that ironic image of a floating, silver Daisy 'safe and proud above the hot struggles of the poor'. 'Daisy and Jordan lay upon an enormous couch, like silver idols weighing down their own white dresses against the singing breeze of the fans.' However, this time weight and solidity are more apparent than magical flight. As in the first scene, Daisy and Jordan are incapable of movement, 'We can't move,' they said together.[71] The relentless beating heat of the day dominates the episode and produces the impression of suffocation which matches the sense of confusion which Daisy expresses.

'But it's so hot,' insisted Daisy, on the verge of tears, 'and everything's so confused. Let's all go to town!'

Her voice struggled on through the heat, beating against it, molding its senselessness into forms.[72]

Just as the barren ash can simulate the appearance of life, so this urge to do something can create a 'nervous gayety' which, like the activities of the guests at Myrtle's party and Gatsby's, can give the appearance of happiness.

It is against this background of confusing heat that Tom realises Daisy loves Gatsby and so the car journey this time is undertaken with the emotions of jealousy and fear uppermost. Although the car is Gatsby's 'splendid car', this time, with Tom driving, the journey to Astoria is not presented as a flight which scatters light. The same road through the ashheaps is followed but this time Carraway feels only an ominous sense of warning. As well as the empty eyes of Doctor T. J. Eckleburg which 'kept their vigil' as always, he also sees Myrtle's eyes 'wide with jealous terror'[73] fixed upon Jordan whom she takes to be Tom's wife. The angry proceedings at the Plaza Hotel recall Myrtle's party and, as on that occasion, it seems that Tom's strength proves decisively superior. Gatsby tries to retain control and talks excitedly to Daisy.

> But with every word she was drawing further and further into herself, so he gave that up, and only the dead dream fought on as the afternoon slipped away, trying to touch what was no longer tangible, struggling unhappily, undespairingly, toward that lost voice across the room.[74]

The episode ends with the return car journey over the bridge. Tom is again the driver and Carraway is sitting next to Jordan Baker. The perspective is vastly different from that sense of 'wild promise' which Gatsby's companionship had produced. Fitzgerald has Carraway become conscious of his age in a way which is the antithesis of hope. 'I was thirty. Before me stretched the portentous, menacing road of a new decade.'[75] This fear of the future is the important point of difference between Carraway's attitude to Jordan and Gatsby's attitude to Daisy on the occasion of that crucial kiss of commitment. This scene in the car on the depressing return from New York recalls that key occasion.

> Thirty – the promise of a decade of loneliness, a thinning list of single men to know, a thinning briefcase of enthusiasm, thinning hair. But there was Jordan beside me, who, unlike Daisy, was too wise ever to carry well-forgotten dreams from age to age. As we passed over the dark bridge her wan face fell lazily against my coat's shoulder and the formidable stroke of thirty died away with the reassuring pressure of her hand.[76]

Carraway turns to Jordan because he needs consolation. There is

no magical moment of intense happiness here; no illusion of
Arcady; only a temporary comfort against the chilling intimations
of future loneliness (from someone who merely happens to be
present). There can be no sense of loss as far as Carraway's attitude
to Jordan is concerned. Unlike Gatsby's kiss of complete commitment, when Carraway first kissed Jordan there was no question at
all of any kind of illusion. In fact their first kiss is characterised by a
lack of emotion.

> We passed a barrier of dark trees, and then the facade of
> Fifty-ninth Street, a block of delicate pale light, beamed down
> into the park. Unlike Gatsby and Tom Buchanan, I had no girl
> whose disembodied face floated along the dark cornices and
> blinding signs, and so I drew up the girl beside me, tightening
> my arms. Her wan, scornful mouth smiled, and so I drew her up
> again closer, this time to my face.[77]

The perfunctory nature of Carraway's action here contrasts strongly with Gatsby's action which was taken with a full appreciation of
the moment's immense significance. In this respect Carraway's
gesture puts him on the same level as all the others who respond
mechanically to social situations following received opinions about
acceptable conduct.

If Carraway's action reveals an essential difference, on other
occasions he also indicates that he shares – albeit on a much lower
level – Gatsby's crucial characteristic: his 'extraordinary gift for
hope'. This, after all, is what is implied in the idea of reserving
judgement. However, as far as Gatsby himself is concerned, the
'infinite hope' concerned his optimistic belief that life could be
guided and controlled. That belief conditioned his struggle to
achieve his first target of a happiness symbolised by Dan Cody's
yacht. Despite Carraway's conventional code of values which
assess the target as ineffably gaudy and the means as morally
corrupt, the impression grows that, misguided as he may have
been, Gatsby's struggle, like Amory Blaine's was 'worth while'.
The major factor which works to achieve that impression is the
vitality and eager sense of purpose which are seen to be the
concomitants of Gatsby's 'infinite hope'. Carraway is seen to have
some small share of this quality and not only on the level of
reserving judgements. His appreciation of the city when seen from
Gatsby's viewpoint suggests more important sympathy. In this

sense the Queensboro Bridge implies a psychological bridge. Significantly, it is when they recross 'the dark bridge' that Carraway's insight into the thinning down process of age, requires him to turn to Jordan for solace. However, even if his awareness of the stark realities of advancing age cuts him off from the radiance consequent upon illusion, he still possesses a vestigial sense of that radiance. His attempt to recapture the 'elusive rhythm', the 'fragment of lost words' suggests that this sense is related to the innocence of childhood.

During the episode at Myrtle's flat, Carraway shows that he still has a child-like sense of life's wonders. On that occasion he draws attention to the way that, when viewed by an outside, innocent eye, even the joyless rituals of a drunken party could assume an enchanting mysteriousness.

Yet high over the city our line of yellow windows must have contributed their share of human secrecy to the casual watcher in the darkening streets, and I saw him too, looking up and wondering. I was within and without, simultaneously enchanted and repelled by the inexhaustible variety of life.[78]

This form of double vision gives Fitzgerald the kind of perspective that his ironical-pessimistic norm required. Through the medium of Carraway's ambivalent narration which is struggling to come to terms with the enchantment/repulsion, Fitzgerald created an artistic form which has a great advantage over his earlier technique. In *This Side of Paradise*, by using imagery to indicate Amory's faulty perceptions, the danger is that the necessary later modification of the norm suggested by the imagery will not be made; it will seem too authoritative. In *The Great Gatsby*, Carraway's innate moral rectitude is continually making judgements, showing ugliness beneath the surface of apparent glamour and, particularly, making very clear that Gatsby – on the basis of everything Carraway has learned – has based most of his life on a terrible mistake. And yet, despite his provincial morality, Carraway is somehow drawn to Gatsby: his narrative requires the reader to defer a final decision about Gatsby.

Once again, Fitzgerald makes use of imagery to suggest this complexity, but in this novel, since the narrator is not the protagonist, the element of doubt and hesitation, the sense of discrepancy between how things seem and how they really are, act as glosses to the opening remarks about the need to reserve judgements. Although it is clear from the descriptions of Gatsby's motivations that Carraway believes he was misguided, there is more than a suspicion that Gatsby's actions can be vindicated. Toward this end Fitzgerald carefully suggests another level of understanding which, because it is implicit, rather than explicit in the narrative, gives the impression that it represents something deeper than Carraway's conscious mind can comprehend. When Carraway listens to Gatsby's description of that crucial moment of the kiss and complete commitment to Daisy he can almost reach back into his own memory to repossess an earlier understanding. He fails at that moment but the impression of a vindicating code remains. The effect of this is to widen the whole story, to take it beyond a kind of anecdote to something much bigger.

Carraway's own personality, then, allowed Fitzgerald to suggest a greater complexity than that of the simple discrepancy between appearance and reality: unlike the omniscient author in *This Side of Paradise*, Carraway is seen to doubt his own perceptions. Fitzgerald is therefore able to exploit the idea of 'the unreality of reality' from the very beginning of the novel. The valley of ashes supplies the best example of this. There the emptiness at the heart of appearance is well expressed but the same essential barrenness underlies the conduct of the Buchanans, and the guests at Gatsby's parties. Carraway's descriptions of these activities suggest that they are mechanical and unemotional rituals. Myrtle's party also offers a good example of this, and, as such, takes its place on this important level in the novel whereby the reality of social behaviour is seen to be made up of empty gestures which proceed from a central nothingness.

Against such a background, Carraway's stated paradox about Gatsby turning out all right at the end can only be intensified. It would at first seem unlikely that a dedication to a double emptiness could be justified, yet that was Fitzgerald's intention. As it was right from the first attempt at the first novel, the key is to be found in the ironic philosophy. Although Amory Blaine's innate confidence that he had been marked out for future glory might have been a delusion, it provided him with a sense of purpose which was marked by a vitality and an eagerness for all life's experiences which sets him apart from all the other characters in the novel and which carried him through all the inevitable humiliations consequent upon his egocentric confidence. Although he would never reach Arcady, the belief that on several occasions he was almost there brought its own temporary Arcadian happiness. In that respect his illusions brought him a greater intensity of pleasure than he would otherwise have had. Gatsby too, experiences pleasure of this illusory kind and, like Amory Blaine, his dedication to the belief that he could so guide and control life that he would eventually reach his particular Arcady can be seen as a naïve reaction to hard reality. But Carraway's ambivalence has the reader join him in an attempt to rediscover a meaning which gives Gatsby's story its true significance.

Carraway's sense of a lost explanation is expressed by a technique which gives the whole story the same kind of inevitability found in fable. Gatsby's story seems to illustrate the operation of a universal truth which ensures that all action will proceed on a predetermined course. In order to achieve this impression Fitzgerald created the strong suggestion of myth and this helps to imply the epic note in the clash between Buchanan and Gatsby. The careful preparation for the crucial death-crash illustrates his method. Behind the conflict lies the myth of Cenomaus who represented Zeus as the incarnate Sun and his queen Hippodameia who represented Hera, the incarnate Moon. Buchanan is clearly associated with the stifling heat of the sun and Daisy with the cold and silvery radiance of the moon. The myth which deals with the way the king agrees to die a mock death has a clear, and ironic, bearing upon the struggle between Buchanan and Gatsby. In the myth the King appoints a surrogate to take his place for a day and to ride in the sun-chariot with the Queen. Towards the end of the day the chariot was raced around a course at the Hippodrome. At a certain point the horses would be scared and, in their maddened flight, a wheel would be detached from the sun-chariot and the surrogate killed in the ensuing crash. In some versions of the myth, the direct cause of the crash is a tree in whose branches the reins become entangled. That death-tree was the Myrtle. Myrtilus who also gave his name to the thirteenth month – the last month of the sacred king's reign – was also said to have tampered with the lynch-pins of the chariot, replacing the original metal ones by waxen pins, so causing the death-crash. On the death of the interrex, the true king emerges from the tomb in which he had been hiding and resumed his rule.

This link with Greek mythology gives Gatsby's story a universality. In this way Fitzgerald's early notion of a wearing down power is associated with a mythic pattern. That background analogy explains the otherwise surprising decision of Buchanan to allow Gatsby to ride with Daisy after the angry argument at the Plaza. It also explains the rather strange preliminary to the last meeting at the Buchanans' house. For that occasion Fitzgerald set the tone by emphasising the suffocating heat. It is that which makes Carraway feel that love is an irrelevance. 'That any one should care in this heat whose flushed lips he kissed, whose head made damp the pajama pocket over his heart!' Then Carraway imagines that the Buchanans' butler answers the telephone in quite an unusual way. '"The master's body!" roared the butler into the mouthpiece. "I'm sorry, madame, but we can't furnish it – it's far too hot to touch this noon!"' [79] In the context of the incarnate Sun, the sacred king who is about to suffer mock death, this prefigures the idea of the ritual removal and appointment of the interrex. The salon offers an immediate extension of this idea because it is 'shadowed well with awnings' and, like a tomb, is 'dark and cool'.[80] Tom warns of the power of the sun. '"I read somewhere that the sun's getting hotter every year," said Tom genially. "It seems that pretty soon the earth's going to fall into the sun –."' [81] Although he qualifies this by not being sure if the opposite is not the case – 'the sun's getting colder every year' – his association with the power of the sun is quite clear. Gatsby, on the other hand is seen to be quite cool. In fact in remarking this characteristic Daisy actually communicates her love to Gatsby. Tom observes this and when Daisy chooses to ride into town in the Buchanans' car, undertakes the drive in Gatsby's car which he calls a 'circus wagon'.[82]

In the terms of the myth, Gatsby has attempted to usurp the sun-king. He has created many of the conditions which suggest that he has equal possessions but when it comes to the point of decision it is clear that he cannot rival the established power of the old king. As in the climax of the myth of seasonal renewal, he has been allowed his one day and one night with the queen. Tom allows him the further privilege of riding with her in the last chariot-race. Ironically, Gatsby's own 'splendid car' becomes the sun-chariot. However, further levels of irony are reached when Myrtle intervenes. Tom appears to be immune to nemesis. Myrtle's power cannot reach him but does effectively destroy Gatsby.

Earlier there had been an intimation of Tom's immunity. Shortly after he married Daisy he survived a car crash at which time his car lost a front wheel. On that occasion he was with 'one of the

chambermaids in the Santa Barbara Hotel'.[83] Owl Eyes also survives a crash in which a car loses a wheel.[84] Gatsby, however,
although not physically harmed by the death-crash proves peculiarly susceptible to the destructive force. Drunken emptiness and
sexual profligacy remain untouched, whereas Gatsby is destroyed.
This suggests that Gatsby's position involves a degree of hubris
which cannot be allowed to pass unpunished. He therefore acts
out the role of the surrogate and is duly destroyed.

In this way Fitzgerald extended his early idea about the wearing
down power which he first wrote about in the pages of *The
Romantic Egotist*. In *The Great Gatsby*, as in the case of the fox who
stood against the bigger animals, that destructive force is especially
directed against Innocence. In *The Great Gatsby*, as in the case of
Amory Blaine, Innocence is related to a susceptibility to the illusion
that, with effort, personal happiness can be achieved. The same
ironic viewpoint informs both novels. Because the hope was based
upon an illusion it was doomed to fail, but the illusion did create
moments of intense happiness and that, it appears, is the nearest a
mortal can come to Arcady. However, Fitzgerald's great achievement in *The Great Gatsby* lies in the way this basic ironic philosophy
was extended to transcend the personal and form a convincing
parable with a wider application. The universalising tendency of
the implied link with Greek mythology assists this movement but
the crucial feature is the way Fitzgerald extended the ironical-tragic
philosophy which Amory Blaine had reached at the end of *This Side
of Paradise*.

The key is to be found in the idea of the kind of 'first-rate
intelligence' which can 'hold two opposed ideas in the mind at the
same time, and still retain the ability to function'. When Gatsby
kissed Daisy he consciously accepted a limitation. He knew he was
cutting himself off from a radiance but the opposing idea which he
also held was that she represented the peak of all his desires. He
was actually luckier than he might have been. He was able to hold
these two opposing ideas in his mind for five more years. Although
he had won Daisy, his enforced separation from her meant that he
was able to retain the intense vitality and emotional sensitivity
which attend the illusion that the road to Arcady is clearly defined.
Unfortunately, not even Gatsby was able to sustain that double
perspective. The sense of loss was too much, even for him. Despite
his determination to succeed, 'the conviction of the inevitability of
failure'[85] pressed too heavily. That moment when Carraway sur-

mised that Gatsby was feeling doubt 'as to the quality of his present happiness'[86] is correct in principle but not in the right time scale. The change had occurred much earlier at the point when expectation became achievement: in that forceful moment the intensity of the 'heightened awareness' began to lessen. On the train from Louisville after he had returned to the city to try to recapture some of the past beauty, Gatsby is shown to be aware of his loss.

> He stretched out his hand desperately as if to snatch only a wisp of air, to save a fragment of the spot that she had made lovely for him. But it was all going by too fast now for his blurred eyes and he knew that he had lost that part of it, the freshest and the best, forever.[87]

What Gatsby had lost was his eager expectation that life would honour its promise and reward him with the happiness for which he had struggled. The illusion that he would be so rewarded had created in him an openness to experience and heightened all his senses so that he would be able to take advantage of any opportunities to reach his personal Arcady. It is this which is characterised as an Innocence. It is well caught in the image of the ladder to the 'secret place above the trees'. In that secret place he would be as close to the source of vitality as it is possible for any mortal to reach: 'once there he could suck on the pap of life, gulp down the incomparable milk of wonder'.[88] That magical refreshment, however, could not be achieved with Daisy and Gatsby's intuition told him so. His energy and vitality might well have been matched with something or someone more equal to it. The fact that he had pinned his hopes upon inadequate targets is not, however, the fact which suggests a tragic aspect. Fitzgerald's statement concerning the nature of his novel is appropriate here. He had said that it was about 'the loss of those illusions that give such color to the world that you don't care whether things are true or false so long as they partake of the magical glory'.[89] The tragic aspect of Gatsby's story comes, not from the fact that he had wasted his enormous potential on worthless ideals, but from the fact that even the 'colossal vitality of his illusion' could not keep alive the 'magic moment' which attends the expectation of happiness. That was because 'life is too strong and remorseless for the sons of men'. In other words, the 'wearing down' power defeats even the most powerful illusions. However, as in *This Side of Paradise*, 'the struggle' is seen to have been 'worth while' because the illusion had created such 'a heightened sensitivity' to all experience that he had lived life more intensely, and more happily, and with a greater sense of purpose, than would otherwise have been the case.

One great advance which *The Great Gatsby* represents over *This Side of Paradise* is to be seen in the way that Fitzgerald extends his ironic-tragic philosophy into an expression of national experience. Carraway's sense of an earlier lost perspective is related to an early stage of the nation's life. This gives a much wider perspective to the idea of innocence. At the close of the novel Fitzgerald imagines the way that America had appeared to the first European explorers. The moment of expectancy is related to Gatsby's vision of the 'secret place' which would feed his intensely receptive mind with 'the incomparable milk of wonder'. That powerful maternal image which first established the intimate link between wonder and innocence is deliberately echoed in the vision vouchsafed the early visitors to the new continent. When the Dutch sailors first glimpsed the 'fresh, green breast of the new world', they too were presented with magnificent promise.

> for a transitory enchanted moment man must have held his breath in the presence of this continent, compelled into an aesthetic contemplation he neither understood nor desired, face to face for the last time in history with something commensurate to his capacity for wonder.[90]

Of course, achievement inevitably fell far short of promise. The trees were felled to make way for the ineffably gaudy world created by Gatsby and those who provided him with his particular notion of beauty and glamour. But 'the moment of glory' had existed and Gatsby's experience repeats the pattern. The moment of expectation born of illusion, is the peak of happiness: no matter if it will eventually be proved to be wrongly based. Fitzgerald recalls the picture of Gatsby with his eyes and his hopes turned towards the light at the end of Daisy's dock.

> his dream must have seemed so close that he could hardly fail to grasp it. He did not know that it was already behind him, somewhere back in that vast obscurity beyond the city, where the dark fields of the republic rolled on under the night.

The novel, then, ends with Fitzgerald's illustration of the attempt to balance 'the conviction of the inevitability of failure' with 'the determination to "succeed"'. The closing image capitalises upon the irony that the happiness which is so much desired has in fact been achieved. The illusion of a complete happiness had created a more limited and short-lived happiness, which seems to be the best that man can hope to achieve. Gatsby's experience is seen to be exemplary.

> Gatsby believed in the green light, the orgiastic future that year by year recedes before us. It eluded us then, but that's no matter – tomorrow we will run faster, stretch out our arms farther . . . And one fine morning –
> So we beat on, boats against the current, borne back ceaselessly into the past.[91]

The important consideration is that 'we' must struggle to keep alive our 'capacity for wonder', even though the world no longer holds anything 'commensurate' with this ability of man. The condition which suggests tragedy is that no one can sustain that capacity. Since it is based upon an illusion, when life's inexorable force reveals the frailty of the hope, 'the magical glory' which attended it disappears. Only the double vision can prolong those moments and give life a radiance, a sense of exciting majesty and the enchanted feeling that anything might happen.

5

The Wise and Tragic Sense of Life

The popularity of a biographical approach to Fitzgerald's work is nowhere more apparent and probably nowhere more misleading than in the present critical consensus about *Tender is the Night*. Although all the elements which had characterised his fiction up to that point are clearly present in this his fourth novel, invariably critical examination focuses upon the author as a way of coming to terms with the work. Crucially, the ironic philosophy centring upon the importance of illusion which had shaped *The Great Gatsby* is ignored in the widespread belief that Fitzgerald's personal difficulties at the time of writing seriously marred *Tender is the Night*. Since such speculations are based upon the premise of Fitzgerald's intellectual naïvety, they are antipathetic to the idea that a conceptual unity, and a corresponding technical continuity, is discernible in all the novels. Thus, earlier dramatisations of conflicts between, on the one hand, a belief that life can be guided and controlled and and, on the other a universal, remorseless, wearing down power are not felt to be relevant to Dick Diver's predicament. Nor is the notion of the attraction of feminine beauty and the apparently mistaken belief that love can lead to Arcady placed in the perspective of the first three novels. Unfortunately, the very context of the biographical approach which so effectively circumscribes an adequate discussion of the tragic aspects of *The Great Gatsby*, is even more inhibiting when applied to *Tender is the Night*.

In the heightened form usually adopted for *Tender is the Night*, the biographical approach turns upon the issue of Fitzgerald's treatment of apparently biographical material. Did he have intellectual and artistic control of his detail or was this novel shaped by the emotional power of remembered experience? In one way or another this kind of questioning finds its way into the literary assessments of all Fitzgerald's major critics. The early naïveties are thought to have been replaced by a slowly developing intellect which gradually produced a greater degree of artistic control. In order to chart this supposed slow growth, reference is invariably made to popular notions of Fitzgerald's real-life difficulties. Thus, in order to 'explain' the sad tones which characterise *Tender is the Night*, the weight falls upon Zelda's schizophrenia, Fitzgerald's deepening depression, growing alcoholism and worsening financial state, rather than upon any consideration of a special notion of the tragic. In other words, criticism is still at the Edmund Wilson standpoint which posits that Fitzgerald's basic writing impulse was emotional and subjective rather than intellectual and objective. Unfortunately, although most critics who follow this line do aim, as Mizener did, to produce a favourable final estimate for Fitzgerald, the actual context of the discussion predisposes only faint praise. Since it concentrates upon Fitzgerald's supposed efforts 'to grasp the nature of the disaster that he felt was then overtaking him',[1] that is, that he was using his fiction in order to probe the meaning of his life, then the question of literary merit tends to become secondary. Under these circumstances the best that is said about the novel exists on an extra-literary dimension where it assumes the role of a documentation of a representative, or even heroic struggle to come to terms with failure.

Curiously enough, critics less favourably disposed towards Fitzgerald's efforts than, say, Mizener or Trilling, exploit the same speculation about the assumed link between Fitzgerald's life and art to reach a different conclusion. Norman Podhoretz, for example, although presenting a different view of the outcome of the struggle, also accepts the idea that Fitzgerald was involved with the problem of coming to terms with the autobiographical bases of *Tender is the Night*. According to Podhoretz, the novel 'fails to come alive' because Fitzgerald could not be 'completely honest with himself'. He claims that:

> Fitzgerald was less than completely honest with himself in conceiving Dick Diver's tragedy. What he tried to get into Dick Diver was his feeling of having been damaged by his marriage to Zelda (Nicole in the novel) and by his weakness for the life of luxurious aristocratic ease.[2]

Within the terms of the biographical approach, this is a perfectly valid assessment. Like Mizener, Podhoretz thinks of the novel as illustrating Fitzgerald's attempt to understand emotionally important real-life circumstances. The difference between the two critics lies in the degree of success which they are willing to ascribe to Fitzgerald in this alleged attempt to come to intellectual terms with reality.

According to Mizener, Fitzgerald's starting point for *Tender is the Night* was what it always was in his writing: it was 'an interest in particular people in particular places'. However, Mizener stresses that the 'logical ordering of this felt experience' would necessarily be inadequate because: 'As always . . . he seems to have felt rather than reasoned his way to an appreciation of what their experience meant.'[3] In the acceptance of the belief that Fitzgerald did not possess a rational understanding of the raw material of the novel, this kind of judgement is very little different from Podhoretz's claim that Fitzgerald lacked honesty in the 'ultimate act of self-confrontation'.[4] In neither case can Fitzgerald be given much intellectual or artistic credit for his creation. In both cases the criticism leads on to suggestions of weakness in what Mizener calls the 'logical ordering' of the 'felt experience'.[5]

Because critics at both ends of the critical spectrum rely upon the same idea concerning Fitzgerald's emotional rather than conceptual understanding of his material, it is not surprising that there is quite widespread agreement about supposed basic artistic flaws in the construction of *Tender is the Night*. The major focus of critical attention has been the portrayal of Dick Diver. Invariably, underlying the criticism of Fitzgerald's fictional character is the belief that he was too much like his author for there to be a strict objective control. This belief is most clearly present in discussions about the inadequacy of Dick Diver's decline. Richard Lehan, for example, claims that the reasons for the decline 'are unclearly entangled in Fitzgerald's concern over Zelda's breakdown, his attitude toward the rich, and his own sense of lost vitality and promise'.[6] The same attitude informs Henry Dan Piper's judgement.

But Fitzgerald was himself implicated in Dick's situation to such an extent that he was unable to deal with it objectively. Instead he lost the necessary aesthetic distance and plunged into a subjective account that at times becomes maudlin with self-pity.[7]

Perhaps the most complete expression of this line of criticism is to be found in the complaint of Albert J. Lubell about 'The Fitzgerald Revival' published in 1955. Lubell refers to what he calls 'the fatal weakness of the novel'. By this he means 'the inability on the part of the author to understand his own creation'. He then goes on to say:

> The reason for Fitzgerald's failure to understand Dick Diver is not far to seek. Dick Diver is a projection of Fitzgerald himself after, say, 1932. About this time he first became conscious of a failing of his powers, of a general depletion of energy, of an emotional exhaustion, which he later likened to the situation of a person who has been spending money recklessly and suddenly finds himself overdrawn at the bank. Beyond that he could not go in giving a reason for his failing powers. Fitzgerald understood Dick Diver no better than he understood himself.[8]

Mizener, of course, had already popularised this idea of a link with the 'Crack-Up' notion of emotional bankruptcy and, clearly, his own judgement that Dick Diver's character is not 'completely coherent'[9] is closely related to Lubell's position.

It would be difficult to over-estimate the important influence of this kind of criticism. By its very nature it has created a critical pattern which effectively pre-determines the attitude to certain crucial issues. The remarkable fact about this pattern is that it is essentially the same one which was produced in Edmund Wilson's 1922 essay, 'Fitzgerald before the Great Gatsby'.[10] Wilson's starting point for that essay was undoubtedly the grudging need to explain how someone whom he regarded as immature could write two novels of some literary excellence. As well as the idea of a 'gift' or 'instinct for graceful and vivid prose' Wilson produced as his main proposition the idea that it was precisely because Fitzgerald was so immature that he was able to enter into the world of his own fictional characters. Since he wrote of characters with whom he had a strong emotional commitment, he was able to capture – albeit unwittingly – a sense of reality which might be denied a more rational approach. Therefore his novels, according to Wilson, although 'he seems never to have planned them thoroughly or to have thought them out from the beginning',[11] nevertheless are 'animated with life'.[12] This quite ingenious explanation of Fitzgerald's literary ability lies behind the work of the many succeeding critics who accept Wilson's fundamental proposition and from this project a second about Fitzgerald's inadequacy when faced with the technical question of the actual structure of the novel. Thus, the belief that the loose form of the 'saturation' novel came naturally to Fitzgerald for *This Side of Paradise* appears as a corollary and leads to the syllogistic conclusion which, at best, can only attempt to present a weakness as a virtue. It is, for example, claimed by James E. Miller that 'in its very immaturity lies its charm'.[13] What the initial proposition can never entertain is the possibility that *This Side of Paradise* proceeded from a coherent intellectual point of view.

Unfortunately, the same critical myopia dominates the approaches to *Tender is the Night* and, therefore, the same kind of false logic is brought to bear upon the structure of the work. Mizener, for example, presses the issue of Fitzgerald's alleged inadequate rationalising abilities into the conclusion that '*Tender is the Night*, though the most profoundly moving of all Fitzgerald's novels, is a structurally imperfect book.'[14]

It is only too clear that a great deal of the critical concern about the structural details of *Tender is the Night* has taken place within the limits of this kind of critical pattern. The tendency towards this criticism has been supported by Fitzgerald's own comments about the narrative order of the novel as it was first published. He did go some way towards a revision of the book by outlining an 'Analysis' in his notebooks. Although Fitzgerald did not complete this plan, his outline which followed his feeling that 'the true beginning . . . is tucked away in the middle of the book'[15] provided Cowley with the major justification for publishing a revised version which gives the novel an uninterrupted chronology. According to Cowley, one great advantage of his version is that it removes what he calls the 'uncertainty of focus' which follows Fitzgerald's decision to have the novel begin with 'Rosemary's Angle'. Although the critical discussion which has followed Cowley's rearrangement of the novel has, ostensibly, been about the technical details of selection and point of view, underlying these discussions is the basic assumption that Fitzgerald did not have a complete intellectual comprehension of the material he was using. Mizener, for example, believes that the impulse to revise the book came from 'his having felt his theme everywhere in his material without always seeing a way to draw these various aspects of it together in a single whole'.[16]

Wayne C. Booth adopts the same position in the explanation of his preference for Cowley's revised version of the novel.[17] Booth believes that Fitzgerald's alleged difficulties in structuring his work would have been 'best solved by using old-fashioned devices'. That is to say by 'developing a clean, direct, old-fashioned presentation of his hero's initial pre-eminence and gradual decline'.[18] For Booth, the crucial factor is the necessity for Fitzgerald to achieve the reader's 'emotional attachment to Dick'[19] as early in the work as possible. He further believes that this would best be done by delaying Rosemary's 'uncertain focus' – he repeats Cowley's words[20] – until the more authoritative impression of 'the reliable narrator'[21] has been established.

> To begin the novel part-way down the slope, as it were, confined to the confused vision of a secondary character, is to sacrifice some of our attachment to Dick and consequently a good deal of the poignant dramatic irony as we watch him move to his doom.[22]

Behind Booth's conclusions lies the feeling that Fitzgerald had not adequately rationalised what it was he wanted to achieve in his presentation of Dick Diver. According to Booth, 'the tragedy Fitzgerald wanted to write'[23] concerned the gradual process of 'the destruction of a man',[24] and this required that the opening of the novel should establish a credible picture of his true qualities. Thus, by choosing to open with Rosemary's 'uncertain focus', Fitzgerald indicated his own uncertainties.

Although Booth's criticism is directed at the novel's narrative order, it too is based upon a supposition about the kind of tragic story Fitzgerald conceived for Diver. In this respect it is hard to avoid the impression that Booth has taken the idea of Fitzgerald's emotional involvement in his own fiction from Mizener. The implicit suggestion is clear: if Fitzgerald had possessed a more rational insight into the concept of tragedy, then he would have been capable of 'a logical ordering' of the material of the novel so as to endow the story of Diver's 'moral destruction'[25] with a tragic sense which would be seen to exist on a plane separate from the author's own personal concerns or 'self-pity'.[26]

In one way or another, either explicitly or implicitly, the idea that Fitzgerald's notion of tragedy was based upon his emotive estimate that his own life was tragic is used as a key explanation of alleged weaknesses in *Tender is the Night*. Like Booth, Cowley, for example, prefers to make the point indirectly. In the following he not only trades upon widely-known details about Fitzgerald's private life – his membership of 'the leisure class', his 'psychotic wife', his loss of vitality – but he also, like Mizener, makes the life-literature link clear by using Fitzgerald's ideas about emotional bankruptcy. The result is an obvious implication that Dick Diver's decline should be seen in terms of Fitzgerald's own.

> Dick fades like a friend who is withdrawing into a private world or sinking to another level of society and, in spite of knowing so much about him, we are never quite certain of the reasons for his decline. Perhaps, as Fitzgerald first planned, it was the standards of the leisure class that corrupted him; perhaps it was the strain of curing a psychotic wife, who gains strength as he loses it by a mysterious transfer of vitality; perhaps it was a form of emotional exhaustion, a giving of himself so generously that he went beyond his resources, 'like a man overdrawing at his bank,' as Fitzgerald would later say of his own crack-up.[27]

Here, not only does Cowley not understand the reasons for Diver's decline, he also implies that neither did Fitzgerald. In this explanation it is the uncertainty itself which makes the decline so credible: an uncertainty which Cowley suggests is highlighted in his re-arranged version which allows 'us merely to guess at the hero's thoughts'.[28] This ingenious explanation is on a par with that approach to *This Side of Paradise* which makes a virtue out of immaturity.

Other critics, like Milton R. Stern, for example, are much more explicit in tying Dick Diver's predicament to Fitzgerald's own. In Stern's case the aim is to vindicate Fitzgerald's sense of his own tragic experience. That is to say, Stern's notion of Fitzgerald's view. For Stern, the sadness which characterises *Tender is the Night* is to be attributed to Fitzgerald's awareness of the gap between 'romantic expectations' and actuality. The resulting 'nostalgic sadness' which Stern identifies in Fitzgerald's writing is thus equated with Keats. Stern actually describes it as 'Fitzgerald's Keatsian nostalgia'. By this he means the mood consequent upon the 'realization of the loss of romantic expectations', and glosses this rather confusedly as follows:

As Keats discovered with his nightingale, Fitzgerald discovered with his dream of the golden moment that the imagination that can create the enormous and deep significance of the desire for the dream in art is overwhelmed by the dissolution of the imaginings in life.

Stern does not, however, suggest that Fitzgerald wrote the novel with an intellectual awareness of the source of his 'nostalgia'. As the following excerpt makes clear, Stern believes that the act of writing was itself the means by which Fitzgerald came to terms with his tendency to sadness:

> *Tender is the Night*, in literary fact, in biographical fact, and in the psychology of Fitzgerald's intentions, is the sign of the morality of art, of Fitzgerald's imagination miraculously preserved within the crack-up of his life. As always, Fitzgerald was feeding his life into a renewal of his literature; but in this book he was also feeding his literature into a renewal of his life. Memory and desire, loss and hope, were the refractors through which Dick's life, as representative of national history, would give Fitzgerald the meaning and uses of his own personal history.[29]

In Stern's view, then, the writing of the novel was part of an investigation into the true meaning of Fitzgerald's experiences. Stern clearly agrees with Wilson's judgement that Fitzgerald did not actually think out his novels or plan them from the beginning.

Stern's explanation of the romantic characteristics of Fitzgerald's temperament is in fact an extension of Mizener's thesis that because Fitzgerald's imagination worked best when it was dealing with personal experience of the most intense kind[30] it can be thought of as romantic. In support of that notion, Mizener quotes the 'taking things hard' note from Fitzgerald's *Notebooks*.[31] In this way, Mizener's concentration on Fitzgerald's own alleged emotional bankruptcy brings him very close to Stern's position. Mizener shows the same propensity to explain that 'though the dazzling Mediterranean sun blazes everywhere in *Tender is the Night*', it is a Keatsian 'no light' and 'verdurous glooms' which dominate the mood.[32] Although Mizener is not explicit about the way he believes Fitzgerald gained his mature awareness, both he and Stern clearly see the process as a slow and painful movement toward a sad truth rather than an intellectual insight gained early.

This tendency to understand Dick Diver's decline in terms of a consideration of his author's personality is responsible for recent attempts which take the issue a stage further. Thomas J. Stavola starts from Miller's idea of the 'story of the losing of a self',[33] and brings the psychoanalytical theory of Erik Erikson to the discussion in order to show that 'a more probing investigation of Dick's psychological state before his marriage, especially his childhood, must be made if we are to clearly understand the basic reasons for his apparently sudden collapse.'[34] Stavola justifies his approach by taking as a fact Mizener's fundamental proposition. After claiming that Fitzgerald 'struggled with the complex dimensions' of the question of 'American cultural identity', Stavola goes on to assert:

> He did this so memorably in his works because his own life was so persistent a search for identity. The subject of his best writing was always his own 'transmuted biography'. It is well documented that Fitzgerald wrote almost exclusively about his own divided nature, the achievement and hopes of the confident, romantic young man who was also fearful of himself and the world.[35]

With this pure Mizener basis Stavola's Freudian-derived theory takes him into a detailed psychoanalysis of Dick Diver and allows him to make a connection between the fictional character and Fitzgerald himself. Apparently, according to Stavola, Fitzgerald suffered at the hands of a spoiling mother:

> the effect of which was Fitzgerald's failure as an infant to establish a basic sense of trust, the foundation of an authentic identity. This inadequacy ... dictated the style of his development through the subsequent stages of life, especially the pivotal crisis of identity.[36]

Although Stavola does not make it clear, it seems that he believes that Fitzgerald had only an intuitive and emotional comprehension of the nature of his 'inadequacy'. Thus, like Stern, *inter alia*, he too thinks of the actual writing as a way of confronting true meaning.

Stavola's interpretation of *Tender is the Night* is one example of a literary approach which could only flourish against a background of accepted fact about Fitzgerald's personality. Central to the accepted facts is the paradox first outlined by Edmund Wilson of a 'rather childlike' intellect which, nevertheless, produced literature of undeniable quality.

This view has attracted several psychoanalytical explanations. John F. Callahan was one of the first critics to offer a full-length explanation based upon the idea that Fitzgerald did indeed struggle with the problem of finding Self.[37] Like Stavola, Callahan relates Fitzgerald's intellectual and artistic struggle to the idea of an American cultural identity but he does it without the aid of a Freudian explanation. Callahan's standpoint comes not from Erik Erikson but from Norman Brown's psychoanalytical theory about the relevance of an historical sense for the individual. According to Brown 'the method of psychoanalytical therapy is to deepen the historical consciousness of the individual . . . till he awakens from his own history as from a nightmare.'[38] Callahan claims that Fitzgerald's novels can work this way for the reader too. In *Tender is the Night* particularly, 'Fitzgerald faces unflinchingly a truth about consciousness, frightening to those of us still searching for a way out, but a truth nevertheless.'[39] Callahan goes on to identify Dick Diver as a paradigm. He believes that Diver's predicament illustrates 'the failure of the American idealist either to integrate himself with or change the course of American history'.[40] In all this Callahan is quite explicit about the link between the fictional character's predicament and Fitzgerald's own problems. He too quotes from *The Crack-Up* essay to indicate that Fitzgerald had himself experienced the same fearful sense of self-consciousness 'during his own period of personal and cosmic uncertainty'.[41]

Psychoanalytical exegeses of Fitzgerald's novels are simply the natural extension of the firmly established biographical approach. Stavola, for example, is able to build upon Mizener's parapsychological explanation of Fitzgerald's allegedly split personality because he has accepted an insecurely based hypothesis as fact. The attempt to explain Dick Diver's predicament in the context of Mrs Fitzgerald's treatment of the infant Scott carries the Mizener-type line of criticism to a logical but ludicrous extreme. Like Mizener, Stavola tries to deflect a Wilsonian form of criticism by revealing deep psychological imports beneath the surface of the novel. Unfortunately, by conceding the accuracy of the early assessment – that Fitzgerald had artistic talent without intellectual appreciation or control – there is very little to be said in praise of Fitzgerald's supposed approach to writing. The only recourse is to emphasise the agonised effort which he allegedly put into the attempt to achieve intellectual and artistic coherence; to see *Tender is the Night* as evidence of the author's continual struggle to view his own experiences objectively. On this basis it has become possible for critics to reach diametrically opposed views. Callahan can claim that 'Fitzgerald faces unflinchingly a truth about consciousness', while Podhoretz asserts that 'Fitzgerald was less completely honest with himself in conceiving Dick Diver's tragedy'.[42] In neither case does the biographical speculation carry literary appreciation very far. To explain the novel as being the unplanned result of a divided nature in search of true meaning and identity is hardly to defend it as a work of real literary merit.

However well-meaning the attempt, any criticism which starts from the 'fact' of Fitzgerald's emotionalising rather than conceptualising understanding invariably tends to praise Fitzgerald's allegedly paradigmatic role. In that way it can be suggested that his failure to reach a complete understanding of complex psychological issues might even be an advantage in his writings. To take this line is to come to the same patronising conclusion which Wilson had reached in 1922: that the novels reveal 'a profounder truth . . . than the author perhaps intended to convey'.[43]

II

The central 'truth' which informs *Tender is the Night* has its origin in the same comprehensive and rational view of life which formed the donnée of even the first work. Far from being the result of a vaguely 'Romantic' predisposition toward a subjective melancholia, the sad tone of all his writings was the artistic consequence of an ironic vision of the world. Proceeding from an intellectual base, the sadness is not of unspecific and unrelieved gloom. In this respect it could usefully be described in the terms used by Matthew Arnold of the poetry of Sophocles. According to Arnold, Sophocles' intellectual overview, his 'true insight', while it left him in no doubt about the 'gravity' of life, also afforded a modified optimism so that the distinctive note of his poetry is a 'serious cheerfulness'.[44] In much the same way, Fitzgerald's ironic vision lightened what would otherwise have been unrelieved pessimism.

The apparently bleak conclusion that hopes of future happiness will always be disappointed is tempered by the ironic perception that the pursuit of illusion can bring temporary happiness. That point of view created *This Side of Paradise* and was the basis of Fitzgerald's mature philosophy of life. It developed into what he later referred to as the 'philosophic concept' of 'the wise and tragic sense of life'. He outlined this in a letter to Scottie. In the following excerpt the kinship of this concept with the 'wearing down' power of his earliest fiction is apparent. After speaking of the way in which the work-a-day world affords no time when one can formulate 'what, for lack of a better phrase, I might call the wise and tragic sense of life', he produces the following definition.

> By this I mean the thing that lies behind all great careers, from Shakespeare's to Abraham Lincoln's, and as far back as there are books to read – the sense that life is essentially a cheat and its conditions are those of defeat, and that the redeeming things are not 'happiness and pleasure' but the deeper satisfactions that come out of struggle.[45]

Although this formulation came late in Fitzgerald's life, it demonstrably lies behind all his fiction. It was surely this concept towards which the 'juvenile indexes' of *The Romantic Egotist* were to have pointed. It is precisely that perception which Amory Blaine finally achieves. The redeeming understanding which replaces his pursuit of happiness is that deeper satisfactions will come from a life of service to others. Luckily for him, his egotism carried him through. Anthony and Gloria Patch were not so blessed: their story charts the decline of those damned in the sense of being merely beautiful and not elect. James Gatz, on the other hand, was one of the elect and his story dramatises the tragic aspects of Fitzgerald's 'philosophic concept'. Gatsby's tragedy was not that he deluded himself with dreams of future happiness with Daisy but that even he with his colossal will and energy could not maintain the illusion. For Dick Diver's story in *Tender is the Night*, Fitzgerald changed the emphasis. Although the same attitude towards the loss of illusion is behind it, there is also an attempt to achieve the balance which the apparently double vision – wisdom and tragedy – requires.

The 'wise and tragic sense', then, should be seen as the key to all Fitzgerald's novels. Once this point has been appreciated, Fitzgerald's true literary perspective becomes clearer. His connection, for example, with Dreiser and Conrad should be seen in terms of his 'philosophic concept' and this will yield much more than biographical speculation has yet achieved. At this point there is much to be gained in considering some of the affinities which exist between Fitzgerald and Conrad, and in particular between *The Great Gatsby* and *Lord Jim*. This is because, although there is a shift in emphasis between *The Great Gatsby* and *Tender is the Night*, the intellectual position and the general technique remains the same and they are, essentially, Conradian.

In the first instance, both titles – *The Great Gatsby* and *Lord Jim* – carry oxymoronic suggestions and thereby signal ironic intentions. From their beginnings both novels create impressions of two levels of judgement: on the one hand there is the world's view, subscribed to in the main by the participating narrators; and on the other hand there are the apparently misguided self-assessments of the protagonists. The ironic resolution to both works is the realisation that, on the basis of a code other than the world's judgements, the protagonists' actions are vindicated: both Jim and Gatsby deserve the ennobling epithets. The effect is to focus attention upon the philosophic codes which determine conduct. On the world's terms both Jim and Gatsby entertain absurd notions of purposive action. How can such notions be justified? Conrad has Mr Stein give the key to the lives of both characters. Although Conrad used the word 'dream' he intends precisely the same meaning as Fitzgerald intends with his word 'illusions'. Here Stein speaks of the way a man can close his eyes and dream he is a saint or a devil.

And because you not always can keep your eyes shut there comes the real trouble – the heart pain – the world pain. I tell you, my friend, it is not good for you to find you cannot make your dream come true, for the reason that you not strong enough are, or not clever enough.[46]

In this Conrad is indicating a non-conventional idea of tragedy with which Fitzgerald could identify. In these two novels, neither author offered the conventional pattern of heroes of great potential doomed to failure because of tragic flaws. For both authors the true tragic perspective is established by the failure of belief in dreams/ illusions: a process which it is implied is inevitable. Gatsby cannot finally be thought to have wasted his life on the dream of a woman who was not worth the effort: neither is Jim to be considered as having wasted his life in a vain search for an arena which would prove his heroic stature. Stein's dictum gives the tragic perspective: despite the world's judgement, a man must immerse himself in his dream. That is exactly what Gatsby and Jim do. It is that which ennobles them. There is, however, an important difference.

The ironic point which *Lord Jim* dramatises is intimately related to the belief that there will always be a discrepancy between the Self's dreams of happiness and the world's more practical views. *Lord Jim* shows that only on the basis of conventional notions of wasted potential can Jim's story be thought to be tragic. On his own terms, as Marlow comes to realise, Jim was 'an extraordinary success'. His 'shadowy ideal of conduct' lifted him above the 'inert life'[47] of the mundane world which he left behind. The real tragedy which he avoided was the realisation that appears to lie in wait for all: that 'you cannot make your dreams come true'. It is at this point that the philosophical difference between Conrad and Fitzgerald becomes apparent. Although Fitzgerald also saw the realisation of the discrepancy between the dream and reality as the basis of life's real tragedy, his intellectual and artistic concern was centred upon the individual who will struggle to achieve the impossible balance between those poles. To Conrad's image of a man trying to hold fast to his dream by keeping his eyes shut, Fitzgerald added the idea of a balance to be struck between illusion and the intuited knowledge of eventual failure. That was his test of a 'first-rate intelligence'. It was on these grounds that he made Gatsby differ from Jim. That is the crucial point conveyed in the scene where Carraway's narrative re-enacts Gatsby's 'incarnation'. 'He knew that when he kissed this girl, and forever wed his unutterable visions to her perishable breath, his mind would never romp again like the mind of God.'[48]

It is this moment of dim awareness which, in Conrad's terms, signals 'the heart pain'. This is why the vision is both tragic and wise. It is the beginning of the understanding that dreams cannot come true and, as Fitzgerald put it when he was explaining what *The Great Gatsby* is about, tragedy is involved whenever the individual suffers 'the loss of those illusions that gave such color to the world that you don't care whether things are true or false so long as they partake of the magical glory'.[49] The great difference between Gatsby and Jim is on this level of awareness. Jim never reached it: he died still immersed in his dream. Gatsby, on the other hand, had the beginnings of an awareness but still struggled to remain immersed. It was that kind of a struggle which Fitzgerald thought of as the modern equivalent of the field for epic action. It was victory in that struggle which made Gatsby 'Great' and, therefore, contrary to the standards of a more realistic world, the illusions did bring some pleasure; they took Gatsby, as they took Amory Blaine, as close to Arcady as is humanly possible. It is that ironic modification of a fatalistic position which gives Fitzgerald's distinctive sad note something of the characteristics of Sophocles' 'serious cheerfulness'.

Even in his first novel Fitzgerald was so consciously organising his material as to be able to encapsulate his ironic intentions within the title. What Amory Blaine has to discover is that, as Wallace Stevens puts it: 'The imperfect is our paradise'.[50] And Anthony Patch's career illustrates a similar point: he was happier and less 'damned' before he possessed the beautiful Gloria. However, the relative failure of that second novel illustrates an important factor about Fitzgerald's ironic vision. The difficulty with *The Beautiful and Damned* as an exposition of that vision arises out of the fact that in it Fitzgerald took the negative way to reach his final level of meaning. Anthony's disillusionment is both lengthy and bitter; moreover he is not the kind of 'first rate intelligence' who can reconcile illusion and reality. There is no nobility in his actions and only the reader is aware of the tragic discrepancy between the dreams and the reality. Furthermore, unlike Amory and Gatsby, Anthony only possesses a dynamic illusion at the beginning of his story when he dreams of eternal happiness with Gloria. It is, therefore, only during this time that, under the terms of the ironic philosophy, he can enjoy a little of the happiness available in an imperfect paradise. For the greater part of the novel his dreams appear rather reflex actions, almost mechanical; certainly not as deeply held beliefs which might bring along some kind of brief joy. It is the reader who reaches the understanding that it is the loss of illusions which creates tragic circumstances, not Anthony: he merely suffers the effects as exemplar. The key factor which *The Beautiful and Damned* should have made clear to Fitzgerald's early critics was that, far from being '100 per cent meaningless',[51] Fitzgerald made it clear that the only time Anthony's life approached meaning and joy was when he was anticipating the happiness of being married to Gloria. That is an important 'meaning'. For Fitzgerald, Love provided the only arena in which the possibilities for tragic action in modern times can exist.

In this respect there is another link with the European novel tradition. At first glance the career of Anthony Patch might seem to illustrate the same kind of fatalistic pessimism which lies behind Flaubert's *Sentimental Education*. Flaubert, after all, offers a powerful suggestion that the happiest time of life is in youth when the individual has all his hopes and illusions intact. However, as Fitzgerald's parody of the Platonic discussion of Love shows, he believes that the kind of approach to Love which a 'first-rate intelligence' might make could create a meaning which, even though it might be illusory, would give a sense of purpose and happiness. This kind of idea is certainly at the heart of *The Great Gatsby* but it received its most complete treatment in *Tender is the Night*. In that work he so extended and developed his ironic interpretation of the importance of the illusions which Love creates as to produce a convincing model of the modern epic. Gatsby's struggle, it is clear, is meant to be seen as essentially heroic, but the narrative method has the effect of making Gatsby so remote as to become almost mythic. Although he is intended to represent a certain kind of intelligence, it is difficult to imagine there could be many more like him. In *Tender is the Night* Fitzgerald attempted to create the conditions which would allow him to present a man who is much less of a mythic character but who, nevertheless, must be seen in an epic context.

Just as *The Great Gatsby* can usefully be compared with *Lord Jim*, so *Tender is the Night* can be illumined by reference to George Eliot's *Middlemarch*. Although George Eliot did not share Fitzgerald's ironic appreciation of the power of illusion, she did share his belief in Love offering the modern arena for epic action. In addition, *Middlemarch* reveals the same preference for an ironic structure to express the philosophical point seen in *The Great Gatsby*.

By beginning her novel by linking Dorothea Brooke to an image of the infant Saint Theresa toddling off to seek martydom and 'an epic life', George Eliot sets in motion the process by which the reader seems to be invited to consider Dorothea as endearingly deluded in her earnest desire for an heroic life. But, by the end of the novel, her devotion to her illusion, to her 'path of hope' is vindicated and she is seen to have lived an epic life. It is, however, not the kind of epic which Saint Theresa experienced. George Eliot makes it clear that the modern world no longer provides the arena for that kind of heroic action. What Dorothea had achieved was a 'home epic'.

Her finely-touched spirit had still its fine issues, though they were not widely visible. Her full nature ... spent itself in channels which had no great name on the earth. But the effect of her being on those around her was incalculably diffusive: for the growing good of the world is partly dependent on unhistoric acts; and that things are not so ill with you and me as they might have been, is half owing to the number who lived faithfully a hidden life, and rest in unvisited tombs.[52]

This idea of a 'hidden life' is a useful way of indicating how someone like Dorothea – or Gatsby or Jim – has their conduct determined by a hidden code. It is, of course, the suggestion of that hidden code which calls into question conventional standards, and that is the major aim of an ironist. Any assessment of *Middlemarch* which underestimates the importance of Dorothea's 'hidden life' and bases its conclusions upon popular notions of success and failure or sentimental notions about what constitutes a happy marriage will miss a fundamental point. In the same way, a failure to be clear about the way Fitzgerald intends Dick Diver's 'hidden life' to be seen will mean that the ironic point about a 'home epic' will almost certainly be missed.

The examples of two classic works in the great tradition of the European novel have the merit of illustrating the way that an ironic point of view can be ideally complemented by an ironic structure. In an important way the technique is itself the philosophy. The essentially *double* vision of the ironist creates what is in effect a double narrative. At every point in the story there is a tension between different levels of understanding, different principles of judgement. Every aspect of the story contributes to a duality, an ambiguity, but once the figure in the carpet has been discerned all the individual parts can be seen to carry the same pattern. If the ironic point of view is the macrocosm, the details of the novel are the microcosm; or, as he put it, the 'juvenile indexes'. In Fitzgerald's case, even the titles carry the pattern of macrocosmic ironic insight. In addition, as *The Great Gatsby* in particular shows, the process can extend toward the names of characters. Not only does Myrtle's name epitomise an extremely relevant mythic story but also Carraway's role in the novel is ironically placed when it is realised that the Carraway seed is a traditional ingredient of love potions. These examples are, however, only minor indications of the fundamental fact that stylistic duality is axiomatic to the double vision of the ironist. The major example is to be found in the strategy of the overall design. It is the careful organisation of the mass of detail in, say, *Middlemarch* and *Lord Jim* which gives the final appearance of complete statements. Because each incident anticipates the final lesson, that final explanation carries the conviction of something which has been already learned subconsciously.

It is because the narrative scheme of *Tender is the Night*, more than any of Fitzgerald's novels, is so intimately related to its ironic philosophy, that the critical preoccupation with an issue about the novel's chronology is so hard to justify. It is not surprising that the other major issue is the question of the nature of Dick Diver's decline. Unless he is seen in the context of another 'first-rate intelligence' engaged in a form of heroic action, then Fitzgerald's ironic point of view will certainly be missed and with that centre gone there will be little hope of appreciating the ironic technique.

The title of the novel which he took from Keats' 'Ode to a Nightingale' illustrates the microcosmic relevance and thus gives a clear indication to the attentive reader that the same 'wise and tragic sense of life' which illuminates the other novels will also be at the centre of *Tender is the Night*. The context suggested by Keats' poem is entirely consistent with the ironic modification of the otherwise fatalistic pessimism which accepts the fact that dreams never can come true. Keats' poem dramatises the way that an intense longing to discover the way to an arcadian world of joyous beauty can actually be the means by which it can be reached. The belief that the approach might be made on 'the viewless wings of Poesy' brings the instant success: 'Already with thee!' And, *therefore*, 'tender is the night'. The context is then, the same one which makes it clear that, as in Gatsby's case, the dream is in a sense its own fulfilment. 'He had come a long way to this blue lawn, and his dream must have seemed so close that he could hardly fail to grasp it. He did not know that it was already behind him.'[53]

There can be no doubt that the meaning Fitzgerald found in Keats' poem complemented his own central belief. He did, however, extend the idea of the momentary and essentially unappreciated transport of happiness into a philosophy which elevated illusion to a high point. Although life cheats everyone by promising more than can be achieved, it is possible to win something back by a wholehearted immersion in the cheating process: by believing in the struggle. This is what lies behind content and technique in all his novels. It is, *pace* Professor Mizener, the basis of the 'logical ordering' of all the novels and, pre-eminently of *Tender is the Night*.

III

Once the centrality of the concept of 'the wise and tragic sense' has been appreciated, the familiar critical concern over the chronology of *Tender is the Night* is obviated. For this novel Fitzgerald adapted the technique he had used so successfully in *The Great Gatsby* and he did so because he was constructing on the same conceptual base. By having Carraway start Gatsby's story 'part-way down the slope',[54] Fitzgerald not only created the impression of an intriguing mystery, he also made it clear, through the narrator's hesitancies, that conventional moral judgements were not to be trusted. Because Carraway's remembered first impressions are shown to be faulty, the existence of a hidden code of behaviour is implied. Although *Tender is the Night* is more ambitious in its scope than *The Great Gatsby*, it too uses the personality of a participator to create a double-story line. In this respect there is a clear kinship with the use of imagery in the first two novels to imply alternative levels of 'truth'. Rosemary is the focal point.

Rosemary appears on the first page of the novel. After two important opening paragraphs from the omniscient narrator she arrives, with her mother, at Gausse's Hotel and almost immediately goes to the beach where she encounters other tourists as well as Dick Diver's group. Her first impressions – registered in a series of approvals and disapprovals – are important factors in the way that the reader's sympathies are engaged. However, before the narrative voice moves into Rosemary's persona, Fitzgerald's technique has carefully placed her high in a framework of approval. This, in view of her naïveties and consequent mistakes, might be thought to be curious but it has the effect of raising interest in the question of what distinguishes her from the other characters. Her difference is anticipated in the novel's first two paragraphs. In particular the second paragraph, which relates the intrusion of the human on a scene of ancient beauty, establishes the kind of background against which Rosemary's radiance will be remarkable.

The hotel and its bright tan prayer rug of a beach were one. In the early morning the distant image of Cannes, the pink and cream of old fortifications, the purple Alp that bounded Italy, were cast across the water and lay quavering in the ripples and rings sent up by sea-plants through the clear shallows. Before eight a man came down to the beach in a blue bathrobe and with much preliminary application to his person of the chilly water, and much grunting and loud breathing, floundered a minute in the sea. When he had gone, beach and bay were quiet for an hour. Merchantmen crawled westward on the horizon; bus boys shouted in the hotel court; the dew dried upon the pines. In another hour the horns of motors began to blow down from the winding road along the low range of the Maures, which sepa-rates the littoral from the true Provencal France.[55]

This is the setting for the entrance of Rosemary and her mother. Their descriptions continue the impression already formed of two worlds: the past and the present co-existing. Here, though, although the older world is represented by the 'fading prettiness' of the mother's face, Rosemary's present appearance is described in terms which are far different from the bather's inelegant ritual. Rosemary

> had magic in her pink palms and her cheeks lit to a lovely flame, like the thrilling flush of children after their cold baths in the evening. Her fine forehead sloped gently up to where her hair, bordering it like an armorial shield, burst into lovelocks and waves and curlicues of ash blonde and gold. Her eyes were bright, big, clear, wet, and shining, the color of her cheeks was real, breaking close to the surface from the strong young pump of her heart.[56]

Clearly, Rosemary belongs to the 'now' world but her presence in this part of an ancient world is treated far more sympathetically than the intrusion of the grunting bather. Also, her youth is strongly emphasised. 'Her body hovered delicately on the last edge of childhood – she was almost eighteen, nearly complete, but the dew was still on her.'[57]

This kind of description, given the authority of the omniscient author's point of view, combines with other details to make it clear that no irony is intended. It is clear that, although Rosemary and her mother are part of the fashionable tourist traffic, there is a note of approval for them which marks them off from the others. In spite of being described as wanting 'high excitement' and being 'obviously without direction and bored by the fact',[58] Rosemary is removed from the implied criticism of others. The distancing is effected in the main by a concentration upon the prevailing ennui and lethargy under the Mediterranean's 'brutal sunshine'. In the following passage the typical mood on the beach – the only place where there is a stir of activity – is given an international aspect. Since the only activity takes place on the 'bright tan prayer rug of a beach'[59] the ironic suggestion of ritual is also added. 'Three British nannies sat knitting the slow pattern of Victorian England, the pattern of the forties, the sixties, and the eighties, into sweaters and socks, to the tune of gossip as formalised as incantation.'[60] Here, not only are the nannies fifty years out of date with their patterns, but the idea of translating 'the slow pattern of Victorian England' into sweaters and socks certainly creates the strong impression of a mechanical and purposeless behaviour.

Significantly, only the children who pursue 'unintimidated fish through the shallows'[61] avoid a mechanical or 'formalized' purposelessness: the children and Rosemary. Unlike the impression given in the description of the first swimmer's efforts, Rosemary's swim is presented sympathetically. 'The water reached up for her, pulled her down tenderly out of the heat, seeped in her hair and ran into the corners of her body. She turned round and round in it, embracing it, wallowing in it.'[62] The sexual connotations of this sensual description are very important. Her youthful vitality becomes associated with a sexuality and thus the first description of her 'on the last edge of childhood' is subtly qualified.

The framework of approval for Rosemary guides the reader's reactions as the narrative voice moves into her persona. The 'vague antipathy'[63] which she forms towards the McKisco group replaces the omniscient author's less obvious but no less attitude-forming descriptions of, for example, Campion's 'tufted chest ... brash navel ... facetious whiskers'.[64] So her preference for and interest in the other group on the beach carries conviction. Thus the reader can sympathise with her judgement: 'She did not like these people'. Significantly, Fitzgerald does not help the reader to come to an independent assessment of Dick Diver's group. The authorial voice, now associated with Rosemary's viewpoint, avoids the kind of adjectival help which suggested disapproval for the McKisco group. The 'esoteric burlesque' of Dick's performance with the rake is described as raising 'hilarious' laughter which attracts the attention of all the beach. Just what it is about is withheld but, from Rosemary's reaction, it is a pleasant and intriguing mystery which is much to be preferred to the company of the McKisco group. Dick Diver as the source of all the 'excitement' becomes the focus of Rosemary's interest.[65] Thus, in a very short time Fitzgerald has succeeded in setting these two characters apart from the others and implying an interesting connection between them.

In the manner in which the reader's interest in the central character is raised there is a similarity between the openings of both *Tender is the Night* and *The Great Gatsby*. In fact the deceptive ease of the narration of *Tender is the Night* marks a considerable advance in the handling of a form of double narrative. Nick Carraway as participating narrator is in effect two persons. He is both the mature one who is telling the story and the relatively naïve earlier one who was trying to understand his experiences. It is essential for Fitzgerald's ironic purpose that the naïve Carraway is seen to transcend his basically conventional, middle-class, middle-western standards and move gradually towards an appreciation of the deeper truths epitomised in Gatsby. In order to indicate the two levels of perception, Fitzgerald has the mature storyteller give an explicit warning at the beginning about the need 'to reserve judgements', and, from time to time, to give other indications that there is more to the story than meets the ingenuous Carraway's eye. For example, attention is drawn to Gatsby's 'appalling sentimentality' but in such a way as to suggest the possibility of 'an elusive rhythm, a fragment of lost words'[66] which could lead to a different scale of values.

In *Tender is the Night* the use of Rosemary gave Fitzgerald the advantage of a naïve observer without the potential confusion of a double identity. Her limited perceptions are balanced by comments from the omniscient author. There is no need for Fitzgerald to have her slowly outgrow initial naïveties. In fact her naïvety offered an excellent base upon which he could construct that essential other narrative if the 'hidden life' of Dick Diver were to be revealed. This is because the omniscient author could much more easily – if just as enigmatically – draw attention to faulty perceptions than could Nick Carraway. The effects aimed for in both novels were the same: to heighten the sense of mystery surrounding the central character and, simultaneously, to offer clues towards resolving that intriguing puzzle. With Rosemary taking on the role of the young Carraway and the omniscient author that of the older Carraway, essential aspects of the inner story are established more soundly than is the case in *The Great Gatsby*.

There is an early example of the balance between Rosemary's subjectivity and the omniscient author's objectivity in Part 4 of Book 1 in which Rosemary reacts to Dick Diver's 'curious garment'.

> Her naïveté responded whole-heartedly to the expensive simplicity of the Divers, unaware of its complexity and its lack of innocence, unaware that it was all a selection of quality rather than quantity from the run of the world's bazaar; and that the simplicity of behaviour also, the nursery-like peace and good will, the emphasis on the simpler virtues, was part of a desperate bargain with the gods and had been attained through struggles she could not have guessed at.[67]

With this kind of a passage the twin aims of heightening the mystery and offering clues towards the final resolution are achieved by making it clear that a deeper level of perception – that is, deeper than Rosemary's – exists. Such passages combine very effectively with those moments when Rosemary, like Carraway, seems to sense something which is just beyond her understanding. Crucially, this nearly always concerns Dick's influence on those around him. Thus, on the beach, looking at the Divers and their friends: 'Even in their absolute immobility, complete as that of the morning, she felt a purpose, a working over something, a direction, an act of creation different from any she had known.'[68] By stressing Rosemary's limited perception and being explicit about a hidden explanation, Fitzgerald induces the reader to reach a higher level of awareness than Rosemary could possibly achieve.

In order to assist the reader along the inner story-line Fitzgerald was careful to place Rosemary – right from the beginning – in a particular perspective of approval. Even on her first appearance on the beach she is seen to be different. Implicit in the background descriptions of an apparently ages-old ennui is a sense of Rosemary's youthful vitality. Her own actions on the beach are neither mechanical nor ritualistic. Significantly, she responds to the sense of purpose she detects in Dick Diver's group. Her own energies and sense of direction came from an idealism which she had learned from her mother. Fitzgerald describes this as a 'somewhat bouncing, breathless and exigent idealism'. Clearly, this idealism is presented within a framework of approval. It marked her out from the purposeless crowd and it helped her to 'sudden success in pictures'.[69] She has an unquestioning belief in her own golden future. She expects fame, fortune and happiness. No doubts about that future, no suggestion that life will prove to be a gradual and inevitable process of disillusionment had yet touched her. It is this more than her physical state which defines her position as hovering on 'the last edge of childhood'. She is poised on that edge which accommodates hopes, dreams and illusions without any suspicion that 'life is essentially a cheat'. This is the force of Fitzgerald's potentially puzzling language which speaks of Rosemary's idealism as 'armour' and a protection; puzzling that is if the centrality of 'the wise and tragic sense of life' is not recognised.

Rosemary, then, with her unalloyed optimism and sense of direction derived from a 'bouncing' idealism, is instinctively attracted to Dick Diver. He is shown to have special powers. He is able to generate excitement and pleasure for others: 'to be included in Dick Diver's world for a while was a remarkable experience: people believed he made special reservations about them, recognizing the proud uniqueness of their destinies, buried under the compromises of how many years.'[70] The first extended example of his abilities comes at the party described in Part 7 of Book 1. Although the individuals around the table are not all entirely sympathetic to one another, under Dick's influence they become united in a magical moment.

> The table seemed to have risen a little toward the sky like a mechanical dancing platform, giving the people around it a sense of being alone with each other in the dark universe, nourished by its only food, warmed by its only lights.

The guests around the table respond to the powerful charm of their hosts.

> And for a moment the faces turned up toward them were like the faces of poor children at a Christmas tree. Then abruptly the table broke up – the moment when the guests had been daringly lifted above conviviality into the rarer atmosphere of sentiment, was over before it could be irreverently breathed, before they had half realized it was there.[71]

Perhaps the most interesting point about this remarkable passage is the gloss it offers to the Keatsian concept which gave the novel its title. A fleeting moment of magical tenderness has been created. 'There' in that bright unity and 'rare atmosphere of sentiment' they experienced a moment of pure pleasure.

> the diffused magic of the hot sweet South had withdrawn into them – the soft-pawed night and the ghostly wash of the Mediterranean far below – the magic left these things and melted into the two Divers and became part of them.[72]

The ability to create such a moment of magical tenderness is made to seem even more remarkable when more details of the actual 'here' as distinct from the 'diffused magic' of the tender Southern night are made known: the Barban/McKisco duel; the grotesqueries of Abe North's drunken confusions; the attempted murder at the Gare Saint Lazare; the discovery of the murdered black man in Rosemary's room; and, finally Nicole's dementia over the blood on the bedspread; all these are part of the real world inhabited by the Divers. Such a preponderance of ugliness and violence suggests a state which should be quite antipathetic to the beauty and calm of the nightingale's tender night. It is surely ludicrous for anyone who inhabits such a reality ever to aspire to transcend 'sole self' and leave behind the ugly '*Here*, where men sit and hear each other groan.' Yet the evocation of Keats clearly implies such a perspective.

The double story-line, then, not only confirms the special qualities of Dick which Rosemary's naïve enthusiasm has discerned, it also makes clear that 'the simplicity of behaviour' and 'the nursery-like peace and good will' was the result of enormous struggle. Not only that, because also hidden from Rosemary was the fact that the 'desperate bargain' was becoming increasingly insecure. The paragraph in which the omniscient author tells of Rosemary's ignorance of the complexity and 'lack of innocence' behind the Diver's 'expensive simplicity' ends with these words: 'in reality a qualitative change had already set in that was not all apparent to Rosemary.'[73] This has the effect of increasing the interest in Dick's position. What is the nature of the struggle in which he is engaged and just how has he changed? In other words the reader is encouraged to think along the lines of the second, hidden narrative; to perceive more than Rosemary could. In this

sense she comes close to being what Henry James described as a
'disponible'.[74] This is mainly because, although by no means the
major character, her special attributes allow Fitzgerald to focus
upon circumstances which go straight to the heart of Dick's
predicament.

In this respect the fact that Rosemary feels herself to have
immediately fallen in love with Dick is most significant. Clearly,
her notion of love is close to the fairy-tale world of the pictures. She
sees Dick rather as a handsome leading man who can so organise
things as to make her happy.

> Afterward she remembered the times when she had felt the
> happiest. The first time was when she and Dick danced together
> and she felt her beauty sparkling bright against his tall, strong
> form as they floated, hovering like people in an amusing
> dream.[75]

Even the moment when she offers herself to him appears like an
episode in a film. 'Suddenly she knew too that it was one of her
greatest rôles and she flung herself into it more passionately.'[76] By
such means Fitzgerald indicates the immature form of love which
Rosemary experiences. Crucial in forming this impression is the
notion of her role as 'Daddy's Girl' in her film of that name.
Ironically her success in that film which ends in 'the vicious
sentimentality' of a 'father complex'[77] came out of character
because as is quite clear from the early pages Rosemary is her
Mummy's girl. That had been the basis of her defences against the
world: she had adopted her mother's idealism as her own and Mrs
Speers now wished that this idealism 'would focus on something
except herself'.[78] With this knowledge the reader easily picks up
the implication that the transfer to Dick – so much older and wiser
than Rosemary – can be seen in the terms of 'Daddy's Girl'. After
she has offered herself to him he actually calls her 'child' and gives
her some fatherly advice. 'So many people are going to love you
and it might be nice to meet your first love all intact, emotionally
too.'[79]

The position which Dick has now reached is indicated in the
following lines which come after he has gently but firmly declined
her offer to give herself to him.

He was suddenly confused, not about the ethics of the matter, for the impossibility of it was sheerly indicated from all angles, but simply confused, and for a moment his usual grace, the tensile strength of his balance, was absent.[80]

Through a combination of Rosemary's point of view and the omniscient author's direct statements, a sense of disparity, a clear idea of the unsuitability of the liaison has been created. Without doubt the reader is meant to see that Dick himself is aware of this fact. The insight into the minds of the two actors given through the manipulation of the dual narrative achieves that.

He kissed her without enjoying it. He knew that there was passion there, but there was no shadow of it in her eyes or on her mouth; there was a faint spray of champagne on her breath. She clung nearer desperately and once more he kissed her and was chilled by the innocence of her kiss.[81]

Immediately following this incident Fitzgerald further emphasises the disparity through the scene in which Rosemary shows her film 'Daddy's Girl'. The narrative voice suggests both objective criticism and Rosemary's own subjective impressions.

There she was – the school girl of a year ago, hair down her back and rippling out stiffly like the solid hair of a tanagra figure; there she was – *so* young and innocent – the product of her mother's loving care; there she was – embodying all the immaturity of the race, cutting a new cardboard paper doll to pass before its empty harlot's mind. She remembered how she had felt in that dress, especially fresh and new under the fresh young silk.

The effect is to show that Rosemary's innocence triumphs over the 'vicious sentimentality' of the screenplay which has the 'tiny fist' of the 'itty-bitty bravekins', 'de tweetest thing' defeat 'the forces of lust and corruption'. In fact, despite having Dick acknowledge the banality of the film, Fitzgerald also has him say 'sincerely' that he believes Rosemary will 'be one of the best actresses on the stage'.[82] However, the distance between Rosemary and Dick is highlighted when Rosemary declares that she has arranged a screen test for Dick. In this way Fitzgerald heightens the mystery as to the nature of Dick's 'effort of the last six years'. What was the 'desperate bargain' struck with the gods and why is it now threatened? In particular, how can it be that a man of such firm purpose and control should lose his poise and become helpless under some force so that he is as 'driven as an animal'? Fitzgerald emphasises Dick's knowledge of the importance of the occasion. 'He knew that what he was not doing marked a turning point in his life – it was out of line with everything that had preceded it.'

The issue is then widened in a remarkable way. The man who had been responsible for 'the expensive simplicity' of the beach activities – behaviour which stood out from the 'formalized' purposelessness of the others – is now metaphorically presented as a machine, a non-sentient mechanism. And then, by a surprising simile with a notion of penitence.

> Dick's necessity of behaving as he did was a projection of some submerged reality: he was compelled to walk there, or stand there, his shirt-sleeve fitting his wrist and his coat sleeve encasing his shirt-sleeve like a sleeve valve, his collar molded plastically to his neck, his red hair cut exactly, his hand holding his small briefcase like a dandy – just as another man once found it necessary to stand in front of a church in Ferrara, in sackcloth and ashes. Dick was paying some tribute to things unforgotten, unshriven, unexpurgated.[83]

Because Fitzgerald has established Diver as a purposive, controlled and dominant person, the effect which this immature, albeit radiant girl has upon him is surprising. Fitzgerald makes it clear just how Diver has been thrown off balance by her. The omniscient author speaks about Diver's 'panic' over the 'loss of control' which Rosemary causes.[84] This is illustrated by his jealousy over Collis Clay[85] and his mistake in using the word 'brooding' when talking to Nicole.[86] The idea of compulsion, present in the machine imagery, is continued throughout Fitzgerald's presentation of Diver as being quite aware that such infatuation is completely out of character. The reader, too, has been made aware of the mistake Diver is making. Rosemary's idea of love is on a much less serious level than his. For her it is closely related to her acting. 'Oh, we're such *actors* – you and I.'[87] And soon after she has offered herself to him she is capable of writing a letter telling her mother she has fallen in love with someone else.[88] As omniscient author Fitzgerald is explicit about the irrational compulsion which drives Diver.

Back at two o'clock in the Roi George corridor the beauty of Nicole had been to the beauty of Rosemary as the beauty of Leonardo's girl was to that of the girl of an illustrator. Dick moved on through the rain, demoniac and frightened.[89]

At this point, he also attempts an implicit reinforcement of the sense of Diver's desperate – and irresistible – error by calling attention to the steady dripping of the rain in a manner which recalls occasions in the first two novels when evil had reached the point where the devil approached. The incident in *The Beautiful and Damned* in which Gloria associates 'the thing' with the visitor, Hull, is heightened by the 'Drip – dri-ip!'[90] of the rain. And in *This Side of Paradise* Amory's nightmarish experience includes the frightening insight that the footsteps which sound 'like a slow dripping'[91] were not following but leading him. Clearly, the notion of a rain-like dripping was associated in Fitzgerald's mind with a sense of horror: the kind of horror reserved for those who are faced with the consequences of a persistent adherence to the wrong standards. In *Tender is the Night*, the earlier kind of horror is absent but in combination with explicit references to Diver's own expressed awareness of fundamental mistakes in *demoniacally* following his emotions, expressions like the following continue to illustrate that this is the wrong path. 'She came over and sat there and while the dripping slowed down outside – drip – dri-i-p, she laid her lips to the beautiful cold image she had created.'[92]

Although Fitzgerald shows that Diver has been knocked off balance by his feelings for Rosemary, he also shows that, in an emergency, the old ability to guide and control to some extent remains. Thus, in the incident involving the murdered negro in Rosemary's room, Diver takes charge and handles everything so that no scandal will follow. And since this follows the drunken complications of Abe North the contrast is clear: Abe, who believes like Maury Noble that 'nothing matters'[93] is incapable of ordering his own life, let alone others; while Diver still retains the ability to function efficiently in the wider world. This factor increases the interest in Dick Diver's code. In particular, since Book 1 ends by recalling the strange scene in the bathroom at Villa Diana, the nature of the 'desperate bargain with the gods'[94] is especially intriguing.

IV

> I am . . . a moralist at heart and really want to preach at people
> in some acceptable form rather than to entertain them.
>
> (Fitzgerald to his daughter 4 November 1939)[95]

The 'form' which was to be the means of conveying Fitzgerald's ideas was, of course, the novel: the basis of the moral preaching was 'the wise and tragic sense'. However, as the use of the word 'acceptable' clearly infers, the preaching should be subtle; the moralising non-didactic. All his novels confirm the accuracy of this description. In each of four completed novels the moral earnestness is present in unobtrusive narrative techniques which create inner stories establishing the serious moral norm. Unfortunately, the habitual critical approach to Fitzgerald cannot accommodate the possibility of a subsuming philosophical concept. Therefore, artistic devices such as the use of imagery to create a hidden level of meaning – particularly in the case of *This Side of Paradise* – are largely unremarked. Usually, as is revealed by the consensus about the use of Rosemary, aspects of the novels which fail to match the notion of Fitzgerald as essentially an emotional rather than a conceptual thinker are cited as evidence of muddled thinking.[96] In fact, as an objective analysis of Rosemary's role in Book 1 shows, Fitzgerald used her in the same way that he used the character of young Carraway: their naïve reactions and first impressions are highly effective in stimulating interest in the crucial perspective of the hidden lives of the chief protagonists.

Although it is possible to consider Rosemary's role simply as a question of technique, to do so is to suggest unhelpful distinctions. Fitzgerald's ironic point of view was such that the method of narration is a crystallisation of the intellectual matter. As with the young Carraway, the device of the fallible narrator is a very important part of the central concept. Rosemary's role is not simply to quicken interest in Dick Diver but also, through her own character, to help focus upon what Fitzgerald felt to be those timeless and universal conditions which provide the field for a modern epic.

In this respect the kinship with the earlier novels is obvious. Book 1 of *Tender is the Night* makes it clear that the importance of love in human relations is going to be a major feature of the novel. Almost immediately Rosemary tells her mother that she 'fell in love on the beach'.[97] She also considers a sexual encounter with Brady – a man she meets for the first time – contemplating 'a surrender with equanimity'.[98] There is also a strong hint of homosexual relationships with Mr Dumphry and Mr Campion.[99] And, as well as the central issue of Dick Diver's love for Nicole and Rosemary, there are glimpses of other aspects of love: there is Mary North's despairing love for Abe; Abe's frightened love for Nicole;[100] Collis Clay's devotion to Rosemary; the 'father complex' of the film *Daddy's Girl*. It is against this kind of background that Dick and Rosemary's love affair develops.

As with the other novels, the concern with love right from the beginning of *Tender is the Night* emphasises one particular aspect. Fitzgerald has Luis Campion indicate this when, in a tearful state over the impending duel he tells Rosemary of the unhappiness of love. 'When you're older you'll know what people who love suffer. The agony. It's better to be cold and young than to love.'[101] And, crucially, as Dick tells Rosemary, love was at the centre of the argument that caused the duel. '"And I mean love," he said, guessing her thoughts. "Active love – it's more complicated than I can tell you. It was responsible for that crazy duel."'[102]

There is also the violent incident at the Gare Saint Lazare where the misery of Abe's 'will to die'[103] is complemented by the shooting of the Englishman by Maria Wallis. Fitzgerald links this incident with the progress of Dick's love for Rosemary. It is the first occasion that Dick's ability to guide events is diminished. He is shown as realising that he was suffering 'a loss of control'.[104] Just as importantly, Fitzgerald tells of the effect of the shooting in imagery which recalls violence on a bigger scale. Speaking of Rosemary and Nicole wanting Dick 'to make a moral comment on the matter', he refers to Rosemary 'who was accustomed to having shell fragments of such events shriek past her head'.[105] The scene closes with the two porters discussing the violence. 'Tu as vu sa chemise? Assez de sang pour se croire à la guerre.'[106]

This linking of love and war is given more extensive treatment earlier. On the occasion of the visit to the First World War trenches Fitzgerald had similarly stressed Rosemary's reliance upon Dick's ability to tell her 'how she should feel' but on this occasion Dick seems to be in complete control. He advises the girl from Tennessee to leave the wreath she bought for her brother's grave on any grave, saying: 'I think that's what he'd have wanted you to do.'[107] In the process of indicating the curious powers of Dick Diver's personality the whole scene is certainly intriguing and, in the main, this is due to his view of the battle of the Somme. He calls it a 'love battle'. 'All my beautiful lovely safe world blew itself up here with a great gust of high explosive love.'[108] And this is followed by Fitzgerald's description of Rosemary's feelings of love for Dick: 'most of all she wanted him to know how she loved him, now that the fact was upsetting everything, now that she was walking over the battle-field in a thrilling dream'.[109]

One of the first potentially violent situations that occurred after Rosemary had declared her love for Dick was the duel between Barban and McKisco. That, as Dick later tells Rosemary, was due to love. Not until the end of Book 1 does Fitzgerald give more explanatory detail about the mysterious occurrence which precipitated the duel. The implication is that Nicole is subject to fits of insanity and that Mrs McKisco had seen and gossiped about one which happened at the Villa Diana. Significantly, Nicole's dementia involves blood. '"It's you!" she cried, "– it's you come to intrude on the only privacy I have in the world – with your spread with red blood on it."' This loss of her control followed the discovery and disposal of the dead negro found on Rosemary's bed in the hotel. Apart from continuing the process of linking the developing love interest with violence – Rosemary 'adored him for saving her'[110] – Fitzgerald creates an interesting allusion. Nicole's horror at the blood is given a special context when it is realised that Fitzgerald gives the manager-owner of the hotel the name of McBeth. This adds another dimension to the relationship of Dick and Nicole. As with references to the First World War, a widening of the story is implied.

The full significance of Nicole's reaction does not become apparent until later. However, by the end of Book 1, several important issues have been made clear. Against the background picture of the unhappy consequences of love, Dick Diver is seen to be helpless against forces which compel him to fall in love with Rosemary. The 'desperate bargain'[111] which had hitherto controlled the ordered world of the Divers is threatened and the details of Nicole's outburst, linked as it is to the leitmotif of love/violence, add to the intriguing mystery which surrounds the Divers. In particular and due largely to the manner of the narration, Dick's compulsion towards the immature and fickle actress is especially puzzling. His own awareness of his position combines with the reader's knowledge that Rosemary thinks of the affair as 'one of her greatest roles'.[112] Thus the strong impression grows that Dick who had seemed to possess magical powers to guide and control events is now in the grip of much stronger powers and is making an awful mistake. Thus, his visit to the film studios in the hope of seeing Rosemary is given in these terms: 'Dignified in his fine clothes, with their fine accessories, he was yet swayed and driven as an animal.' And, standing in front of the studios he is described as 'paying some tribute to things unforgotten, unshriven, unexpurgated'.[113]

The effect is to increase the desire to know more about Dick Diver's life before this 'turning point': to discover what it was in the past that made this compulsion – presented as an act of penance – necessary. In fact and quite in keeping with his wish to have his 'preaching' in an acceptable form, Fitzgerald continually offers assistance with the puzzle. As he had struggled to do even with 'The Romantic Egotist' he aimed to plant 'indexes' to the final point of view rather than expressing it directly from the beginning. The effect aimed for was a gradual dawning of understanding gained through a series of events consistently presented in a context which would inevitably lead to only one possible 'explanation': the writer's own view of the way things are. Certainly, that method can be an effective and acceptable form of preaching. In *The Great Gatsby* for example, the reader's understanding follows Nick Carraway's growing awareness that his middle-class, middle-American standards are inadequate when faced with Gatsby's code: he was functioning on the basis of principles which were much older than Carraway's.

For all his novels Fitzgerald followed the basic artistic strategy outlined in 'The Romantic Egotist'. He wished for a slowly deepening appreciation of a point of view not immediately apparent in the entertaining events of the surface story. The gradual awareness of a deeper level of meaning is achieved as much by the presentation of incidents as by the nature of the incidents selected. In *This Side of Paradise* for example, imagery – of travel and music – consistently implies Amory's moral decline and prefigures his descent to the 'labyrinth' of despair. Imagery, the patterning of events and particularly the consistently sad tone of the narrative are as effective as the actual incidents chosen in hinting at the 'indexes' to the controlling ironic vision. The effect aimed for is similar to the sense Nick Carraway had when listening to Gatsby's amazing story. 'I was reminded of something – an elusive rhythm, a fragment of lost words, that I had heard somewhere a long time ago.'[114] The technique can be highly effective. A moral position which is slowly discerned rather than didactically imposed is likely to be quite persuasive. This is what lay at the heart of Fitzgerald's idea of an acceptable form for his preaching.

In fact, such was the nature of his own point of view that the form of slow revelation was axiomatic. The ironic belief that illusion is the source of both pain and pleasure is adequately presented in a narrative which continually implies real pain behind apparent pleasure. In the case of *Tender is the Night*, by starting with the outwardly successful and happy circumstances of the Divers, through a careful manipulation of the narrative voice Fitzgerald succeeds in making Book 1 place the reader in Gatsby's position when he contemplated his past: 'if he could once return to a certain starting place and go over it all slowly, he could find out what the thing was'.[115] In Book 1, Fitzgerald aimed not only to dramatise Dick Diver's surprising loss of poise and control but also to imply the reasons. In that way the preaching would exist in an acceptable form.

The continual reference to the First World War in Book 1 is most apparent in Book 2 which opens with details of Dick Diver's involvement. After being a Rhodes Scholar at Oxford in 1914 he returned to Johns Hopkins and took his degree in 1915. In 1916 'he managed to get to Vienna under the impression that, if he did not make haste, the great Freud would eventually succumb to an aeroplane bomb.'[116] In 1917, at the age of twenty-six he was in Zurich following the instruction of his local draft board to complete his studies there. After graduating he was attached to a military neurological unit in France where his duties were 'executive rather than practical'. In 1919, at the age of twenty-eight, he was discharged. He returned to Zurich. These details are, however, considerably conditioned by one important factor: he seems to be a man of potential greatness. Indeed, he is likened to Grant 'lolling in his general store in Galena, . . . ready to be called to an intricate destiny'.[117] That, and the fact that Fitzgerald immediately tells how Dick has plenty of illusions, should suggest a kinship with Amory Blaine and Gatsby. The same concept of egotism linked to a sense of immense potential lies behind the presentation of Dick Diver. In the terminology of the early work, Dick – unlike Anthony Patch – is one of the elect. One of the marks of his election is the strong impression that he knows where he is going; of confident purposive movement. He can, for example, burn 'almost a hundred textbooks' for fuel in Vienna's winter, 'with an assurance chuckling inside him'[118] that he had thoroughly digested each word and could recall them later if needed. In this he is unlike Amory Blaine who stumbled along many paths without a sense of purpose and more like Gatsby who knew early that the 'drums of his destiny' led him to the faithful 'service of a vast, vulgar, and meretricious beauty'.[119] The difference in the presentation of Dick is that although Fitzgerald again emphasises the call 'to an intricate destiny',[120] in Dick's case the narrative voice offers neither criticism nor praise to the notion.

The controlling macro-vision has the important effect of implying an inevitability about the story but in the matter of creating indexes to that final point of view the danger is that the micro-detail can be puzzlingly enigmatic. That is perhaps the case with the early reference to 'Lucky Dick' needing to be 'less intact, even faintly destroyed'.[121] However, even if not yet fully appreciated, such statements add the suggestion of painful experience to the 'intricate destiny'.

Section 2 of Book 2 moves in, as it were, from the opening long-shot to give the impression of Dick embarking on the path to his destiny. Significantly, Fitzgerald uses the kind of imagery he had created for Amory and Gatsby when they contemplated Arcady. In contrast to the feeling in France of 'finite' lanes, in Zurich there seems something more: 'the roofs upled the eyes to tinkling cow pastures, which in turn modified hilltops further up – so life was a perpendicular starting off to a postcard heaven.'[122] This is remarkably like Gatsby's view of a ladder formed by 'the blocks of the sidewalks'[123] and Amory's sense of the magical pathway which Myra's presence had created by the steps of the Country Club.[124] In this case the imagery indicates Dick's confident optimism in regard to his ambition 'to be a good psychologist – maybe to be the greatest one that ever lived'.[125] That, however, is not his only ambition. Fitzgerald supplies an important piece of information which has a bearing upon the cryptic description of 'Lucky Dick' being 'less intact': 'he used to think that he wanted to be good, he wanted to be kind, he wanted to be brave and wise, but it was all pretty difficult. He wanted to be loved, too, if he could fit it in.'[126] The reference to the desire to be loved is crucial. As far back as the story of Uncle George[127] Fitzgerald had made this the source of pleasure/pain. With Amory it signalled his

Achilles' heel which made him vulnerable to evil; with Gatsby, although his 'appalling sentimentality'[128] forced him into a colossal mistake, his suffering was vindicated. At this stage of Dick's journey, with the reader already knowing of the compulsive need for Rosemary, a danger signal should be heard.

An important part of the narrative technique assisting this warning note is to be observed in the way that Fitzgerald associates love with illness or wounding. The whole of the sequence which introduces Nicole is given against a background of the war. And when Dick first goes to Dohmler's clinic to see Franz Gregorovius Fitzgerald draws attention to 'the white flag of a nurse waving beside a patient on a path'.[129]

In view of what is related later, this linking of love with battle is highly significant. Nicole's psychological 'wound' is diagnosed as schizophrenia caused by an act of incest with her father. Dick has been encouraged to correspond with Nicole: the act of 'transference' seems to have aided her recovery. Clearly, falling in love with Dick has been a major element in the improvement. Knowing of the dangers in such a relationship, Dick attempts to end it but is represented as missing her badly. In fact he is unable to resist the pull of his emotions. Fitzgerald shows Dick's vulnerability by describing his sensations at Cauz after the accidental meeting with Nicole in the funicular – prefigured in the early idea of the 'perpendicular starting off to a postcard heaven'.[130]

> He wheeled off his bicycle, feeling Nicole's eyes following him, feeling her helpless first love, feeling it twist around inside him. He went three hundred yards up the slope to the other hotel, he engaged a room and found himself washing without a memory of the intervening ten minutes, only a sort of drunken flush pierced with voices, unimportant voices that did not know how much he was loved.[131]

There are two important aspects of Fitzgerald's treatment of the Nicole–Dick relationship: first, the immediate concentration is upon her love for him; and secondly, war imagery is used even at the point of their first kiss. The last point is especially noteworthy. Their first embrace begins in an atmosphere of contest because Nicole is demanding the right to be loved. After the kiss she felt triumphantly: 'I've got him, he's mine.' And Fitzgerald makes her attempt to take stock of the situation. 'Nicole was up in her head now, cool as cool, trying to collate the sentimentalities of her childhood, as deliberate as a man getting drunk after battle.'[132] This kind of coolness, complemented by the absence of any declaration of love by Dick and linked as it all is to impressions of battle, suggests a less than ideal love. Attentive readers will also note the similarities between the second kiss and the earlier kiss just before Rosemary discovered the body in her room.

> He breathed over her shoulder and turned her insistently
> about; she kissed him several times, her face getting big every
> time she came close, her hands holding him by the shoulders.
> 'It's raining hard.'[133]

Some of this is almost word-for-word like the kiss with Rosemary and the effect is to highlight the patterning of experience. Of course, the fact of the rain too, recalls the devil scene in *The Beautiful and Damned* and this reinforces the impression that Fitzgerald is implying that the wrong path is being followed. However, no outside knowledge is really needed because so much has been accomplished by means of careful patterning. By having Rosemary appear first as 'Daddy's Girl', and then introducing Nicole, who had been in a different sense her Daddy's girl, Fitzgerald created suggestive ironies. With both Rosemary and Nicole Dick is drawn against his will into love affairs. Both women are presented as being in love with him and actively pursuing their desires; Rosemary as an actress indulging in 'one of her greatest roles',[134] and Nicole coolly, as a contestant. Dick's wish to be loved appears to render him helpless to these assaults. However, the inescapable fact about the patterning Fitzgerald created is that Dick's role in both affairs is surrogate Daddy. The unsatisfactory nature of this stamps both affairs as fundamental mistakes.

The patterning then, together with a form of narrative which is continually indicating the unsatisfactory nature of Dick Diver's love affairs, plays a major part in the creation of an inner story-line. Not only is the method characteristic, so is the underlying notion of basic issues. Like Gatsby, like Amory, like Anthony, Dick Diver is shown to be helpless before female beauty. In *Tender is the Night*, although the narrative voice is not confined to the persona of a participating narrator, the artistic aim is similar to that used for *The*

Great Gatsby. By the end of Book 1 the reader should have sensed –
as the young Carraway did of Gatsby's story – that certain clues
which could resolve the mystery of the events related have already
been given.

As part of the process of linking love with violence/pain,
Fitzgerald created the incident on the battlefield of the Somme at
which time he had Dick Diver describe the fighting as 'the last love
battle'. The visit takes place at a time when Rosemary's love for
him is beginning to make her 'unhappy . . . desperate'. Dick claims:
'This kind of battle was invented by Lewis Carroll and Jules Verne
and whoever wrote Undine.'[135] The fantasies of the first two
writers – of fairy-story and science-fiction lands respectively – are
easily understood as implying the fantastic nature of war; but the
Undine reference is not so obvious. Anthough *Undine*, like *Alice in
Wonderland* deals in magical characters, it also tells of an unhappy
love story. The knight Huldbrand falls in love with the sylph
Undine. In marrying him she receives a human soul. Although
they are at first happy he begins to neglect her in favour of another
beautiful girl. Undine has to return to her own family beneath the
water. As Huldbrand prepares to marry again, Undine rises from a
well and kisses him whereupon he dies. It could be that Fitzgerald
considered a symbolic link with the story of Dick Diver: certainly
the marriage to Nicole brought her back into the world from
insanity; but there are other more helpful implications. Friedrich,
Baron de la Motte Fouqué was inspired to write *Undine* by a
passage in Paracelsus and when once the idea of this man has been
raised interesting connections are suggested.

Paracelsus – Philippus Aureolus Theophrastus Bombastus ab
Hohenheim – was born near Zurich in 1493. As a kind of doctor he
wandered Europe practising magic, alchemy and astrology. He
was credited with amazing cures and was appointed to a chair of
physic and surgery at Basel. He was so sure of his own abilities that
he burnt the works of his predecessors Galen and Avicenna. He
did, however, lose favour and was pronounced a quack. He
returned to his wanderings around Europe and died, still disre-
garded. Even this brief outline suggests a link with Dick Diver,
particularly in the burning of the books, but the link becomes quite
significant when that version of the story which Fitzgerald is most
likely to have known is considered.

Browning's dramatic poem 'Paracelsus', published in 1835 draws
upon the actual life of the legendary Paracelsus and presents him

as a man early aware of his election 'which marked [him] out/apart from men'. His 'certain aim' was to discover

> the secret of the world,
> Of man, and man's true purpose, path and fate.

He sets out on this quest despite the entreaties of his friends and, after searching and though learning a great deal, the secret still eludes him. In Constantinople he meets a poet Aprile who is also dedicated to a quest. Whereas Paracelsus aspires 'to know' all, Aprile 'would love infinitely, and be loved!'

Paracelsus realises that to pursue knowledge while excluding love was his fundamental error. He resolves to put the balance right.

> Still thou hast beauty and I, power.
> We wake:
> What penance canst devise for both of us?

Appointed to the teaching position at Basel he is still unhappy: he cannot enjoy the adulation he receives against a background of quackery and willing credulity because he still cannot reconcile beauty and knowledge. Thus his new quest is 'to know and to enjoy at/once'. His dissatisfaction causes his dismissal as a quack and he resumes his wandering. He dies in apparent degradation and failure. Browning's 'Paracelsus' illustrates the characteristic Romantic concern with the quester whose very intensity brings about his own destruction. The 'Alastor' figure was clearly intriguing to Fitzgerald: particularly in the idea of love being at once delusion and the source of happiness. His variations on the Romantic preoccupation with a psyche-epipsyche strategy as seen in *This Side of Paradise*;[136] his version of Plato's 'Symposium' in *The Beautiful and Damned*:[137] and his ironic treatment of Gatsby's dedication to Daisy's image,[138] all indicate his sympathy for the Romantic's concern with human love. However, Browning's influence probably extended beyond the basic idea concerning the vital role of love.

At the end of Book 1 of *Paracelsus*, Browning has the quester describe his task by means of an extremely interesting image: it is the simile of a pearl-fisher.

> Are there not, Festus, are there not,
> 　　dear Michal,
> Two points in the adventure of the
> 　　diver:
> One – when, a beggar, he prepares to
> 　　plunge?
> One – when, a prince, he rises with
> 　　his pearl?

In this, not only was there an ideal name offered for Fitzgerald's hero, there was also an extremely helpful plotting suggestion. Inherent in the image is the opportunity for irony. As Paracelsus shows, his attainment has not brought him the perfect joy he had hoped for: success brought a form of 'degradation'. However, failure could be seen as a form of success. *The Great Gatsby* in particular shows Fitzgerald's interest in that kind of structural irony. Carraway's story also shows Fitzgerald's predilection for a non chronological narration. Gatsby is first seen as 'a prince' and only then as 'a beggar' before he took his plunge'. The effect is to concentrate attention upon his true 'starting point'. That is clearly shown to have been the time he perceived 'all the beauty and glamour in the world' to be founded upon the 'fairy's wing' of material possessions.[139] The wish to find an acceptable form for the 'preaching' was served by first dramatising Gatsby in his apparent success: in that way his real motivations could be highlighted and, apparently, placed in a moral perspective. This paved the way for Fitzgerald's special vision of the epic struggle to perpetuate illusion. *Tender is the Night* utilises the same general approach usefully indicated in Browning's image of the pearl-diver. As with *The Great Gatsby* and true to his wish to convince his readers by means of a slowly developing understanding, he chose to present Dick Diver as an apparent success some years after his first plunge and only then to show him at his true 'starting point'.

In Rosemary's first view of the people on the beach Nicole is twice characterised as the woman wearing a 'string of pearls'.[140] Dick Diver is the leader and director of his group's activities. Rosemary is attracted to 'the expensive simplicity of the Divers'.[141] Indeed, the privileged affluence of the Divers' group is a far cry from any notion of beggars, yet such is Fitzgerald's presentation that Dick's present 'princely' state is continually called into question. In keeping with his early idea about indexes to a final point of view, Fitzgerald sows the narrative of Book 1 with seeds of strong doubt. Thus, when in Book 2 he goes back in time to the young Dick Diver, there is a natural focusing upon the special characteristics of Diver's personality.

In the first instance, because the reader has already seen the kind of life enjoyed by the Divers after several years of marriage, the aspirations of Dick up to the age of twenty-eight are placed in definite perspective. Although Rosemary is impressed by his dominant control, the trivial purposiveness seems a poor achievement beside the potential of 'an intricate destiny'.[142] The comments from the omniscient author also support this view and, overall, the sad tone of the narrative voice continually implies disappointment. By illustrating the modifications to the sense of election even before that election has been referred to, the claim that 'life is a cheat' has already been proved.

There is, however, a further aspect of the patterning of experience which has a crucial bearing on the issue of Fitzgerald's intellectual control over his material. Fitzgerald's allusive technique which associates Romantic characteristics with Dick Diver's predicament goes much further than this. Elements from Keats' 'Ode to a Nightingale', from Browning's 'Paracelsus', and from Shelley's 'Alastor' intermingle with Fitzgerald's materials – in content and technique – thereby widening the whole story and suggesting a universality in much the same way as the Greek mythology and references to early explorers expanded *The Great Gatsby*. Yet there is a further range of allusion which adds even more to the story. The point can be illustrated from the incident outside the Film Studios towards the end of Book 1 in which Dick Diver is represented as 'swayed and driven as an animal' in his growing obsession for Rosemary.

> . . . Dick's necessity of behaving as he did was a projection of some submerged reality: he was compelled to walk there, or stand there, his shirt-sleeve fitting his wrist and his coat sleeve encasing his shirt-sleeve like a sleeve-valve, his collar molded plastically to his neck, his red hair cut exactly, his hand holding his small briefcase like a dandy – just as another man once found it necessary to stand in front of a church in Ferrara, in sackcloth and ashes. Dick was paying some tribute to things unforgotten, unshriven, unexpurgated.[143]

In this powerful and initially puzzling description the first emphasis is upon the mechanical behaviour: some 'submerged reality' forces Dick to respond, as would a machine, to some, preprogramming. The necessity is then linked, surprisingly, with a notion of penitence.

Although the analogy is not immediately clear, the overall effect is to place Dick's compulsion on a high level of seriousness. The historical/religious connotations widen the implications of his behaviour. At this point in the novel – shortly before the end of Book 1 – it could appear that to create a context of religious penitence for a love affair risked bathetic exaggeration. However, if Gatsby's commitment to Daisy is recalled, it will be seen that not only is the technique characteristic of Fitzgerald but that such passages offer the clearest insights into the controlling power of 'the wise and tragic sense'.

When Carraway is made to recall Gatsby's commitment to Daisy, he tells of Gatsby's understanding that once he kissed her 'his mind would never romp again like the mind of God'. Like Gatsby, Dick Diver is shown to be aware that his behaviour constituted a 'turning point'. Although, for him, there was no 'incarnation', the serious religious perspective is suggested in the idea that his act is one of contrition; that he is suffering for sins 'unshriven, unexpurgated'. Both episodes, then, make apparently minor incidents in the progress of love affairs assume wide-ranging significance. There is, though, an important difference. Even though the same basic 'philosophical concept' can be shown to lie behind them both, Gatsby's starting point is placed in the past while Dick Diver is shown to be making a second commitment in the present. This is a crucial distinction. The compulsive attempt to see Rosemary is not Dick Diver's starting place: it is a 'turning place' and it is to be seen in a carefully controlled structure which, by its patterning, the use of imagery, and a form of dual narration, supplies a framework of meaning. Above all, the decision to begin with the affair with Rosemary gives Fitzgerald the opportunity to introduce those elements which will most assist his aim of non-didactic preaching. The story of her involvement with Diver establishes the crucial perspective against which his true starting place can be seen and it combines with the chronologically earlier love affair in offering Fitzgerald the ideal form for the expression of his ironic-pessimistic philosophy.

Of course to begin a novel with a love affair which is so

integrated with later events that its full meaning is delayed is to risk misunderstanding. On a superficial level the Rosemary Hoyt/ Dick Diver love story can be explained as a fairly typical occurrence: after several years of marriage an older man falls in love with a young and beautiful girl. However, the interplay between Rosemary's subjective impressions and the omniscient author's authoritative statements is always tending to an intriguing gravity which implies a more complex situation. Imagery which associates love with wounding and pain assists this process. But the most powerful conditioning factor is Fitzgerald's allusive technique which, as the story develops, combines with the other elements to create a subtle framework. It is this hidden structure which contains the 'explanation' of Dick Diver's predicament. Not surprisingly, in the light of its centrality to the three earlier novels, the sense of inexorable universal forces at work on humanity – the 'wearing down power of the universe' – is a key issue. Nor is it surprising that love should provide the illustrative examples. In *Tender is the Night*, mainly by association with Romantic ideas of questing, the spiritual pilgrimage which is so characteristic of the Fitzgerald hero, invests Dick Diver's journey through life with epic characteristics. Typically, his sense of election is conditioned by his need to be loved. That is his starting place, and, as with Gatsby, is the source of all his pleasure and pain. References like the penitent at Ferrara widen the issue by implying that, throughout the ages, men have discovered this sad truth. Although the reference is usually thought to allude to the humiliation of Henry IV at Canossa in 1077,[144] the specific mention of Ferrara inevitably brings to mind the tragic story of the poet Tasso. Although he was never literally a penitent before a church in Ferrara, he did suffer imprisonment there over his obsessive love, made a formal repentance and, after banishment, wandered through Europe. Byron's poem 'The Lament of Tasso' and Goethe's 'Torquato Tasso' were almost certainly known by Fitzgerald and, along with the Paracelsus legend, they provided further impressions of the universality of the destructive power of love.

Important as it undoubtedly was in forming a persuasive illustration of the universality of the 'wearing down power', this linking with older stories is not the major part of the narrative structure. There is another element which not only determined that the novel should begin with Rosemary rather than Nicole but also shaped the ironic resolution. It was, of course, the philosophic concept of the wise and tragic sense but in *Tender is the Night* it appears in a form which contemporaries ought to have recognised.

From the beginning of his novel writing career, Fitzgerald made an idea of Egotism a central issue. It was, for example, the basis of the structural irony in *This Side of Paradise*. Amory Blaine's egotism – first appearing as narcissism – initially worked against his innate sense of election. Later, after a series of negative experiences in pursuit of an illusory Arcady, he achieved a better understanding of his egotism and, thus, of achievable happiness. Almost certainly because of a fixed opinion of the nature of Fitzgerald's intelligence, the correspondence with Freud's theories is never remarked. Specifically, Freud's early explanation of the duality in the human mind refers to erotic impulses derived from ego impulses on the one hand and reproductive impulses on the other. He also attached great importance to the human wish for pleasure, believing it was the dominant principle in mental life. Without wishing to press too heavily on the connections with Fitzgerald's early work, it should be clear that in Freud's theories he would have found much that corresponded with his own point of view.

When *Tender is the Night* is considered with these possible connections in view, significant patterns can be discerned. Attitudes to love provide the key.

It will be recalled that Dick Diver went to Vienna in 1916, 'under the impression that, if he did not make haste, the great Freud would eventually succumb to an aeroplane bomb'.[145] After the successful completion of his studies and brief war service he returned to Zurich in pursuit of his ambition 'to be a good psychologist – maybe to be the greatest one that ever lived'.[146] Part 2 of Book 2 tells of Nicole's 'transference' to Dick. After the letters written to Dick, Fitzgerald supplies details of the incestuous incident which seems to have provoked the schizophrenia. Throughout this background information about Nicole's history there is an emphasis upon love. The letters for example strongly suggest a need for (as well as a fear of) love. This seems explicable when the transfer from 'wonderful father and daughter' to 'lovers'[147] is related. It seems entirely plausible that her return to sanity should be through her love for Dick. He, recognising that marriage would mean devoting his life to her, and realising that the Warrens were actually proposing to find 'some good doctor'[148] who would marry Nicole, attempts to avoid the commitment. Then in the kind of kiss by which Gatsby 'wed his unutterable visions to

[Daisy's] perishable breath'[149] the commitment is made.[150] The wedding and the first years of marriage are compressed into the short Part 10 of Book 2, mainly in a stream-of-consciousness narrative from Nicole. In that, a clear impression of her mental instability is given. It is also clear just what effect Dick's devotion is having on his career: he is not writing. Their life suggests that their only motivation is a concern for her health. It is at this point that the narrative returns to the events of the present: it is the morning after Dick has stage-managed the disposal of the body found in Rosemary's room. Dick now admits to Mrs Speers that he is in love with Rosemary. The scene recalls Dick's conversation with Nicole's sister, for Mrs Speers' 'detachment'[151] is as impressive as Baby's practicality.

It is not only this last similarity which links Dick Diver's two love affairs. Rosemary's success as 'Daddy's Girl' is an essential prerequisite for an understanding of the hidden story-line. Throughout Book 1, Fitzgerald's narrative method has stressed the child-like naïvety, freshness and charm of Rosemary. It has also strongly implied that Dick would be making a mistake if he were to allow himself to love her. By having Nicole's early story presented in a very similar way, it would at first seem that Fitzgerald is using the incest motif to form the plane of meaning by which the love for Rosemary must be judged. In fact, although superficially there is that link, almost the reverse is true. In a very important way, Rosemary's role in Book 1 offers a meaning for Nicole's role in the novel.

From the very beginning Rosemary is presented in terms which imply her sexuality. Although 'her body hovered delicately on the last edge of childhood',[152] the description of her first swim emphasises her sensuality. Although she soon decides she has fallen in love with Dick Diver, such is her naïvety that this could be thought to be a mere 'crush' on an older man were it not for the fact that Fitzgerald shows she is capable of thinking about a sexual 'surrender'[153] to Earl Brady and that she is 'deeply moved'[154] by the idea of Nicole and Dick arranging to make love. Crucially, it is she who makes all the early advances and, despite the fact that she is conscious of acting, she offers herself to him. At that moment, after being 'chilled by the innocence of her kiss',[155] Fitzgerald makes the gulf between them clear. He tells how Dick 'recovered his paternal attitude'.[156] The scene ends with Dick saying: 'Good night, child.'[157] In these ways Fitzgerald invests Rosemary with a naïvety which contains a definite sexuality and deliberately places her relationship with Dick on the implied level of incest. The danger with this technique is that when the later details about Nicole's incest are given it might at first appear that the warning note which is so clearly sounded for Dick against involvement with Rosemary as it was with Nicole should be thought to have been played on that specific moral scale. That would be only part of the book's moral preaching. Not enough attention would have been paid to Rosemary's sexual awareness.

Writing of Freud's changing views regarding incest, Ernest Jones points out that, first, 'he held the opinion that the essential cause of hysteria was a sexual seduction of an innocent child on the part of some adult, most often the father'. Later, however, he was forced to accept the 'truth':

> that irrespective of incest wishes of parents toward their children, and even of occasional acts of the kind, what he had to concern himself with was the general occurrence of incest wishes of children toward their parents.[158]

It is this vital 'truth', as Jones calls it, that would be less easy to discern were Nicole's story to begin the novel. Her sexual awareness – seen in the letters to Dick and her determined pursuit of him – are not to be thought to be the result of her incestuous act: as with Rosemary's pursuit of Dick they are manifestations of the 'truth' of Freud's later observations.

In point of fact, Fitzgerald's use of Rosemary to provide the correct frame of reference for Dick Diver's predicament goes beyond the obvious implication of a father/daughter relationship and in this demonstrates both the complexity of Fitzgerald's structural framework and his use of Freud's essays. After the incident at the Villa Diana which precipitated the duel, Rosemary appears to be helplessly in love with Dick. The nature of her infatuation is suggested in a manner which emphasises Dick's power and authority and places Rosemary in the role of supplicant. The bathroom incident had destroyed the magic of the dinner table where the guests took on the appearance of 'poor children at a Christmas tree'.[159] For Dick, 'the space between heaven and earth had cooled his mind',[160] and he tries to disengage himself from Rosemary. 'She was stricken. She touched him, feeling the smooth cloth of his dark coat like a chasuble. She seemed about to fall to her knees.'[161] This religious imagery prefigures the similar imagery indicating the nature of Dick's compulsion before the Film Studios. However, Rosemary's obsession is given a specific framework and, given Fitzgerald's earlier use of Plato's notions of love in *The Beautiful and Damned* as well as the influence of Freud, the consequence might have been expected. In the first instance he emphasises the erotic nature of this naïve love for a father/priest figure. In her bed that night Rosemary suffered insomnia. 'Cloaked by the erotic darkness she exhausted the future quickly, with all the eventualities that might lead up to a kiss.' But then Fitzgerald breaks the narrative of the present to give information about the way Rosemary had been brought up, ending with a speech implied by Mrs Speers after Rosemary had, presumably, told of her love.

You were brought up to work – not especially to marry. Now you've found your first nut to crack and it's a good nut – go ahead and put whatever happens down to experience. Wound yourself or him – whatever happens it can't spoil you because economically you're a boy, not a girl.[162]

Apart from the notion of wounding, this passage is interesting in the description of Rosemary as being 'economically' a boy. This certainly qualifies the impression of the developing relationship.

Immediately after this scene, Rosemary meets Luis Campion. 'He was weeping hard and quietly and shaking in the same parts as a weeping woman.'[163] He, the homosexual, tells her of the 'agony' which the 'people who love' suffer.[164] He also tells of the proposed duel: an occasion which could well cause physical wounding. Thus, very subtly, Fitzgerald has implied a link between Rosemary's desire for Diver and homosexuality; and, the subsuming notion of love's pain. Within only a few lines he has had Rosemary described as a boy and Campion exhibiting female characteristics: Rosemary who is in love with Diver and Campion in love with Dumphrey.

In order to understand Fitzgerald's purpose in this it is necessary to recall Freud's theories: specifically, his notion of the development of the libido and the Oedipus complex. Rosemary, although having the public persona of 'Daddy's Girl' is, in another sense, definitely her mother's girl. Mrs Speers' implied speech to Rosemary is described as the 'final severance of the umbilical cord'.[165] Up to this point hovering 'delicately on the last edge of childhood'[166]

Rosemary had been completely dependent upon her mother. In Freud's terms, the loss of her father meant that Rosemary passed through the pregenital and phallic stages with her developing libido fixed upon her mother. Instead of a girl's *Electra complex* – attachment to father – she retains the Oedipus complex rather like an immature boy. Fitzgerald's use of the word 'economically' in this context is interesting and revealing. Freud specifically used the word 'economic' in order to explain a factor which he differentiated from 'topographical' ones and 'dynamic' ones in describing the mental processes at work upon the actions of individuals. The word was especially important in his description of the demands made by 'the pleasure principle'.

> In the theory of psychoanalysis we have no hesitation in assuming that the course taken by mental events is automatically regulated by the pleasure principle. We believe, that is to say, that the course of those events is invariably set in motion by an unpleasurable tension, and that it takes a direction such that its final outcome coincides with a lowering of that tension – that is, with an avoidance of unpleasure or a production of pleasure. In taking that course into account in our consideration of the mental processes which are the subject of our study, we are introducing an 'economic' point of view into our work.[167]

By having Rosemary described as 'economically' a boy, and particularly because this saves her from being spoiled, Fitzgerald supplied a crucial frame of reference for her behaviour. Her pursuit of 'the pleasure principle' would always be conditioned by the early fixation upon her mother. 'Economically' she is still a boy: it would require the painful transition of an Electra complex before she could pass from infantile sexuality to adult sexuality. Thus, her love for Diver could only be a stage of her development.

There can be little doubt that in Freud Fitzgerald would find authoritative corroboration for the point of a view which had informed all his fiction; even from the days of 'The Romantic Egotist'. It is, however, important not to overstate the influence. *Tender is the Night* does not rest ultimately on foundations supplied by Freud: as with much else, Fitzgerald draws upon the undoubtedly widespread knowledge of psychoanalytical theories in order to add to the essential truths of his own insights. Freud's view of the development of the libido gave plausibility – and a sense of universality – to Fitzgerald's moral preaching. Above all, as with other cryptic allusions, it supplied the impression of a de facto illustration that there is indeed an inexorable 'wearing down' force in the universe.

There is one further aspect of Freud's influence which should be mentioned. His method of approaching psychological problems was to investigate the past with his patients; then, through abreaction, present problems could be removed. Like Gatsby searching for 'a certain starting place', the psychoanalyst would probe the past for a key to the present, and, just as it did for Carraway, that impulse gives the reader the most helpful way into Dick Diver's story. In fact, for *Tender is the Night* psychotherapy acts as an implicit metaphor with the reader placed more firmly in the role of informed observer than is the case with *The Great Gatsby*: more informed by reason of the greater number of helpful, allusive references but also in the form of the narrative which, importantly, makes Rosemary begin the story.

Even when the correspondences – and differences – between the Rosemary/Dick love and the Nicole/Dick love are appreciated, Dick's own predicament might initially seem more puzzling. He is, after all, a good psychologist and should appreciate his own position better than the lay observer. However, it is his helplessness against certain forces – given religious/romantic/psychological overtones – which is most emphasised. The impression is given that even a man who possesses to a high degree the ability to control events is powerless against such forces. This has the effect of heightening the interest in Dick Diver himself and in particular why he should need the two love affairs which as the narrative style is continually implying cannot bring him what he requires.

Although it should not be thought of as an essential prerequisite, an understanding of Amory Blaine's position at the end of *This Side of Paradise* can be used to illustrate what Fitzgerald was dramatising through Dick Diver's story. Throughout his journey to self-discovery Amory suffered a series of negative experiences. Although he grows up 'to find all Gods dead, all wars fought, all faiths in man shaken',[168] the major illusion which had prevented his correct progress had been the feeling that he would find the road to Arcady through the love of a lovely girl. He finally realises the true nature of his egotism, and that, it seems, was the real prize; the only Arcady available on this side of Paradise, rather than the achievement of some glorious ambition.

In the constant failure of his dreams, Amory was continually having to face the fact that 'life is essentially a cheat and its conditions are those of defeat'. Fitzgerald, of course, wrote those words much later but they exactly match the pattern of that first novel. There was, in fact, a remarkably similar point of view given widespread currency in the years when *This Side of Paradise* was enjoying great popularity. Freud's essay 'Beyond the Pleasure Principle' appeared first in its German text in 1920 and in English in 1922 – the year in which *This Side of Paradise* was published. Not only would the title of the essay serve as an excellent subtitle for Fitzgerald's novel, but also Freud's identification of 'the reality principle' which is always working against the pleasure principle provides the right terminology to describe Amory's experience.

More importantly, Freud's essay marked a change in his attitude to that duality of mind which Amory's career dramatises: namely the reproductive instincts and the ego impulses. After observations of First World War veterans who suffered war dreams Freud came to the conclusion that there was another principle to be considered. He called this 'repetition-compulsion' and meant by it that phenomenon he had observed in which patients were compelled to relive unpleasant experiences over and over again. Amory Blaine's life-journey certainly shows this tendency but in *Tender is the Night* the deliberate use of war imagery as the major framework for the love story suggests a clear understanding of those principles identified by Freud.

What the careful use of allusions seeks to achieve is that kind of widening of Dick Diver's predicament which will introduce the sense of an epic struggle. If the forces which determine the story are timeless, universal and irrevocable, then the attempt to resist them – as in the story of the small animals fighting the big animals[169] – can be considered heroic. Freud's theories join with allusions to Paracelsus and Tasso to suggest that kind of perspective. In particular, references to the First World War illustrate the large-scale canvas on which Fitzgerald was working. The conversation at the trenches of the Somme illustrates the process.

It will be recalled that Fitzgerald has Dick Diver describe the fighting as 'the last love battle'.[170] This strange remark can only be explained by reference to Freud's essay 'Beyond the Pleasure Principle'. For in that work, not only did he name the 'reality principle' he also identified a new duality of the mind. To the earlier concept of the libido he added part of the instinct towards self-preservation and called the combined force the Life instinct or Eros. The opposing force – a Death instinct or Thanatos – was a new formulation. To it Freud linked the tendency towards repetition and described it as 'demonic' in character. The Death instinct signified the force by which mankind seeks always to return to the original state of inorganic matter and a complete freedom from the tensions of pleasure-unpleasure struggles.

Interestingly, immediately after Diver has described the war as a love battle Abe North parodies the seriousness. 'The war spirit's getting into me again. I have a hundred years of Ohio love behind me and I'm going to bomb out this trench.'[171] Soon after this – at the Gare Saint Lazare – North's companions are presented as being afraid of him: 'they were frightened at his survivant will, once a will to live, now become a will to die.'[172] The reference is clearly intended to give the suggestion of Freud's classifications. In fact the whole of Book 1 performs the important task of dramatising the effects of the Eros/Thanatos duality. Given that framework, the opening story of Rosemary Hoyt's effect on Dick Diver is extremely important.

At the end of *This Side of Paradise* Amory Blaine has learned of the great gulf between his illusions and actuality. He has 'grown up to find all Gods dead, all wars fought, all faiths in man shaken'.[173] In particular he has discovered that there was no road to Arcady through the love of a lovely girl. In fact what he illustrates in his final position was described by Freud. In view of Fitzgerald's later formulation of the double vision thesis – 'the ability to hold two opposed ideas in the mind at the same time'[174] – out of which grew the 'wise and tragic sense', it is extremely illuminating to note Freud's treatment of relevant issues.

According to Freud's biographer, Ernest Jones, Freud's first ideas on the pleasure-unpleasure principle were modified as he became more concerned with a duality.

> He was in all his psychological work ... seized with the conception of a profound conflict within the mind, and he was very naturally concerned to apprehend the nature of the opposing forces. For the first twenty years or so of his work Freud was content to state the terms of mental conflict as being erotic impulses, derived from what biologists call the reproductive instinct, on the one hand, and ego impulses, including notably the instinct of self-preservation, on the other.[175]

Freud identified the most obvious modifier of the pleasure principle as 'the reality principle'.

> This . . . principle does not abandon the intention of ultimately obtaining pleasure, but it nevertheless demands and carries into effect the postponement of satisfaction, the abandonment of a number of possibilities of gaining satisfaction and the temporary toleration of unpleasure as a step on the long indirect road to pleasure.[176]

This notion of duality is extremely helpful when Rosemary's role is considered. In particular the kind of things she stands for – to the American public as well as Dick Diver – are of great relevance to Fitzgerald's purpose. His description of her as she appears in the film is specially revealing. 'There she was – embodying all the immaturity of the race, cutting a new cardboard paper doll to pass before its empty harlot's mind.' As 'Daddy's Girl' she is a powerful force against the forces of evil. 'Before her tiny fist the forces of lust and corruption rolled away; nay, the very march of destiny stopped; inevitable became evitable.'[177] The unreality of this sentimental portrayal is clear but the implied comment is also powerfully present. Mummy's girl has skilfully presented an enormously popular – if viciously sentimental – image of the world. The crucial point is that this image of infantile innocence defeating lust and corruption is patently an invention: one which is entirely welcome to the 'empty harlot's mind' of the public. Later, in the beginning of Book 2 Fitzgerald makes an important thematic connection with Dick Diver on this level. Speaking of the illusions which Diver took with him to Zurich he says that there were plenty: 'illusions of a nation, the lies of generations of frontier mothers who had to croon falsely, that there were no wolves outside the cabin door'.[178] Of course, that kind of falsehood is very different to the one perpetrated by 'Daddy's Girl' and suggests a difference in the quality of innocence. 'Daddy's Girl' trades upon a sentimental wish to revert to a world where love momentarily kept everything safe: that world which existed in childhood before the reality principle overtook the pleasure principle. The world referred to by Dick Diver on the Somme where he laments its passing. 'All my beautiful lovely safe world blew itself up here with a great gust of high explosive love.'[179] Book 1 presents a world which has been overtaken by the reality principle. Love is shown as a destructive, wounding force. Dick Diver alone seems to be able to stand against it but even he so manipulates the power of his personality that the 'fascinated and uncritical love' he inspires in most people is described as creating 'carnivals of affection' upon which he reflects 'as a general might gaze upon a massacre he had ordered to satisfy an impersonal blood lust'.[180]

Into Diver's world comes Rosemary Hoyt and, despite himself, he loses control and is irresistibly drawn to her. In the passage in which Fitzgerald attempts a universalising aspect by invoking Tasso and by using religious terminology, he also extends his allusions to imply Freud's important theory of Eros and Thanatos. In the shop windows on the way to the Film Studios are advertisements for shirts. But then Fitzgerald goes on:

> On either side he read: 'Papeterie,' 'Pâtisserie,' 'Solde,' 'Réclame' – and Constance Talmadge in 'Déjeuner de Soleil,' and farther away there were more sombre announcements: 'Vêtements Ecclésiastiques,' 'Déclaration de Décès' and 'Pompes Funèbres.' Life and death.[181]

Although the allusion to Freud is clear, it would be a mistake to press the connection too heavily. True to his early belief that 'life is too strong and remorseless for the sons of men'[182] and consistent with his early practice of identifying female beauty as a major agent of the destructive force, Fitzgerald exposed Dick Diver to the same remorseless power which had tested Amory, destroyed Anthony and, ultimately, ennobled Gatsby. In order to give credence to his idea that love lay at the centre of the issue, he associated Diver's journey towards understanding with a Romantic notion of a quest which makes love the key. He gave the impression that the force he had identified had existed since time began. He did this by invoking the legend of men like Tasso and also by using religious terminology which has the additional effect of consolidating the high level of seriousness on which the matter is placed. The allusions to Freud also work to that end. His theories deal with the human condition and attempt to isolate and describe various forces which compel various forms of behaviour. As such, they too served Fitzgerald's purpose.

If Browning's 'Paracelsus' gave Fitzgerald's protagonist a name and the novel a basic form, it was Freud's essay, 'Beyond the Pleasure Principle' that gave it the resolution which shaped the

end. The reason why this was possible is almost certainly because
the essay gave Fitzgerald the opportunity for a natural extension of
the ironic position he had early reached and from which viewpoint
he had written *This Side of Paradise*. To understand the connections
and the use made of them it is best to consider the way that battle
imagery conditions the whole novel.

The novel is in fact controlled by imagery of war in the same way
that *This Side of Paradise* establishes its philosophic norm by means
of imagery of travel and music. Consistently, love is presented as a
battleground. The Europe of the novel is a Europe dominated by
the recent memory of the First World War. Fitzgerald's timescale is,
however, vaster than the twentieth century. The characteristically
sad tone of the omniscient narrator is always implying an eternal
problem and specific references such as the one linking Dick Diver
with Grant 'lolling in his general store in Galena',[183] give the
impression that war – all wars – not just the 1914–18 war, is to be an
essential part of the novel.

Freud, of course, came to think of war as a national attempt at
psychological self-preservation. In that sense it was part of the Life
instinct. That is the underlying meaning beneath Diver's description of the battle of the Somme as a 'love battle': nations enacted on
a world scale what individuals are compelled to do on the level of
human relationships. Looked at from that point of view, Diver's
manipulation of others in 'carnivals of affection' seems to have
been the chief outlet for his Eros tendencies up until the time he
met Rosemary. Although his compulsive need for her matches
Freud's analysis, it is important to note that it also matches
Fitzgerald's idea about the power of illusion. The danger in trying
to interpret *Tender is the Night* completely in Freudian terms is that
the crucial ironic justification of illusion which shaped *The Great
Gatsby* will be missed. Fitzgerald certainly used the notion of
repetition-compulsion as Freud would have understood it in this
novel of battleground imagery, but it was his own ironic point of
view which gave that principle its full meaning. In being drawn to
Rosemary Dick Diver is repeating the conditions of his earlier
compulsive need for Nicole. By repeating the experience he is not
to be thought of as one of Freud's patients acting out an unpleasant
experience in order to come to terms with it. As with all other cases
in the earlier novels Dick Diver is drawn by the illusion that the
love of a beautiful girl will bring Arcadian happiness. Starting with
Uncle George,[184] Fitzgerald had made it clear that this was a

delusion. Starting with Gatsby, he also made it clear – following Conrad – that the struggle to sustain the illusion created epic conditions. For the tragedy is that even the most magnificent effort is doomed to fail: such is the wearing down force in the universe.

At the beginning of the novel where Dick Diver is presented as the prince with his pearl, the implied story-line tells of a man with great potential passing his time in trivial pursuits. Purposeless as his activities seem, they do in fact indicate an energy which is missing in others. Significantly, his powers are consistently expressed through images associated with violence. Meeting his guests at the party at the Villa Diana, he carries his coat 'like a toreador's cape'.[185] And in the description of the way he can give others a sense of special unity there is a similar reference to bull-fighting, because 'by destroying the outsiders softly but permanently with an ironic coup de grâce',[186] the insiders are brought together. This kind of imagery combines with other details illustrating Diver's power to control so that the impression is given of him as being a redoubtable adversary in any love battle. This makes it so surprising when he is represented as being helpless when faced with Rosemary. Surprising, that is, until the detail for the possible psychoanalysis is given: Diver's true Achilles' heel was that 'he wanted to be loved'.[187]

In *The Great Gatsby* Fitzgerald created a powerful character who had kept his illusion about Daisy alive over a period of years. Like Diver and later Munroe Stahr he made a second plunge for his pearl, that is to say for his illusion of happiness. As in the story of the 'Pierian Springs', for Diver the associated idea is of refreshment, of revitalisation. And, as it was for Gatsby, so for Diver there was the suppressed awareness that such dreams were delusions. Interestingly, by choosing the name of a herb – Rosemary – for this particular image of feminine beauty, Fitzgerald achieved a similar ironic comment as that attaching to the name Carraway in *The Great Gatsby*. Rosemary has been traditionally thought to possess the power to reinvigorate and strengthen. It is the illusion that Rosemary, the character, will possess such properties which is part of the forces which impel Dick Diver to her. Of course, what she really represents – the reality principle – has been made clear by the use of the incest motif and by putting the affair in that context Fitzgerald widens the issue to an interesting comment on contemporary America. Despite the fact that Diver is aware of the vicious sentimentality of her Daddy's Girl image, he, like the rest of her vast audience is irresistibly drawn to her.

In this last respect the kind of America which Nicole stands for is important. Early in Book 1 she is portrayed as an important cog in the capitalist society's wheel: a privileged consumer. For her 'the whole system swayed and thundered onward'. However, Fitzgerald ends that particular passage in a rather cryptic sentence which also owes much to Freud. 'She illustrated very simple principles, containing in herself her own doom, but illustrated them so accurately that there was grace in the procedure.'[188] The 'certain place' in Nicole's story which psychoanalysis would uncover as a key point in her development was the time when she and her father became lovers. In Fitzgerald's terms she was wounded on the battlefield of love. That wounding turned her in upon herself. She too experiences repetition compulsion: in fact, as the novel is patterned to suggest, her marriage to Dick, in a sense, repeats the experience. Her periodic dementia is related to the instinctive wish to return to the first traumatic incident: in other words, the Death wish. It is this which is implied in the idea of 'containing in herself her own doom'. She is to be seen as possessing inwardly-directed aggression. Since all this is presented in a context which suggests her deeply-rooted Americanness, Dick Diver's growing paresis and need of Rosemary takes on an added meaning. The impression grows that Fitzgerald's moral preaching extends to the whole continent.

When, towards the end of Part 10 of Book 2 the narrative returns to the present, the surface story of Dick Diver chronicles the events which illustrate the loss of balance and control consequent upon his need for Rosemary. His 'wound' tends to make him less able to direct his aggression/love outwards. And, as Freud believed, the inwardly-directed aggression easily turned to eroticism. In the Swiss Alps at Christmas for example, he is attracted to a 'special girl' sitting at a table behind him.[189] And then, back at the clinic 'after a long dream of war'[190] he feels something like sexual attraction for the woman suffering with nervous eczema. She, incidentally, is quite literally scarred after her love battles. Fitzgerald has her drive the point home in terms of subsuming imagery. 'I'm sharing the fate of the women of my time who challenged men to battle.'[191] Diver kisses her. Interestingly enough, Freud specifically warned Ferenczi not to kiss patients because a kiss 'signifies a certain erotic intimacy'.[192] However, at this point in the hidden story the kiss was between two wounded combatants.

Soon after this incident the effect of Diver's diminishing control is seen in the madness of Nicole at the Agiri Fair and the subsequent car crash. There are crucial indications of the thematic patterning of the whole novel to be seen in this section. One confirms the impression that Nicole's behaviour is prompted by the Death wish and the other offers an important clue to the way in which the inner story line concerning Diver's true development will be resolved. The former is indicated in Nicole's jeer after the crash. '"You were scared, weren't you?" she accused him. "You wanted to live."'[193] This suggests that although he is moving towards Thanatos, he still retains the Life instinct. The second point is contained in the following description of his sense of responsibility for Nicole's condition. 'He had a sense of guilt as in one of those nightmares where we are accused of a crime which we recognize as something undeniably experienced, but which upon waking we realize we have not committed.'[194] It is this sense of guilt which extends the concept of the wise and tragic sense beyond the point which Amory Blaine reached when, after his final 'renunciation of beauty'[195] he can accept the loss of illusions and still 'retain the ability to function'.[196]

Once again, Freud's theories can illustrate Fitzgerald's intellectual position. Up to this point in Dick Diver's story, Freud's conclusions outlined in 'Beyond the Pleasure Principle' have supplied the authority for presenting aggression as the consequence of the quest for love. Now Freud's later idea contained in 'Civilization and Its Discontents' supplies the key. In that work Freud faced the issue of man's innate aggressiveness and suggested that individuals internalised their aggression into a superego of conscience. Ernest Jones has well described the result of this internalising process. He claims that the conscience

> exercises the same propensity to harsh aggressiveness against the ego that the ego would have liked to exercise against others. The tension between the two constitutes what is called the sense of guilt. A sense of guilt begins not from an inborn sense of sin but from the fear of losing love.[197]

This is a good description of Diver's situation as the pressures of the reality principle force him to abandon the pleasure principle. Not only does he feel guilt about his infidelity towards Nicole but his increasing eroticism – 'he was in love with every pretty woman he saw now'[198] – is seen as belittling his years of fidelity. The news too of his father's death makes him wish 'he had always been as good as he had intended to be'.[199] In fact the tensions within him now that he can no longer externalise his aggressions in 'carnivals of affection', make his relationships with others extremely difficult. Even to Rosemary he is a disturbing force. '"I guess I'm the Black Death," he said slowly. "I don't seem to bring people happiness any more."'[200]

The depths of his self-disgust are reached after the sordid fracas with the taxi-drivers has resulted in the even uglier scene at the police station. He is in the same kind of position as Amory Blaine was when he moved closer to the labyrinth of disillusion and loneliness.

> Dick's rage had retreated into him a little and he felt a vast criminal irresponsibility. What had happened to him was so awful that nothing could make any difference unless he could choke it to death, and, as this was unlikely, he was hopeless. He would be a different person henceforward, and in his raw state he had bizarre feelings of what the new self would be. The matter had about it the impersonal quality of an act of God.[201]

It will be recalled that when Amory considered saving Alec Connage from the shame of a scandal he realised 'the great impersonality of sacrifice'. The insight is given religious significance: 'sacrifice ... was like a great elective office'.[202] Amory's perception is accompanied by the sensation of God speaking to him and the evil 'gossamer aura' disappears. When this notion of the assumption of guilt is recalled, then the true nature of Dick Diver's attempt to make a speech to the crowd confessing that he had 'raped a five-year-old girl'[203] can be appreciated. Not only is it, in Freud's terms, an illustration of the way that repressed aggressiveness turns into a heightened sense of guilt, but also it fits into a pattern already established by the incest motif.

The obviously false confession cannot, of course be taken seriously but it is an important pointer to Fitzgerald's moral lesson. The crucial factor is the way that the concept of guilt and sacrifice is made to take on an increasing religious significance. In this, again, there is a strong link with Amory Blaine for, it should be noted, that out of his 'attempted sacrifice' came true understanding. 'He found something that he wanted, had always wanted and always would want – not to be admired, as he had feared; not to be loved, as he had made himself believe; but to be necessary to people, to be indispensable.'[204] Dick Diver's impulsive confession of guilt is, like Amory's attempted sacrifice, done impersonally, almost arrogantly. Like Amory, Dick Diver acts through a mis-apprehension of his true Self. Fitzgerald presents Diver's thoughts at this time and indicates the same perspective. He is considering the segmented nature of life.

> His love for Nicole and Rosemary, his friendship with Abe North, with Tommy Barban in the broken universe of the war's ending – in such contacts the personalities had seemed to press up so close to him that he became the personality itself – there seemed some necessity of taking all or nothing; it was as if for the remainder of his life he was condemned to carry with him the egos of certain people, early met and early loved, and to be only as complete as they were complete themselves.[205]

Of course, Monsignor Darcy had already warned Amory of the danger: 'Beware of losing yourself in the personality of another being.'[206] But Diver's final insight in this passage indicates the reality principle at work on the need to be loved which characte-rises both him and Amory: 'so easy to be loved – so hard to love'.[207] Not until both characters can transcend Self and move to a life of self-abnegation can they achieve the balance they require.

In Dick Diver's case he has moved some way along this path. When he kissed the patient imprisoned in the nervous eczema caused by neuro-syphilis he indicated a non self-seeking love but, as Freud had pointed out, such behaviour indicated a form of eroticism and what is increasingly implied is a love which should be free from such implications.

Ironically, Nicole's father's illness is presented within a framework which presses religious impressions. He is, for exam-ple, nursed by a nun because he had become 'very religious'.[208] And when he abruptly leaves, the description is that 'the old boy took up his bed and walked'.[209]

While Amory Blaine was under the impression that 'sacrifice should be eternally supercilious',[210] he saw only ugliness in New

York. Similarly, Diver's world is unpleasant and his behaviour denies all his previous attempts to create beautiful moments. Even towards Nicole his behaviour is ugly: ugly because he is 'detached'.[211] The effect is to make her feel free of him. Her progress to freedom is given in the language of combat. The climax comes when she struggles to free herself from the power of his intelligence, 'fighting him with her small, fine eyes . . . she fought him with her money . . . fighting bravely . . . And suddenly . . . she achieved her victory.' The effect is to leave him leaning 'his head forward on the parapet',[212] like a soldier after battle. The difference is that his 'defeat' has left him at liberty.

After this there is one more occasion when he exhibits some of the control and power which he had possessed when his aggression was channelled into making people love him. He goes out to help get Mary North and Caroline Sibley-Biers out of jail, 'because it had early become a habit to be loved'.[213] Significantly, their escapade adds another measure to the already extensive catalogue of sexual experiences. The episode ends with Diver conscious that he could once more employ charm but he resists the temptation and his final act is to make a blessing. 'He raised his right hand and with a papal cross he blessed the beach from the high terrace.'[214] After this he disappears back to America but seems to wander around and Nicole finally loses touch with him.

That final act strongly suggests that Fitzgerald's controlling vision was closer to Plato rather than Freud. Although it was an ironic gesture, the 'papal cross', coming as it does as the climax of a movement towards self-abnegation and the attempt to learn to love others, suggests an embracing compassion which mixes notions of physical love with a mystic religiosity very like that shown by Diotima in the *Symposium*. For her the way to complete understanding involved a pilgrimage inspired by ideas of love. Although Fitzgerald changed her notion of the 'sole object' of the pilgrimage from awareness of 'absolute beauty' to something more like Freud's notion of freedom from tensions, the steps of the pilgrimage made by Dick Diver are seen to be analogous. According to her he should begin with

> examples of beauty in this world, and using them as steps to ascend continually with that absolute beauty as one's aim, from one instance of physical beauty to two and from two to all, then from physical beauty to moral beauty, and from moral beauty to

the beauty of knowledge, until from knowledge of various kinds one arrives at the supreme knowledge whose sole object is that absolute beauty, and knows at last what absolute beauty is.[215]

Like Diotima's vision, like all mystical experiences, Dick Diver's is essentially ineffable: it can only be communicated by technical devices like imagery, thematic patterning and allusions. By these means a moral framework is created which points to the same ironic-pessimistic point of view which conditioned and controlled even Fitzgerald's earliest novel. Once again, as in *The Great Gatsby*, religious imagery is used to show the importance and the universality of a particular force. The key to Gatsby's predicament is to be seen in the fact that although making the commitment to Daisy made him incarnate it did bring him as close to the Arcady he wanted as he could ever hope to get. And for Dick Diver his apparent mistake in sacrificing his career for Nicole turned out all right in the end because thanks to the miseries caused through his affair with Rosemary he was eventually able to understand how to love. Certainly, Freud's writings add to the plausibility of the action: they lend weight to the early diagnosed sense of a universal wearing down force; but elements of Romantic legends also testify to the similarly universal need to find love. Overall, however, the novel is shaped by that same ironic philosophy which preferred an indirect expression of a moral vision. Fitzgerald's use of the Keats' poem from which he took his title is quite typical; as with the other titles, it encapsulates the whole philosophic concept. In the novel, as in the poem, the wish to join the nightingale's beautiful world is accomplished as soon as it is made in the right context. In Dick Diver's case, his first 'plunge' had been a sacrifice born, not out of love, but a need to be loved. After marriage and until he met Rosemary he lived with that sacrifice, devotedly creating Nicole's world. Rosemary reawakened that need to be loved and, in powerful imagery of penitence it is suggested that Diver had been denying what amounts to a religious truth.

Fittingly, the novel draws to a close by returning to the Riviera sunshine and the beach Dick Diver had created. Clearly, the circularity was plotted by Fitzgerald: the end is prefigured in the sad tones of the opening opposition between the old and the contemporary. The significance of the description of the 'bright tan prayer rug of a beach'[216] has become apparent. Fitzgerald has skilfully blended religious elements, popular philosophic assessments and hints of earlier literary forms to create the strong impression of a universality of experience. Against the background of an inevitable and irresistible wearing down force, Dick Diver's struggle to create a universe based upon love is seen to be deluded for it is doomed to failure. It is, however, in a deep sense successful because his desperate search for love, as well as giving him distinctive purpose, gives him a Paraclesian nobility: the same kind of ironic and epic greatness achieved by Gatsby and Lord Jim. In a very important sense Dick Diver's two plunges following the compulsive delusions of Love have allowed him to achieve the understanding which the greatest psychologist must have: 'the sense that life is essentially a cheat and its conditions are those of defeat, and that the redeeming things are not "happiness and pleasure" but the deeper satisfactions that come out of struggle'.[217]

It is that philosophic concept which determines the whole creation of *Tender is the Night* as it did all Fitzgerald's novels. In that, his most complete expression of the philosophy, he achieves for Dick Diver the same kind of success George Eliot created for Dorothea Brooke. Indeed the closing lines of *Middlemarch* are equally applicable to Fitzgerald's feelings about Dick Diver.

But the effect of her being on those around her was incalculably diffusive: for the growing good of the world is partly dependent on unhistoric acts; and that things are not so ill with you and me as they might have been, is half owing to the number who lived faithfully a hidden life, and rest in unvisited tombs.[218]

Like Eliot, Fitzgerald returns his protagonist to anonymity. The contemporary world is not the stage for a 'new Theresa' or a 'new Antigone' but by invoking those names Eliot implies universality. Similarly, Fitzgerald deliberately implies a world-wide stage by locating Diver in small American towns like Batavia and Geneva and also by returning to the idea of Grant in Galena he implies an insight into an age-old story. It is indeed remarkable that such care in the creation of this literary form in order to produce an acceptable piece of moral preaching should ever have been thought to be a muddled search for meaning through personal experiences.

From the first attempts to achieve the correct form in 'The Romantic Egotist' to the mature complete expression of *Tender is the Night*, there is a remarkable consistency in Fitzgerald's thought.

Even if his 'philosophic concept' is not thought to be startingly innovative, it did give his work intellectual coherence and its presence at the heart of all his artistic concerns should have obviated any suggestion of a lack of control.

Notes and References

Since many of the critical essays are contained in the Kazin collection, Kazin, Alfred, *F. Scott Fitzgerald: The Man and His Work* (ed.) Kazin, A. (New York: Collier), is referred to as *F. S. F.*

1 Scott Fitzgerald's Novels

1. Arthur Mizener, *The Far Side of Paradise: A Biography of F. Scott Fitzgerald* (New York: Vintage Books ed., 1959).
2. Ibid., p. xvii Introduction.
3. Ibid., p. viii Preface.
4. Ibid., p. vii, my italics.
5. Lionel Trilling, *The Liberal Imagination* (London: Secker & Warburg, 1955) p. 244.
6. Ibid., p. 243.
7. F. R. Leavis, Introduction to Marius Bewley, *The Complex Fate* (London: Chatto and Windus, 1968) pp. x–xi.
8. Milton R. Stern, *The Golden Moment: The Novels of F. Scott Fitzgerald* (Urbana: University of Illinois Press, 1970).
9. Ibid., p. 462.
10. Robert Sklar, *F. Scott Fitzgerald: The Last Laocoön* (New York: OUP 1967).
11. Ibid., p. 341–2.
12. Henry Dan Piper, *F. Scott Fitzgerald: A Critical Portrait* (New York: Holt, Rinehart & Winston, 1965) p. 25.
13. Alfred Kazin, 'All the lost Generation' in *On Native Grounds* (New York: Doubleday Anchor, 1956) pp. 242–9.
   Malcolm Cowley, see especially 'Third Act and Epilogue' reprinted in *F. Scott Fitzgerald: The Man and His Work* ed. Alfred Kazin (Collier Books edn, 1962) pp. 147–54.
14. Piper, op. cit., p. 22.
15. Edmund Wilson to F. Scott Fitzgerald, 21 November 1919. Quoted by Mizener, op. cit., p. 113.
16. Edmund Wilson, 'Fitzgerald Before *The Great Gatsby*', reprinted in Kazin ed., *F. S. F.*, pp. 78–84.
17. See Jackson R. Bryer, *The Critical Reputation of F. Scott Fitzgerald: A Bibliographical Study* (Hamden: Archon Books, 1967) particularly pp. 4–12.
18. Ibid., p. 25.
19. Kazin ed., *F. S. F.*, p. 78.
20. Norman Podhoretz, *Doings and Undoings* (London: Rupert Hart Davis, 1965) p. 65.
21. Ernest Hemingway, *A Moveable Feast* (London: Jonathan Cape, 1964) p. 128.
22. Kazin ed., *F.S.F.*, p. 84.
23. Mizener, op. cit., p. xiii Foreword.
24. Mizener, op. cit., p. xix Introduction.

25. Kazin ed., *F. S. F.*, p. 25.
26. Mizener, op. cit., p. xix Introduction.
27. Mizener, op. cit., p. 65.
28. Kazin, *On Native Grounds*, pp. 244–5.
29. Malcolm Cowley, 'Third Act and Epilogue', Kazin ed., *F. S. F.*, p. 150.
30. Piper, op. cit., p. 236.
31. John Kuehl, 'Scott Fitzgerald's Critical Opinions' in Modern Fiction Studies vol. VII no. 1 (Spring, 1961), pp. 3–18.
32. James E. Miller, *F. Scott Fitzgerald His Art and His Technique* (New York University Press, 1964).
     Sergio Perosa, *The Art of F. Scott Fitzgerald* (Ann Arbor: University of Michigan Press, 1965).
33. Miller, op. cit., p. 161.
     Perosa, op. cit., p. 46.
34. See Kazin ed., *F. S. F.*, p. 25.
35. R. D. Lehan, *F. Scott Fitzgerald: The Man and his Works* (Toronto: Forum House, 1969). p. 82.
36. Kazin, *On Native Grounds*, p. 245.
37. K. G. W. Cross, *Scott Fitzgerald* in 'Writers and Critics' series (Edinburgh: Oliver and Boyd, 1964) p. 20.
38. Wilson, Kazin ed., *F. S. F.*, p. 82.
39. Miller, op. cit., p. 45.
40. Perosa, op. cit., pp. 46–7.
41. Stern, op. cit., p. 114.
42. Cross, op. cit., pp. 35–6.
43. Mizener, op. cit., p. 155.
44. James R. Mellow, *Invented Lives: F. Scott and Zelda Fitzgerald* (London: Souvenir Press, 1985) pp. 148–9.
     André Le Vot, *F. Scott Fitzgerald* (London: Allen Lane, 1984) p. 104.
45. Wilson, Kazin ed., *F. S. F.*, p. 79.
46. Miller, op. cit., p. 25.
47. Miller, p. 44.
     Edmund Wilson, John O'Hara and Alan Ross are the writers Miller mentions.
48. Sklar, op. cit., p. 37.
49. Cross, op. cit., p. 24.
50. Stern, op. cit., p. 37.
51. *The Letters of F. Scott Fitzgerald* ed. Andrew Turnbull (Bodley Head, London 1964) p. 96.
52. Wilson, Kazin ed., *F. S. F.*, p. 79.

2 From The Romantic Egotist to This Side of Paradise

1. *The Romantic Egotist*, Princeton Papers, Rare Book Department, Princeton University Library. Of the original 23 chapters which Fitzgerald claimed to have written, only 5 chapters from the revised version are known to exist. All the quotations which follow are taken from this material.

2. Wilson, 'Fitzgerald before *The Great Gatsby*', see Kazin ed., *F. S. F.*, p. 81.
3. Princeton University Library, Rare Book Department.
4. Mizener, *The Far Side of Paradise*, p. 7.
5. Piper, *F. Scott Fitzgerald*, p. 49.
6. Mizener, op. cit., p. 68.
7. It is reprinted in its original form in John Kuehl, *The Apprentice Fiction of F. Scott Fitzgerald 1909–1917* (New Brunswick: Rutgers University Press, 1965) pp. 105–14.
8. Op. cit., p. 107.
9. Ibid., p. 109.
10. Ibid., p.114.
11. Mizener, *Scott Fitzgerald and his World* (London: Thames & Hudson, 1972) p. 26.
12. Ibid., p. 26.
13. Kuehl, op. cit., p. 112.
14. Ibid., p. 114.
15. Ibid., p. 105.
16. Ibid., p. 111, p. 108.
17. Ibid., p. 111.
18. Ibid., p. 107.
19. Ibid., p. 112.
20. Letter to John Grier Hibben, dated 3 June 1920, published in *The Letters of F. Scott Fitzgerald*, ed. Andrew Turnbull (London: The Bodley Head, 1964) p. 462.
21. Reported by Thomas A. Boyd, 'Scott Fitzgerald Speaks at Home', *St. Paul Daily News*, 4 December 1921. See James E. Miller, *F. Scott Fitzgerald: His Art and His Technique* (New York University Press, 1964), p. 46.
22. H. L. Mencken, 'Theodore Dreiser' from *A Book of Prefaces* printed in Alastair Cooke, *The Vintage Mencken* (New York: Vintage Books, 1955), p. 48.
23. Ibid., p. 48.
24. Above p. 24.
25. Mencken, op. cit., p. 48.
26. See Kuehl, op. cit., p. 144–59.
27. Ibid., p. 154.
28. Kuehl, op. cit., pp. 163–74.
29. Kuehl, p. 165, p. 167, p. 173.
30. Ibid., p. 174.
31. *This Side of Paradise* (Scribner's, New York paper back edn) p. 55.
32. Ibid., p. 17.
33. Ibid., p. 89.
34. Ibid., p. 54.
35. Ibid., p. 72.
36. Ibid., p. 77.
37. Ibid., p. 81.
38. Ibid., p. 83.
39. Ibid., p. 85.

40. Ibid., p. 87.
41. Ibid., p. 54.
42. Ibid., p. 41.
43. Ibid., p. 78.
44. Ibid., p. 40.
45. Ibid., p. 186.
46. Ibid., p. 136.
47. Ibid., p. 18.
48. Ibid., p. 106.
49. Ibid., p. 14.
50. See above pp. 25–6.
51. *This Side of Paradise*, p. 30.
52. Ibid., p. 31.
53. Ibid., pp. 32–3.
54. Ibid., p. 69.
55. Ibid., p. 70.
56. Ibid., pp. 81–2.
57. Above p. 43.
58. *This Side of Paradise*, p. 109–10.
59. Ibid., p. 110.
60. Ibid., p. 113.
61. Ibid., pp. 114–15.
62. Ibid., p. 116.
63. Ibid., p. 115, p. 116.
64. Ibid., p. 45.
65. Ibid., p. 115.
66. Ibid., p. 117, p. 118.
67. Ibid., p. 118.
68. Ibid., p. 136.
69. Ibid., p. 123.
70. Ibid., p. 125.
71. Ibid., p. 146.
72. Ibid., pp. 146–7.
73. Ibid., p. 147.
74. Ibid., p. 150.
75. Ibid., p. 148.
76. Ibid., p. 147.
77. Ibid., p. 150.
78. Ibid., p. 154.
79. Ibid., pp. 186–7.
80. Ibid., p. 194.
81. Ibid., p. 196.
82. Kuehl, op. cit., p. 150. *This Side of Paradise*, p. 177.
83. *The Crack-Up* (Penguin Books, 1965), p. 39.
84. *This Side of Paradise*, p. 186.
85. Ibid., p. 202.
86. Ibid., p. 220.
87. Ibid., p. 219.
88. Ibid., p. 24.

89.   Ibid., p. 25.
90.   Ibid., p. 103.
91.   Ibid., p. 105.
92.   Ibid., p. 220.
93.   Ibid., p. 219.
94.   Ibid., p. 220.
95.   Ibid., p. 106.
96.   Ibid., p. 222.
97.   Ibid., p. 220.
98.   Ibid., p. 228.
99.   Ibid., p. 232–3.
100.   See above p. 51.
101.   *This Side of Paradise*, p. 229.
102.   Ibid., p. 233.
103.   Ibid., p. 234.
104.   Ibid., p. 239.
105.   Ibid., p. 240.
106.   Ibid., p. 236.
107.   Ibid., p. 245.
108.   Ibid., p. 247.
109.   Ibid., p. 248.
110.   Ibid., p. 19.
111.   Ibid., p. 248.
112.   Ibid., p. 33.
113.   Ibid., p. 69.
114.   Ibid., p. 186.
115.   Ibid., p. 232.
116.   Ibid., p. 45.
117.   Ibid., p. 255.
118.   Ibid., p. 248.
119.   Ibid., p. 256.
120.   Ibid., p. 263.
121.   Ibid., p. 265.
122.   Ibid., p. 266.
123.   Ibid., p. 266. N.B. 'self' is misprinted as 'elf'.
124.   See above, p. 57.
125.   *This Side of Paradise*, p. 266.
126.   Ibid., pp. 266–7.
127.   Ibid., p. 273.
128.   Ibid., p. 271.
129.   Ibid., p. 73.
130.   Ibid., p. 278.
131.   Ibid., p. 280.
132.   Ibid., p. 280.
133.   Ibid., p. 282.
134.   Ibid., p. 278.
135.   Ibid., p. 281.
136.   Ibid., p. 280.
137.   Ibid., p. 54.

138.   Ibid., p. 282.
139.   Ibid., p. 265.
140.   Ibid., p. 266.
141.   Ibid., p. 282.
142.   Ibid., p. 282.
143.   Ibid., p. 278.

3   **The Beautiful and Damned**

1.   *This Side of Paradise*, p. 18.
2.   *The Beautiful and Damned* (Scribner's New York paper back edn) p. 3, my emphasis.
3.   Ibid., p. 55.
4.   Ibid., pp. 54–5.
5.   Ibid., p. 56.
6.   *This Side of Paradise*, pp. 280–1.
7.   Ibid., p. 265.
8.   Ibid., p. 266.
9.   Ibid., p. 265.
10.   Ibid., p. 266.
11.   Ibid., p. 281.
12.   *The Beautiful and Damned*, p. 54.
13.   Ibid., p. 284.
14.   *This Side of Paradise*, p. 272.
15.   *The Beautiful and Damned*, p. 285.
16.   Ibid., pp. 11–12.
17.   Ibid., p. 17.
18.   Ibid., pp. 18–19.
19.   Ibid., p. 3.
20.   *This Side of Paradise*, p. 222.
21.   Ibid., p. 226.
22.   See Plato's *Symposium* (Penguin Classics, 1979), p. 92.
23.   E. A. Poe, 'Ulalume' in *Selected Writings*, ed. Galloway (Penguin), pp. 81–3.
24.   *This Side of Paradise*, p. 240.
25.   Ibid., p. 233.
26.   Ibid., p. 13.
27.   Ibid., p. 282.
28.   Ibid., p. 266.
29.   *The Beautiful and Damned*, p. 57.
30.   Ibid., p. 101.
31.   Ibid., p. 102.
32.   Ibid., p. 107.
33.   Ibid., pp. 114, 115, 116.
34.   Ibid., p. 148.
35.   Ibid., p. 149.
36.   Ibid., p. 137.
37.   Ibid., pp. 149–50.
38.   Ibid., pp. 70–73.

39. Edmund Wilson in 'Fitzgerald before *The Great Gatsby*' see Kazin ed., *F. S. F.*, op. cit., p. 84.
40. *The Beautiful and Damned*, p. 11.
41. Ibid., pp. 126–7.
42. Ibid., p. 191.
43. Plato, op. cit., p. 86.
44. Ibid., p. 85.
45. *The Beautiful and Damned*, p. 251.
46. Ibid., p. 255.
47. Ibid., p. 259.
48. Plato, op. cit., p. 70.
49. *The Beautiful and Damned*, p. 196.
50. Ibid., p. 202.
51. Plato, op. cit., p. 87.
52. Ibid., pp. 56–7.
53. *The Beautiful and Damned*, pp. 203–5.
54. Ibid., p. 257.
55. Ibid., pp. 213–14.
56. Ibid., pp. 237–40.
57. Ibid., pp. 241–2.
58. Ibid., pp. 243–4.
59. *This Side of Paradise*, p. 114.
60. *The Beautiful and Damned*, p. 225. p. 226.
61. Ibid., p. 217.
62. Plato, op. cit., p. 83.
63. *This Side of Paradise*, p. 280.
64. Plato, op. cit., p. 42.

4 The Great Gatsby

1. Norman Podhoretz, *Doings and Undoings* (London, Hart Davis, 1965), p. 62.
2. Richard D. Lehan, *F. Scott Fitzgerald: The Man and his Works* (Toronto, Forum House, 1969), p. 49.
3. Arthur Mizener, *The Far Side of Paradise* (Vintage Books), p. 66.
4. Henry Dan Piper, *F. Scott Fitzgerald: A Critical Portrait* (New York: Holt, Rinehart & Winston, 1965), pp. 291, 295.
5. Mizener, op. cit., p. 193.
6. Podhoretz, op. cit., p. 62.
7. Piper, op. cit., p. 148.
8. Fitzgerald, *The Great Gatsby* (New York, Scribner's paper back edn) p. 112, p. 111.
9. Ibid., p. 112.
10. Piper, op. cit., p. 150.
11. *This Side of Paradise*, p. 282.
12. See above p. 22 onwards.
13. See above p. 33 onwards.
14. *This Side of Paradise*, Book 1, 'A Kiss for Amory', pp. 8–15.
15. Op. cit., p. 13.

16. *The Great Gatsby*, p. 112.
17. Piper, op. cit., p. 106. From Princeton Papers, undated letter to Ludlow Fowler.
18. *This Side of Paradise*, p. 282, pp. 271–2.
19. *The Crack-Up* (Penguin Books), p. 39.
20. Ibid., p. 39.
21. Ibid., p. 55.
22. Ibid., pp. 55–6.
23. *The Great Gatsby*, p. 2.
24. Ibid., p. 40.
25. Ibid., p. 46.
26. Ibid., pp. 46–7.
27. Ibid., p. 48.
28. Ibid., p. 50.
29. Ibid., p. 56.
30. Ibid., p. 20.
31. Ibid., p. 18.
32. Ibid., p. 49.
33. Ibid., p. 1.
34. Ibid., pp. 6–7.
35. Ibid., p. 8.
36. Ibid., p. 9.
37. Ibid., p. 17.
38. Ibid., p. 18.
39. Ibid., pp. 20–21.
40. Ibid., p. 21.
41. Ibid., p. 10.
42. Ibid., p. 21.
43. Ibid., pp. 7–8.
44. Ibid., p. 21.
45. Ibid., p. 22.
46. Ibid., p. 23.
47. Ibid., p. 28, p. 29, p. 34.
48. Ibid., p. 37.
49. Ibid., pp. 37–8.
50. Ibid., p. 37.
51. Ibid., p. 29.
52. Ibid., p. 58.
53. Ibid., p. 2.
54. Ibid., p. 2.
55. Ibid., p. 99.
56. Ibid., p. 100. See also *This Side of Paradise*, p. 17.
57. *The Great Gatsby*, p. 99.
58. Ibid., pp. 99–100.
59. Ibid., p. 79.
60. Ibid., p. 9.
61. Ibid., p. 120.
62. Ibid., p. 90.
63. Ibid., p. 97.

64. Ibid., pp. 100–1.
65. Ibid., p. 112.
66. Ibid., p. 150.
67. Ibid., p. 100.
68. Ibid., p. 148.
69. Ibid., p. 59.
70. Ibid., pp. 68–9.
71. Ibid., p. 115.
72. Ibid., pp. 118–19.
73. Ibid., p. 124, p. 125.
74. Ibid., p. 135.
75. Ibid., p. 136.
76. Ibid., p. 136.
77. Ibid., p. 81.
78. Ibid., p. 36.
79. Ibid., p. 115.
80. Ibid., p. 115.
81. Ibid., p. 118.
82. Ibid., p. 121.
83. Ibid., p. 78.
84. Ibid., pp. 54–6.
85. *The Crack-Up*, p. 40.
86. See above, pp. 113–14.
87. *The Great Gatsby*, p. 153.
88. Ibid., p. 112.
89. See above, p. 99.
90. *The Great Gatsby*, p. 182.
91. Ibid., p. 182.

5   The Wise and Tragic Sense of Life

1.   K. G. W. Cross, *Scott Fitzgerald*, p. 79.
2.   Norman Podhoretz, *Doings and Undoings*, p. 63.
3.   Mizener, *The Far Side of Paradise*, p. 264.
4.   Podhoretz, op. cit., p. 63.
5.   Mizener, op. cit., p. 264.
6.   Richard Lehan, *F. Scott Fitzgerald: The Man and His Works*, p. 148.
7.   Henry Dan Piper, *F. Scott Fitzgerald: A Critical Portrait*, p. 209.
8.   Albert J. Lubell, South Atlantic Quarterly, LIV (Jan. 1955) pp. 103–4. Extract printed in Matthew J. Bruccoli, *The Composition of Tender is the Night* (University of Pittsburgh, 1963), pp. 12–13.
9.   Mizener, op. cit., p. 263.
10. Edmund Wilson, 'Fitzgerald before *The Great Gatsby*', 1922. Reprinted Alfred Kazin, *F. Scott Fitzgerald: The Man and His Work*, (Collier paperback edn., 1962) pp. 78–84.
11. Kazin, ed., *F. S. F.*, p. 84.
12. Ibid., p. 79.
13. James E. Miller, *F. Scott Fitzgerald: His Art and His Technique*, 1964, p. 44.

14. Arthur Mizener, 'F. Scott Fitzgerald 1896–1940: The Poet of Borrowed Time', 1946 reprinted in Kazin, ed., *F. S. F.*, pp. 23–45, p. 39.
15. *Tender is the Night* (Penguin, 1961) p. 9, quoted by Malcolm Cowley.
16. Mizener, 'The Poet of Borrowed Time', Kazin, ed., *F. S. F.*, p. 38.
17. Wayne C. Booth, *The Rhetoric of Fiction* (Chicago: University of Chicago, 1961. Paperback edn., 1968) pp. 189–90.
18. Ibid., pp. 189–90, p. 195.
19. Ibid., p. 194.
20. Ibid., p. 195.
21. Ibid., p. 190.
22. Ibid., p. 194.
23. Ibid., p. 195.
24. Ibid., p. 192.
25. Ibid., p. 192.
26. See Piper's assessment p. 129 above.
27. Cowley, Introduction to *Tender is the Night*, p. 15.
28. Ibid., p. 15.
29. Milton R. Stern, *The Golden Moment: The Novels of F. Scott Fitzgerald*. All quotations from pp. 380–2.
30. Mizener, *The Far Side of Paradise* pp. 65–6.
31. Ibid., p. 66.
32. In Kazin, ed., *F. S. F.*, pp. 39–40.
33. Thomas J. Stavola, *Scott Fitzgerald: Crisis in an American Identity*, (London: Vision, 1979) p. 149.
34. Ibid., p. 147.
35. Ibid., p. 11.
36. Ibid., p. 159.
37. John F. Callahan, *The Illusions of a Nation: Myth and History in the Novels of F. Scott Fitzgerald* (University of Illinois Press, 1972).
38. Ibid., p. 24.
39. Ibid., p. 25.
40. Ibid., p. 24.
41. Ibid., pp. 25–6.
42. Podhoretz, op. cit., p. 63.
43. Kazin ed., *F. S. F.*, p. 84.
44. 'On the Modern Element in Literature', in *Matthew Arnold: Selected Prose* (ed.) with Introduction by P. J. Keating (Penguin, 1970) pp. 73–4.
45. *The Letters of F. Scott Fitzgerald*, ed. Andrew Turnbull (London: Bodley Head, 1964) p. 96.
46. Joseph Conrad, *Lord Jim* (Dent, London, 1948) p. 213.
47. Ibid., p. 416.
48. *The Great Gatsby*, p. 112.
49. See Chapter 5 above, p. 99.
50. *Collected Poems of Wallace Stevens* (London: Faber & Faber, 1959) 'The Poems of our Climate', p. 194.
51. See above, pp. 11 ff.
52. George Eliot, *Middlemarch* (Norton edition, London, 1977) p. 578.

53. *The Great Gatsby*, p. 182.
54. Wayne C. Booth, op. cit., p. 194. See above, p. 132.
55. *Tender is the Night* (Scribner's paperback edn., 1962), p. 3.
56. Ibid., pp. 3–4.
57. Ibid., p. 4.
58. Ibid., p. 4.
59. Ibid., p. 3.
60. Ibid., p. 4.
61. Ibid., p. 4.
62. Ibid., p. 5.
63. Ibid., p. 6.
64. Ibid., p. 5.
65. Ibid., p. 8, p. 6.
66. *The Great Gatsby*, p. 112.
67. *Tender is the Night*, p. 21.
68. Ibid., p. 19.
69. Ibid., p. 13.
70. Ibid., p. 27.
71. Ibid., p. 34.
72. Ibid., p. 35.
73. Ibid., p. 22.
74. Preface to *The Portrait of a Lady*, Henry James (Riverside edn, 1963) p. 5.
75. *Tender is the Night*, p. 77.
76. Ibid., p. 64.
77. Ibid., p. 69.
78. Ibid., p. 13.
79. Ibid., p. 66.
80. Ibid., p. 65.
81. Ibid., pp. 63–4.
82. Ibid., all quotations from pp. 68–9.
83. Ibid., p. 91.
84. Ibid., p. 85.
85. Ibid., p. 88.
86. Ibid., p. 95.
87. Ibid., p. 105.
88. Ibid., p. 95.
89. Ibid., p. 104.
90. *The Beautiful and Damned*, p. 242.
91. *This Side of Paradise*, p. 114.
92. *Tender is the Night*, p. 105.
93. Ibid., p. 61.
94. Ibid., p. 21.
95. *The Letters of F. Scott Fitzgerald*, ed. Andrew Turnbull (Bodley Head, London, 1964) p. 63.
96. See above Chapter 5 Part (I) pp. 127 ff.
97. *Tender is the Night*, p. 12.
98. Ibid., p. 24.
99. Ibid., p. 21.

100. Ibid., p. 81.
101. Ibid., p. 41.
102. Ibid., p. 75.
103. Ibid., p. 83.
104. Ibid., p. 85.
105. Ibid.
106. Ibid., p. 86.
107. Ibid., p. 58.
108. Ibid., p. 57.
109. Ibid., p. 58.
110. Ibid., p. 112.
111. Ibid., p. 21.
112. Ibid., p. 64.
113. Ibid., p. 91.
114. *The Great Gatsby*, p. 112.
115. Ibid., pp. 111–12.
116. *Tender is the Night*, p. 115.
117. Ibid., p. 118.
118. Ibid., p. 116.
119. *The Great Gatsby*, p. 99.
120. *Tender is the Night*, p. 118.
121. Ibid., p. 116.
122. Ibid., p. 118.
123. *The Great Gatsby*, p. 112.
124. *This Side of Paradise*, p. 13.
125. *Tender is the Night*, p. 132.
126. Ibid., p. 133.
127. See Chapter 2 above, pp. 33 ff.
128. *The Great Gatsby*, p. 112.
129. *Tender is the Night*, p. 121.
130. See above, p. 161.
131. *Tender is the Night*, p. 150.
132. Ibid., p. 155.
133. Ibid., p. 155.
134. Ibid., p. 64.
135. Ibid., p. 57.
136. See Chapter 3 above, pp. 74 ff.
137. See Chapter 3 above, pp. 83 ff.
138. See Chapter 4 above, pp. 96–8.
139. *The Great Gatsby*, p. 100.
140. *Tender is the Night*, p. 6.
141. Ibid., p. 21.
142. Ibid., p. 118.
143. Ibid., p. 91.
144. See for example John F. Callahan's reference in *The Illusions of a Nation*, p. 129.
145. *Tender is the Night*, p. 115.
146. Ibid., p. 132.
147. Ibid., p. 129.

148. Ibid., p. 152.
149. *The Great Gatsby*, p. 112.
150. *Tender is the Night*, p. 155.
151. Ibid., p. 164.
152. Ibid., p. 4.
153. Ibid., p. 24.
154. Ibid., p. 54.
155. Ibid., p. 64.
156. Ibid., p. 64.
157. Ibid., p. 66.
158. Ernest Jones, *The Life and Work of Sigmund Freud*, abridged version Penguin Books, 1984, pp. 278–9.
159. *Tender is the Night*, p. 34.
160. Ibid., p. 38.
161. Ibid., p. 38.
162. Ibid., pp. 39–40.
163. Ibid., pp. 40–1.
164. Ibid., p. 41.
165. Ibid., p. 40.
166. Ibid., p. 4.
167. Freud, 'Beyond the Pleasure Principle' in The Pelican Freud Library, vol. 11, p. 275.
168. *This Side of Paradise*, p. 282.
169. See Chapter 2 above, pp. 21 ff.
170. *Tender is the Night*, p. 57.
171. Ibid., pp. 57–8.
172. Ibid., p. 83.
173. *This Side of Paradise*, p. 282.
174. *The Crack-Up*, Penguin Books p. 39.
175. E. Jones, op. cit., p. 505.
176. Freud, 'Beyond the Pleasure Principle', vol. 11, p. 278.
177. *Tender is the Night*, p. 69.
178. Ibid., p. 117.
179. Ibid., p. 57.
180. Ibid., p. 27.
181. Ibid., p. 91.
182. See Chapter 2 above, p. 29.
183. *Tender is the Night*, p. 118.
184. See Chapter 2 above, pp. 33 ff.
185. *Tender is the Night*, p. 28.
186. Ibid., p. 52.
187. Ibid., p. 133.
188. Ibid., p. 55.
189. Ibid., p. 174.
190. Ibid., p. 179.
191. Ibid., p. 184.
192. E. Jones, op. cit., p. 606.
193. *Tender is the Night*, p. 192.
194. Ibid., p. 190.

195. *This Side of Paradise*, p. 280.
196. *The Crack-Up* p. 39.
197. E. Jones, op. cit., p. 596.
198. *Tender is the Night*, p. 201.
199. Ibid., p. 204.
200. Ibid., p. 219.
201. Ibid., p. 233.
202. *This Side of Paradise*, pp. 247–8.
203. *Tender is the Night*, p. 235.
204. *This Side of Paradise*, p. 266.
205. *Tender is the Night*, p. 245.
206. *This Side of Paradise*, p. 220.
207. *Tender is the Night*, p. 245.
208. Ibid., p. 247.
209. Ibid., p. 251.
210. *This Side of Paradise*, p. 248.
211. *Tender is the Night*, p. 273.
212. Ibid., pp. 301–2.
213. Ibid., p. 302.
214. Ibid., p. 314.
215. Plato's *Symposium* (Penguin Books) p. 94.
216. *Tender is the Night*, p. 3.
217. *Letters*, op. cit., p. 96.
218. George Eliot, *Middlemarch* (Norton edn) p. 578.

Selected Bibliography

Works by Fitzgerald

As far as possible all references have been made to those editions most easily available.

The Apprentice Fiction of F. Scott Fitzgerald, 1909–1917, ed. with an introduction by John Kuehl (New Brunswick: Rutgers University Press, 1965).
This Side of Paradise (New York: Scribner's (reset version), 1960).
The Beautiful and Damned (New York: Scribner's, 1950).
The Great Gatsby (New York: Scribner's, 1953).
Tender is the Night (New York: Scribner's, 1962).
Tender is the Night (London: Penguin (Cowley's revised version), 1961).
The Letters of F. Scott Fitzgerald ed. A. Turnbull (London: Bodley Head, 1964).
The Crack-Up with Other Pieces and Stories (London: Penguin, 1965).

For a complete listing of Fitzgerald's published works see
PIPER, HENRY, DAN, 'F. Scott Fitzgerald: A Check-List'. *Princeton University Library Chronicle 12:4* (Summer 1951) pp. 196–208.

In addition to all Fitzgerald's published work I have had unrestricted access to the collection of The Fitzgerald Papers in the Rare Book Department in the Firestone Library at Princeton, New Jersey. For a description of that collection see
MIZENER, ARTHUR, 'The F. Scott Fitzgerald Papers'. *Princeton University Library Chronicle 12:4* (Summer 1951) pp. 190–5.

Biography and Criticism

ALDERMAN, TAYLOR, 'The Begetting of *Gatsby*', *Modern Fiction Studies*, vol. 19 no. 4 (Winter 1973–4), pp. 563–5.
ALLEN, JOAN, M. *Candles and Carnival Lights* (New York University Press, 1978).
BEWLEY, MARIUS, 'Scott Fitzgerald and the Collapse of the American Dream', in his *The Eccentric Design: Form in the Classic American Novel* (London: Chatto and Windus, 1959), pp. 259–87.
— 'Scott Fitzgerald: The Apprentice Fiction', in *Masks & Mirrors: Essays in Criticism* (Atheneum Publications, 1970).
BIGSBY, C. W. E., 'The Two Identities of F. Scott Fitzgerald', In *The American Novel and the Nineteen Twenties* (Stratford On Avon Studies, Edward Arnold, 1971), pp. 129–49.
BOOTH, WAYNE, C., *The Rhetoric of Fiction* (Chicago: University of Chicago Press, 1961), pp. 190–5.
BRUCCOLI, MATTHEW, J., *The Composition of Tender is the Night* (University of Pittsburgh Press, 1963).
— *The Last of the Novelists: F. Scott Fitzgerald and The Last Tycoon* (S. Illinois Press, 1977).

204

— *Scott and Ernest: The Authority of Failure and the Authority of Success* (London, The Bodley Head, 1978).
— *Some sort of Epic Grandeur: The Life of F. Scott Fitzgerald* (London: Hodder and Stoughton, 1981).
BRYER, JACKSON, R., *The Critical Reputation of F. Scott Fitzgerald: A Bibliographical Study* (Hamden: Archon Books, 1967).
BUFKIN, E. C., 'A Pattern of Parallel and Double: The Function of Myrtle in *The Great Gatsby*', *Modern Fiction Studies*, vol XV no.4 (Winter 1969–70), pp. 517–24.
CALLAGHAN, MORLEY, *That Summer in Paris* (New York: Coward-McCann, Inc, 1963).
CALLAHAN, JOHN, F., *The Illusions of a Nation: Myth and History in the Novels of F. Scott Fitzgerald* (University of Illinois Press, 1972).
CARLISLE, E. FRED, 'The Triple Vision of Nick Carraway', *Modern Fiction Studies*, vol. XI, no. 4 (Winter 1965–6), pp. 351–60.
CHASE, RICHARD, 'The Great Gatsby' in *Modern American Fiction: Essays in Criticism* (ed.) A. Walton Litz (New York: OUP, 1963).
COWLEY, MALCOLM, 'Third Act and Epilogue' (1945), in Kazin (ed.) *F.S.F.*, pp. 147–54.
— 'Introduction', *The Stories of F. Scott Fitzgerald* (New York: Scribner's, 1951), pp. vii–xxv.
— *Exile's Return: A Literary Odyssey of the 1920's* (New York: Viking Press, 1951).
— 'Introduction', *The Great Gatsby* in *Three Novels of F. Scott Fitzgerald* (New York: Scribner's, 1953).
— 'Introduction', *Tender is the Night*, revised version (Penguin Books, 1955).
CROSS, K. G. W., *Scott Fitzgerald*, in 'Writers and Critics' series (Oliver and Boyd, 1964).
DOS PASSOS, JOHN, 'A Note on Fitzgerald' (1941) in Kazin (ed.) *F.S.F.*, pp. 155–60.
FIEDLER, LESLIE, 'Some Notes on F. Scott Fitzgerald' (1951) in his *An End to Innocence* (Boston: Beacon Press, 1955), pp. 174–82.
GEISMAR, MAXWELL, 'F. Scott Fitzgerald: Orestes at the Ritz', in his *The Last of the Provincials: The American Novel*, 1915–25 (Boston: Houghton Mifflin, 1943), pp. 287–352.
GRAHAM, SHEILA and GERALD, FRANK, *Beloved Infidel* (New York: Bantam Books, 1959).
GRAHAM, SHEILA, *The Rest of the Story* (New York: Bantam Books, 1964).
College of One (New York: Viking Press, 1966).
HARDING, D. W., 'Scott Fitzgerald', *Scrutiny*, XVIII, Winter 1951–2, pp. 166–74.
HINDUS, MILTON, F. Scott Fitzgerald: An Introduction and Interpretation, in 'American Authors and Critics' series (Holt, Rinehart & Winston, Inc.), 1968.
HOFFMAN, FREDERICK, J., *The Modern Novel in America, 1900–1950* (Chicago: Henry Regnery, 1951), pp. 120–30.
KAZIN, ALFRED, *F. Scott Fitzgerald: The Man and his Work* (New York: Collier Books, 1962 edn).

— *On Native Grounds: An Interpretation of Modern American Prose Literature* (Anchor Books edn, 1956), pp. 242–9.
— 'Fitzgerald: An American Confession' (1945), in Kazin (ed.), *F.S.F.*, pp. 173–82.
KUEHL, JOHN, *The Apprentice Fiction of F. Scott Fitzgerald 1909–1917* (New Brunswick: Rutgers University Press, 1965).
— 'Scott Fitzgerald: Romantic and Realist', *Texas Studies in Literature and Language*, I (Autumn 1959), pp. 412–26.
— 'Scott Fitzgerald's Critical Opinions', *Modern Fiction Studies*, vol VII, no. 1 (Spring 1961), pp. 3–18.
— 'Scott Fitzgerald's Reading'. *Princeton University Library Chronicle*, vol XXII, no. 2 (Winter 1961), pp. 58–89.
LAHOOD, MARVIN, J., *Tender is the Night: Essays in Criticism* (ed.) LaHood (Bloomington: Indiana University Press, 1969).
LATHAM, AARON, *Crazy Sundays: F. Scott Fitzgerald in Hollywood* (Viking edn, 1971).
LAUTER, PAUL, 'Plato's Stepchildren: Gatsby and Cohn', *Modern Fiction Studies* vol IX, no. 4 (Winter 1963–4), pp. 338–46.
LEHAN, RICHARD, D., *F. Scott Fitzgerald: The Man and his Works* (Toronto: Forum House, 1969).
LE VOT, ANDRE, *F. Scott Fitzgerald: A Biography*, English trans. by William Byron (London: Allen Lane, 1984).
LONG, ROBERT EMMET, *The Achieving of The Great Gatsby* (London: Associated University Press, 1979).
MARSHALL, MARGARET, 'On Rereading Fitzgerald' (1941), in Kazin (ed.), *F.S.F.*, pp. 112–14.
MATTHEWS, T. S., 'Taps at Reveille' (1941), in Kazin (ed.), *F.S.F.*, p. 107.
MELLOW, JAMES R., *Invented Lives: F. Scott and Zelda Fitzgerald* (London: Souvenir Press, 1985).
MILLER, JAMES, E., *F. Scott Fitzgerald: His Art and his Technique* (New York University Press, 1964).
MIZENER, ARTHUR, 'F. Scott Fitzgerald: The Poet of Borrowed Time' (1946) in Kazin (ed.), *F.S.F.*, pp. 23–45.
— *The Far Side of Paradise: A Biography of F. Scott Fitzgerald* (New York: Vintage Books, 1959).
— Introduction and Notes, *Afternoon of an Author: A Selection of Uncollected Stories and Essays* (Princeton, University Library, 1957).
— 'Introduction', *Flappers and Philosophers* (New York: Scribner's, 1959), pp. 11–16.
— 'The Maturity of Scott Fitzgerald', *Sewanee Review*, LXVII (Autumn 1959), pp. 658–75.
— *Scott Fitzgerald and his World* (London: Thames and Hudson, 1972).
PEROSA, SERGIO, *The Art of F. Scott Fitzgerald* (Ann Arbor: University of Michigan, 1965).
PIPER, HENRY, DAN, *F. Scott Fitzgerald: A Critical Portrait* (New York: Holt, Rinehart & Winston, 1965).
— 'Fitzgerald's Cult of Disillusion', *American Quarterly*, III (Spring 1951), pp. 69–80.
— 'F. Scott Fitzgerald: A Check List', *Princeton University Library Chronicle*, XII (Summer 1951), pp. 196–208.

— 'F. Scott Fitzgerald and the Image of his Father', *Princeton University Library Chronicle*, XII (Summer 1951), pp. 181–6.

PODHORETZ, NORMAN, *Doings and Undoings* (London: Rupert Hart Davis, 1965).

POWERS, J. F., 'Dealer in Diamonds and Rhinestones' (1945), in Kazin (ed.), *F.S.F.*, pp. 183–7.

PRIESTLEY, J. B., 'Introduction', *The Bodley Head Scott Fitzgerald* (London: The Bodley Head, 1958), pp. 7–16.

RIDDEL, JOSEPH, N., 'F. Scott Fitzgerald: The Jamesian Inheritance and the Morality of Fiction', *Modern Fiction Studies*, vol. XI, no. 4 (Winter 1965–6), pp. 331–50.

ROBBINS, J. ALBERT, 'Fitzgerald and the Simple Articulate Farmer', *Modern Fiction Studies*, vol. VII, no. 4 (Winter 1961–2), pp. 365–9.

ROSENFELD, PAUL, 'Fitzgerald before *The Great Gatsby*' (1925), in Kazin (ed.), *F.S.F.*, pp. 72–7.

SCHULBERT, BUDD, 'Fitzgerald in Hollywood' (1941), in Kazin (ed.), *F.S.F.*, pp. 108–11.

— 'Old Scott: The Mask, the Myth, and the Man', *Esquire*, LV (January 1961), pp. 96–101.

SCHORER, MARK, 'Fitzgerald's Tragic Sense' (1945), in Kazin (ed.), *F.S.F.*, pp. 170–2.

SKLAR, ROBERT, *F. Scott Fitzgerald. The Last Laocoön* (New York: OUP, 1967).

STALLMAN, R. W., 'Gatsby and the Hole in Time', *Modern Fiction Studies*, vol. I, no. 4 (November 1955), pp. 1–16.

STANTON, ROBERT, 'Daddy's Girl: Symbol and Theme in *Tender is the Night*', *Modern Fiction Studies*, vol. IV, no. 2 (Summer 1958), pp. 136–42.

STAVOLA, THOMAS, J., *Scott Fitzgerald: Crisis in an American Identity* (London: Vision, 1979).

STERN, MILTON, R., *The Golden Moment: The Novels of F. Scott Fitzgerald* (Urbana: University of Illinois Press, 1970).

TOMKINS, CALVIN, *Living Well is the Best Revenge* (New York: Signet Books, 1972).

TRILLING, LIONEL, 'F. Scott Fitzgerald', in his *The Liberal Imagination* (London: Secker and Warburg, 1955), pp. 243–54.

TROY, WILLIAM, 'Scott Fitzgerald – the Authority of Failure' (1945), in Kazin (ed.), *F.S.F.*, pp. 188–94.

TURNBULL, ANDREW, *Scott Fitzgerald* (London: The Bodley Head, 1964).

WANNING, ANDREWS, 'Fitzgerald and his Brethren' (1945), in Kazin (ed.), *F.S.F.*, pp. 161–9.

WEIR, CHARLES, Jr., 'An invite with Gilded Edges' (1944), in Kazin (ed.), *F.S.F.*, pp. 133–46.

WESCOTT, GLENWAY, 'The Moral of F. Scott Fitzgerald' (1941), in Kazin (ed.), *F.S.F.*, pp. 115–29.

WHITE, EUGENE, 'The Intricate Destiny of Dick Diver', *Modern Fiction Studies*, vol. VII, no. 1 (Spring 1961), pp. 55–62.

WHITLEY, JOHN, S., *F. Scott Fitzgerald: The Great Gatsby*, in 'Studies in English Literature' series, no. 60 (London: Edward Arnold, 1976).

WILSON, EDMUND, 'Fitzgerald before *The Great Gatsby*' (1925), in Kazin (ed.), *F.S.F.*, pp. 78–84.

— 'The Delegate from Great Neck' (1926), in Kazin (ed.), *F.S.F.*, pp. 54–66.
— (ed.), *The Crack-Up* (New York: New Directions, 1945).

For a complete listing of critical works on Fitzgerald see:

BEEBE, MAURICE and BRYER, JACKSON R., 'Criticism of F. Scott Fitzgerald: A Selected Checklist', in *Modern Fiction Studies*, vol. VII, no. 2 (Summer, 1961), pp. 82–94.
BRYER, JACKSON, R., 'F. Scott Fitzgerald and His Critics: A Bibliographical Record', *Bulletin of Bibliography*, Meckler Publishing, vol. 23, no. 1 (January–April 1962), pp. 154–207.
BRUCCOLI, MATTHEW, J., *The Fitzgerald Newsletter* (ed.) Bruccoli (Columbus: Ohio State University Press, 1958–64). Each number contains a bibliography.
BRUCCOLI, MATTHEW, J., *F. Scott Fitzgerald: A Descriptive Bibliography* (Pittsburgh: University of Pittsburgh Press, 1972).
— *Supplement to F. Scott Fitzgerald: A Descriptive Bibliography* (Pittsburgh: University of Pittsburgh Press, 1980).

Index

Agathon, 83
Agiri Fair incident, The, 183
Alastor, 165, 167
Alice in Wonderland, 164
Animal fight, *Ledger* story of, 21–2,
   25, 95, 123, 176
Arcady, 58, 59, 60, 63, 67, 75, 78,
   79, 83, 97, 118, 121, 123, 124,
   127, 141, 161, 170, 175, 177,
   180, 187
Arnold, Matthew, 137
Asbury Park, 41, 87
Ashes, The Valley of, 108, 109, 115,
   116, 120
Astarte, 75, 76
Astoria, 116, 117
Austen, Jane, 37

Barban, Tommy, 151, 158, 185
Beautiful and Damned, The, 6, 7, 8, 9,
   11, 12, 13, 66–89, 91, 99, 141,
   155, 163, 165, 173
Bishop, John Peale, 8
Blaine, Amory, 6, 14, 15, 16, 37,
   38–66, 67–70, 71, 74–6, 78, 82,
   84, 86, 88, 89, 95, 96–8, 99, 100,
   101, 112, 114, 118, 119, 120,
   121, 123, 138, 141, 155, 159,
   160, 161, 163, 170, 175–6, 177,
   179, 183, 184
Bloeckman, 85
Booth, Wayne C., 132, 133
Brooke, Dorothea, 142, 143, 188
Brooke, Rupert, 54, 66
Brown, Norman, 136
Browning, Robert, 164, 165, 167,
   179
Buchanans, 101, 104, 105, 107, 108,
   120, 122

Callahan, John F., 136, 137
Campion, Luis, 147, 157, 173
Canossa, 169

Carraway, Nick, 98, 101–23, 125,
   140, 143, 145, 148, 149, 156,
   159, 163, 166, 168, 175, 181
Carroll, Lewis, 164
Cenomaus (Zeus), 121
Civilisation and its Discontents
   (Freud), 183
Clara, 49
Cody, Dan, 100, 114, 118
Connage, Alec, 57, 114, 184
Conrad, Joseph, 29, 30, 35–6, 138,
   139–40, 181
Cowley, Malcolm, 5, 8–9, 131, 132,
   133
Crack-Up, The, 2, 16, 24, 99, 100,
   130, 136
Cross, K.G.W., 11, 12, 14

Daddy's Girl, 152, 153, 157, 163,
   171, 173, 178, 181
Damp Symbolic Interlude, The, 35,
   36, 50
Daisy (Buchanan/Fay), 92, 93, 94,
   97, 98–100, 105–7, 108, 109,
   110, 113–17, 120, 121, 122, 123,
   124, 125, 138, 165, 168, 171,
   181, 187
Darcy, Monsignor, 43, 52, 53, 54,
   58, 59, 60, 61, 64, 65, 185
Dedalus, Stephen, 61
Demonic, 155, 177
Devil, The, 42–7, 48, 50, 52, 54, 57,
   68, 70, 75, 86, 88, 155, 163
Diotima, 82, 84, 89, 186, 187
Diver, Dick, 127–88 *passim*
Don Juan, 54, 55, 60
Dreiser, Theodore, 29, 30, 138
Dumphrey, Royal, 157, 173

Eckleburg, Dr T. J., 108, 117
Eleanor, 54, 55, 56, 57, 59, 72, 74,
   75, 84, 96
Electra complex, 174

Eliot, George, 142, 188
Epipsychidion, 74
Erikson, Erik, 135, 136
Eros, 177, 179, 180, 183
Eryximachus, 84

Far Side of Paradise, The, 1, 2
Ferenczi, Sandor, 182
Ferrara, 154, 167, 169
Ferrenby, 40, 62
First World War, The, 49, 157, 158, 160, 162, 164, 176, 180
Fitzgerald, F. Scott (themes)
  admired/loved, wish to be, 61, 69, 70, 76, 161, 162, 163, 169, 181, 185, 187
  beauty linked with evil, 43, 48, 54, 69–73, 74, 80, 179
  egocentricity, 16, 17, 18, 25, 32, 37, 38, 53, 54, 56, 57, 58, 59, 60, 61, 62, 63, 120
  egotism, 20, 21, 38, 53, 64, 68, 112, 138, 160, 170, 175
  egotist, 24, 58, 95
  inartistic sixth act, 33, 34, 78, 81, 84, 92, 96, 99
  juvenile indexes, 18, 31, 66, 96, 97, 107, 138, 143, 159, 161, 166
  sixth sense, 43, 45, 48, 53, 55, 59, 64, 67, 68, 69
  wearing down power, 22–3, 25, 26, 28, 29, 30, 34, 35, 70, 73, 84, 95, 99, 100, 121, 123, 124, 126, 127, 138, 169, 175, 179, 181, 187, 188
  wise and tragic sense, the, 15, 138, 145, 150, 156, 183
Flappers and Philosophers, 6
Flaubert, Gustave, 142
Freud, Sigmund, 135, 136, 160, 170, 172, 173–4, 176–9, 180, 182, 183–4, 185, 186, 187

Gatsby, The Great, 5, 9, 10, 90, 91–126, 127, 139, 140, 142, 143, 145, 148, 149, 159, 163, 166, 167, 175, 180, 181, 187
Gatsby, Jay, 91–4, 96, 97, 98, 99, 100–5, 107, 108, 110, 111–26, 138–88 *passim*

Gatz, James, 112, 138
George, Uncle, 33, 34, 35, 36, 38, 78, 81, 95, 96, 98, 99, 161, 180
Gloria (Patch), 76, 77, 78, 79, 80, 81, 83, 84, 85, 86, 87, 88, 89, 98, 138, 141, 155
Grant, General Ulysses, 160, 180, 188

Hemingway, Ernest, 7
Henry IV, 169
Hibben, President John Grier, 29, 30
Hippodameia (Hera), 121
Hippodrome, 121
Holiday, Burne, 48–9, 50
Hubris, 55, 74, 123
Huckleberry Finn, 19, 32
Hull (Devil), 86, 88, 155
Humbird, Dick, 39, 40, 41, 42, 47, 52, 62

Incest, 162, 170, 171, 172, 181, 184
Interrex (sun-king), 121, 122
Isabelle, 39, 40, 59, 96

James, Henry, 14, 15, 152
Jones, Ernest, 172, 177, 183
Jordan (Baker), 105–6, 111, 113, 115, 116, 117, 118, 119

Kazin, Alfred, 5, 8, 10
Keats, John, 9, 133, 134, 144, 151, 167, 187
Kuehl, John, 9

Leavis, F.R., 3
Ledger, The, 21
Lehan, Richard, 129
Le Vot, André, 13
Libido, 173, 176
Lincoln, Abraham, 15, 138
Little Millionaire, The, 43, 45
Locksley Hall, 49
Longest Journey, The, 114
Lord Jim, 139, 140, 142, 143, 144, 188
Lubell, Albert J., 130

McBeth, 158

McKee (Mr and Mrs), 109
McKisco (Mr and Mrs), 147, 148, 151, 158
Mackenzie, Compton, 11, 12, 21
Mann Act, The, 57
Maury (Noble), 82, 83, 85, 86, 87, 89, 155
Meaninglessness of Life, The, 71, 89, 141
Mellow, James R., 12
Mencken, H.L., 13, 29, 30, 31
Middlemarch, 142, 143, 144, 188
Miller, James E., 9, 10, 11–12, 13, 131
Mizener, Arthur, 1, 2, 3, 4, 8, 10, 11, 12, 17, 27, 28, 91, 92, 128, 129, 130, 131, 132, 133, 134, 135, 136, 145
Myra, 43, 45, 47, 75, 96, 161
Myrtilius, 121
Myrtle (Wilson), 108, 109, 110, 111, 115, 116, 117, 119, 120, 121, 122, 143

Nassau Literary Magazine, 27, 36
New York, 28, 29, 35, 46, 59, 60, 62, 105, 107 , 109, 117, 185–6
Nicole (Warren/Diver), 151, 154, 155, 157, 158, 162, 163, 164, 166, 169, 170, 171, 172, 175, 180, 182, 183, 184, 185, 186, 187
North, Abe, 151, 155, 157, 177, 185
North, Mary, 157, 186

Ode to a Nightingale, 144, 167
Oedipus complex, 173, 174
Owl eyes, 102, 123

Palms, Stephen, 18–27, 30, 32, 37, 66
Paracelsus (Robert Browning), 164, 165, 166, 167, 169, 176, 179, 188
Paradise (Arcady), 66, 95, 96, 175
Paradise, This Side of, 5, 10–18, 27–38, 51, 66–101 *passim*, 112–38 *passim*, 155–9, 165, 170, 175–7, 180
Patch, Anthony, 67–74, 76–81, 84,

85, 88, 89, 96, 98, 99, 138, 141, 142, 160, 163, 179
Pausanias, 84
Pegasus, 34, 95, 97
Perosa, Sergio, 9, 12
Phaedrus, 89
Phoebe, 46, 86
Pierian Springs and the Last Straw, The, 33, 34, 35, 38, 95, 181
Piper, Henry Dan, 5, 9, 91–100, 129
Plato, 74, 75, 81, 83–6, 89, 142, 165, 173, 186
Pleasure Principle, Beyond the, 174, 176, 177, 179, 183, 184
Podhoretz, Norman, 3, 7, 92, 128–9, 137
Poe, Edgar Allen, 55, 74, 75
Pride and Prejudice, 37
Princeton, 22, 23, 25, 27, 28, 29, 38, 39, 40, 41, 45, 47, 48, 49, 57, 59, 61, 62, 63, 95
Psyche (Soul), 74, 75, 78, 82
Psyche-Epipsyche, 74, 75, 76, 77, 78, 165
Psychotherapy, 174–5, 181

Queensboro Bridge, The, 116, 119

Reality Principle, The, 176–8, 181, 184, 185
Repetition-compulsion, 176, 180, 182
Romantic, A, 51, 54, 61, 65, 80
Romantic Egotist, The, 17–27, 30, 31, 32, 35, 36–8, 43, 66, 93, 95, 100, 123, 138, 159, 174, 188
Rosalind, 50–53, 59, 96
Rosemary (Hoyt), 131–2, 145–59, 162, 163, 164, 166, 167, 168, 169, 171–5, 177–82, 184, 185, 187

Saint Theresa, 142, 188
Schizophrenia, 128, 162, 170
Scottie (Fitzgerald), 15, 138
Sentimentality, 51–3, 55, 59
Sentiment and the use of Rouge, 32–4, 51
Shakespeare, 15, 56, 138
Shelley, Percy B., 55, 74, 167

Sklar, Robert, 4–5, 13–14
Socialism, 62, 64
Socrates, 82, 84
Somme, Battle of, 158, 164, 176, 178, 180
Sophocles, 137, 141
Speers, Mrs, 171, 173
Spire and the Gargoyle, The, 27–9, 31–4, 38, 48
Spires and Gargoyles, 38–48, 53, 63, 65
Stavola, Thomas T., 135, 136
Stein (in *Lord Jim*), 139, 140
Stern, Milton R., 4, 12, 14, 133–5
Stevens, Wallace, 141
Sun-chariot, 121, 122
Swinburne, A.G., 49, 55
Symposium (Fitzgerald), 74, 75, 81, 82, 83, 86, 89, 165, 186
Symposium, The (Plato), 81, 82, 83, 89, 186
Syneforth, Lieutenant, 32, 33

Tarkington, Booth, 21
Tasso, 169, 176, 179
Tender is the Night, 9–10, 90, 127–37, 138, 139, 142, 143, 144, 145–89 *passim*

Tennyson, Alfred Lord, 49, 50
Thanatos, 177, 179, 182, 183
Tiare Tahiti, 66
Tom (Buchanan), 105–10, 115, 117, 118, 121, 122
Tom (Parke D'Invilliers), 50, 88
Town Tattle, 109, 110
Trilling, Lionel, 2, 3, 128
Tycoon, The Last, 10

Ulalume, 74, 75
Undine, 164

Verne, Jules, 164

Wallis, Marie, 157
Walpole, Hugh, 30, 31
Warren, Baby, 171
Wilson, Edmund, 5–8, 11–15, 17, 35, 91, 128, 130, 131, 134, 135, 136, 137
Wonderful Girl, Incident of, 43, 46

Yale, 22, 95

Zelda (Fitzgerald), 93, 128, 129
Zeus, 121
Zurich, 160, 161, 164, 170, 178